Resistance
PSYCHODYNAMIC AND BEHAVIORAL APPROACHES

Resistance
PSYCHODYNAMIC AND
BEHAVIORAL APPROACHES

Edited by
Paul L. Wachtel

City College of the City University of New York
New York, New York

PLENUM PRESS • NEW YORK AND LONDON

Library of Congress Cataloging in Publication Data

Main entry under title:

Resistance, psychodynamic and behavioral approaches.

  Bibliography: p.
  Includes index.
  1. Resistance (Psychoanalysis) 2. Psychotherapy. I. Wachtel, Paul L., 1940 –
RC489.R49R47   616.89'14   81-23494
ISBN 0-306-40769-8   AACR2

© 1982 Plenum Press, New York
A Division of Plenum Publishing Corporation
233 Spring Street, New York, N.Y. 10013

Printed in the United States of America

This book is dedicated
to the memory of my father,
Nathan Wachtel

Contributors

Michael Franz Basch, M.D., Suite 3605, 55 East Washington Street, Chicago, Illinois

Sidney J. Blatt, Ph.D., Departments of Psychiatry and Psychology, Yale University, New Haven, Connecticut

Paul A. Dewald, M.D., Department of Psychiatry, St. Louis University School of Medicine, St. Louis, Missouri

H. Shmuel Erlich, Ph.D., Department of Psychology, Hebrew University, Jerusalem, Israel

Allen Fay, M.D., Department of Psychiatry, Mount Sinai School of Medicine, City University of New York, New York, New York

J. Barnard Gilmore, Ph.D., Department of Psychology, University of Toronto, Toronto, Ontario, Canada

Marvin R. Goldfried, Ph.D., Department of Psychology, State University of New York, Stony Brook, New York

Arnold A. Lazarus, Ph.D., Graduate School of Applied and Professional Psychology, Rutgers — The State University, New Brunswick, New Jersey

Donald Meichenbaum, Ph.D., Department of Psychology, University of Waterloo, Waterloo, Ontario, Canada

Victor Meyer, Ph.D., Academic Department of Psychiatry, Middlesex Hospital Medical School, London, England

Herbert J. Schlesinger, Ph.D., Denver V. A. Medical Center, Department of Psychiatry, University of Colorado School of Medicine, Denver, Colorado

Ira Daniel Turkat, Ph.D., Departments of Psychology and Medicine, Vanderbilt University and School of Medicine, Nashville, Tennessee

Paul L. Wachtel, Ph.D., Department of Psychology, City College of the City University of New York, New York, New York

Contents

Introduction

RESISTANCE AND THE PROCESS OF THERAPEUTIC CHANGE

Paul L. Wachtel

Psychotherapy, whether practiced from a psychodynamic or a behavioral point of view,[1] is rarely as straightforward as textbooks and case reports usually seem to imply. More often the work proceeds in fits and starts (and often does not seem to be proceeding at all, but rather unraveling or moving backward). The "typical" case is in fact quite atypical. Almost all cases present substantial difficulties for which the therapist feels, at least some of the time, quite unprepared. Practicing psychotherapy is a difficult—if also rewarding—way to earn a living. It is no profession for the individual who likes certainty, predictability, or a fairly constant sense that one knows what one is doing. There are few professions in which feeling stupid or stymied is as likely to be a part of one's ordinary professional day, even for those at the pinnacle of the field. Indeed, I would be loath to refer a patient to any therapist who declared that he almost always felt effective and clear about what was going on. Such a feeling can be maintained, I believe, only by an inordinate amount of bravado and lack of critical self-reflection.

But the therapist trying to get some ideas about how to work with

---

[1] These are, of course, not the only two points of view in psychotherapy; nor do I believe they are the only two of value. They are however the two dominant points of view in individual psychotherapy, and the exploration of their interface has been, and will continue to be, of considerable value.

Paul L. Wachtel ● Department of Psychology, City College of the City University of New York, New York, New York 10031.

a "difficult"—read "typical"—patient is likely to find the literature of the field disappointing. Almost every case is likely to present at least some moments when everything one has learned seems irrelevant—or when one feels one has learned nothing at all. At such moments one would like to know, "What would X do in this instance?" This book is meant to illustrate what some of the most highly regarded "X's" in both the psychodynamic and behavioral traditions do when the going gets rough.

The focus of this book is on "resistance," but the reader will notice that quite a few of the chapters do not really limit themselves to discussions of resistance alone. Perhaps more accurately, what they reject (as I do myself) is the idea that resistance can be understood in terms of particular, specific disruptions in what is otherwise a smoothly flowing process of change. Resistance is instead, as Herbert Schlesinger suggests in his chapter, a *point of view* on phenomena, a way of looking at the entire process that is complementary to other points of view. Particular dramatic or difficult instances make this point of view prepotent at times, but it is relevant throughout as a guide to understanding what it is that the therapist is participating in.

The concept of resistance originated, of course, within the psychoanalytic tradition. It is for all analysts a central notion in understanding how the therapeutic process proceeds. In the behavioral literature, references to resistance are scant. If one only *reads* about behavior therapy, one is likely to conclude either that behavior therapists do not understand or do not notice resistance or that their methods overcome resistance or make it irrelevant. Such an illusion is likely to disappear quite rapidly if one sits down face to face with a behavior therapist and gets to talking cases.

I still recall quite vividly my first few experiences in presenting my own emerging ideas about psychotherapy to an audience that was largely behavioral in orientation. My training had originally been in the psychoanalytic tradition, but a variety of clinical and theoretical considerations had led me to the conclusion that an attempt to integrate psychodynamic and behavioral approaches would be fruitful. I had presented some of these ideas to psychoanalytic groups and although my innovations had hardly been embraced with open arms, I had received a respectful and attentive reception. The questions raised were difficult and piercing, but they were *familiar*. I was on home territory, and I knew what to expect. After all, my turn toward a consideration of behavioral methods and points of view, and toward questioning whether they needed to be totally excluded from the approach of the dynamically oriented therapist, had arisen from dissatisfactions and questions about traditional psychodynamic theories and practices. I *knew* why I thought that dynamic approaches alone were often insufficient. I had been struggling for a good long time with just that question.

But approached from the reverse, the questions were at first unfamiliar. In telling behavior therapists why *they* might find it useful to consider ideas and practices deriving from a *psychodynamic* approach, I was on virgin territory. I had persuaded myself that an exclusively psychodynamic approach was insufficient. Now I had to demonstrate—to myself and to the (at that point unfamiliar) behavioral audience—that the insufficiency held from the other direction as well. I have rarely been as nervous in addressing an audience as I was on that first occasion of presenting my ideas about psychotherapy to an audience consisting largely of behavior therapists and their students—and rarely have I been as pleasantly surprised. I had felt as if I was going into the lion's den. But my opening question seemed to suggest that, like Daniel, I had come to remove a thorn, and like Daniel the response I received was warm and welcoming.

The question I asked was: "Do you not find that frequently you feel you have analyzed the case correctly, have set up a program of experiences which if carried out would help the patient to change, but find that the patient either does not carry out the suggested procedures or does so over and over in peculiarly idiosyncratic ways that are not quite what you had in mind?" I believe that I had lots of useful and interesting things to say in the remainder of my talk that I would like to think accounted at least in part for the warm response I received. But I know that the battle was largely won with my opening question. In that talk and in other talks to behavioral audiences that followed, numerous members of the audience indicated to me afterward that I was raising an issue that had been of great concern to them but which they had felt largely constrained to suppress in what was the prevailing zeitgeist of their institution. I heard this admission particularly from students, but from a good number of faculty members as well. I am under no illusion that I removed all the thorny problems of helping living and complicated human beings to change; but at least the thorn of silence had been plucked.

The situation has changed substantially in recent years. Students hear far less frequently from their teachers of behavior therapy the evasive position that their job is simply to prescribe the appropriate interventions and that if the patient or client does not make use of them, that is not their responsibility. Behavior therapy has changed considerably as behavior therapists have encountered a wider range of patients and problems and as they have felt more secure about the value of their approach, and hence more open to expanding and revising their thinking. Some of the authors in this volume have been among the most important contributors to the increasing clinical relevance and sophistication of behavior therapy.

Today the student who reports to his behavioral supervisor that his patient did not carry through on what was suggested is more likely to be told that he has not conducted an adequate behavioral analysis, that the patient's failure to follow through reflects the therapist's insufficient understanding of the variables governing the patient's difficulties. That is, to my mind, a vast improvement over "we did our part; he didn't do his." It is, in fact, unassailable. But it is unassailable in part because it is so abstract. The question remains precisely what kind of further understanding will enable the therapist to make his interventions in such a way that he achieves not merely a moral victory but actual and effective participation by the patient.

Thus far few behavior therapists—even those in the avant-garde—have made much use of psychoanalysis in their efforts to achieve such an understanding. "Cognitive" perspectives seem to predominate at the front lines of the clinical advance of behavior therapy. Psychodynamic perspectives still seem to lie well beyond the frontier, and appear even to most enlightened behavior therapists to be too foreign to ever incorporate. I had hoped that this book would contribute—from both sides—to a spirit of détente and to the recognition that psychodynamic and behavioral perspectives could be mutually facilitative. As the reader will discover, this hope has been largely unrealized. Although the chapters are excellent and valuable clinical contributions, they are primarily inward looking rather than reaching to incorporate from outside the pale. This fact is reflected as well in the commentary chapters, a number of which are defenses of the virtue of the writer's own point of view rather than efforts to see what can be learned from the other side of the boundary.

In retrospect, this outcome was probably to be expected. The contributors were, to be sure, chosen because each has shown, in a general way at least, a tendency to reach beyond and/or to examine critically his own approach. But all are, as well, admired and established clinicians and teachers who, one is safe in assuming, have experienced not only the dark nights of the therapist's soul but a good deal of success as well. It is only human to defend the means by which one has achieved such hard-fought victories. That in the commentary chapters the defenses seem to be about equally vociferous from each side may be, for the reader, a metacommentary on the clinical value of each approach.

It will be for the reader more generally to put together the hints and guidelines from various directions and see what help they give in fashioning an approach to the problems of clinical work. Although it will be clear that I have not completely refrained from editorializing here—I am, after all, the "editor"—I have tried not to engage in Monday-morning quarterbacking. I chose contributors with both strong reputations and strong opinions, and to expect both those properties and an agreement with my own views as well would not be reasonable. The reader who is familiar with the positions I have taken on these issues will have no difficulty seeing where the contributors depart. I differ as well from some of them in their evaluations of their cocontributors' accounts. Having placed them at each other's tender mercies, I feel some responsibility for how they are treated. I will resist the temptation to intervene here as well, however, and trust to the solidity of all of their reputations to withstand the critical scrutiny of their colleagues.

I remain committed to the synthesis of psychodynamic and behavioral approaches I described in *Psychoanalysis and Behavior Therapy*. The use of both psychodynamic and behavioral methods described there differs substantially from much of what is described in this book. But one chooses to edit a book for different reasons than one chooses to write one. I wrote my first book largely to teach. I edited this one in order to learn. As I presented my ideas about a psychodynamic-behavioral synthesis, it became clear that it was particularly with regard to dealing with resistance that the synthesis made a contribution. I was tempted to write a sequel further explicating how my approach deals with resistance in particular. Someday I may. But just because the topic of resistance was so central to what I was up to, it seemed to me useful to get a clearer bead on just how resistance is dealt with by those who have been most successful in applying just one of the two approaches I felt were complementary. The results have encouraged me on two counts. To my own idiosyncratic reading, the chapters demonstrate both the riches that have been mined from both traditions and the limits of an exclusive approach. The therapists who have written the following chapters have clearly helped their patients a good deal. My guess is that they could do so even more if they would pay greater attention to each other. Perhaps in putting them between the same covers I may contribute to that end. In any event I hope that the reader will find valuable hints for his clinical work in the chapters not only by those whose orientation is closest to one's own but in those of the "others" as well.

Part of the difficulty in getting therapists to look beyond their own paradigms lies in the strong identifications held by therapists with a particular tradition and its own particular language and philosophy. The therapist agrees to accept someone else's painful and seemingly intractable dilemmas as the subject matter of his life's work. The responsibilities and the difficulties that are thereby encountered can be rather overwhelming if one is not rather thoroughly immersed in a supportive community. Add to that the centrality of their own personal therapy in the training of many therapists and you have a formula for almost unshakeable commitment not only to a particular approach but to a particular way of talking about what one does. As a consequence, convergence may in fact be considerably greater than is recognized because different language is used by different therapists to describe roughly the same thing.

This is particularly the case with regard to the concept of resistance. Behavior therapists have tended to bristle at the term because to many of them it has seemed to imply blaming the patient's lack of cooperativeness rather than looking to where the therapist has fallen short. Moreover, they have understood the concept to mean that the patient does not really want to get better after all and/or is stubbornly opposing the therapist and refusing to do what is necessary to make the therapy work. This misunderstanding is ironic since, as noted earlier, at one time such an attitude was particularly prevalent among behavior therapists, many of whom saw their responsibility as solely to outline what was in effect an idealized treatment program and placing the burden of actually *participating* in the program on the patient.

Now in some respects *most* successful therapists do something like that. Existential therapists, dynamic therapists, family therapists, behavior therapists—indeed most effective therapists of most orientations—wisely refrain from placing themselves in the untenable position of trying to force the patient to do what needs to be done, of chasing after the patient, cajoling him, "making him" do what he is so good at not doing. The patient must, in important ways, take responsibility for his own treatment. But that does not mean that the *therapist's* responsibility is limited to a simple take-it-or-leave-it explication of what is to be done. The therapist's responsibility includes, very importantly, helping make it more likely that the patient *will* decide to take up the cudgel from his end.

It is in the very nature of most psychological problems that the patient is hampered from doing what must be done to make things better. The very problems the patient comes to therapy to try to solve make it difficult for him to cooperate in their solution. This dilemma is the heart of the concept of resistance. The concept refers not to any willful malevolence or opposition on the patient's part but instead to the difficulties inherent in attempting to encounter and master feelings and experiences that have previously seemed so overwhelming they must be avoided and denied at all costs. Freud recognized early that the task of free association he set his patients could not be achieved as he posed it, though it could be approximated to varying degrees by different patients at different times. The plan he developed for helping patients despite their inability to do what originally seemed necessary involved, on the one hand, making use of that degree of cooperation or success in the task that they could manifest, and on the other making use of efforts to understand *how and why they fell short*. Thus, from very early (and increasingly as Freud's experience with his method developed and broadened), psychoanalysis as a therapeutic procedure became very centrally concerned with phenomena (the resistances) that at first were merely annoying distractions from the "real" task of psychoanalysis. Unlike the popular slogan of the sixties—"If you're not part of the solution, you're part of the problem"—for psychoanalysis the motto became, in essence, "You're inevitably part of the problem, and taking this fact into account is the only way to be part of the solution."

Resistance was easier to address from a psychodynamic point of view because that view was so focally concerned with *conflict*. Even today, as behavior therapists are increasingly recognizing the problem of resistance (if not always so naming it), and as they are developing new and effective ways of dealing with it (as the following chapters illustrate), they are hampered, I believe, by their lack of attention to conflict. In important ways, in fact, the concepts of resistance and of conflict are almost identical. Resistance is not something that periodically comes up to disrupt the therapy. It is the track of the patient's conflict about changing, the way in which the sincere desire to change confronts the fears, misconceptions, and prior adaptive strategies that make change difficult.

It is my guess that the single greatest change that will occur in the practice of behavior therapists in the next decade will be a great increase in concern with phenomena of conflict—a concern that I expect will be motivated most of all by an increasingly sophisticated understanding of phenomena of resistance. It is also my guess that behavior therapists *already* concern themselves with conflict considerably more than one would gather from their writings. It is hardly a state secret that therapists tend to practice in ways that differ considerably from the formal version of the theory they identify with. Most therapists who are contributors to the literature acknowledge in private that their actual practice can at times be quite different from what they describe in print. What is described tends to be an ideal model. As such it has value: It enables the writer (and the reader) to articulate the principles underlying the work and provides a coherent rational model that is at least in principle capable of being refined and tested. It is also easier to teach to a neophyte than is the more complex truth with which he will eventually have to come to terms.

In daily practice, however, an enormous variety of "exceptions" arise, and they require, almost daily, deviations from the idealized model. Beginning therapists who try to adhere strictly to the model they are learning and who take seriously its taboos often find themselves stymied when they confront actual clinical problems that have led them (as they almost always do) out of safe, predictable waters. Experienced therapists tend to hew less strictly to the party line, but most of us remain hampered to some degree by the blinders we were taught to wear as students. The chapters that follow vary in the degree to which they present ideas and techniques that the authors could not have readily shared with their supervisors. But all of them represent the distillation of the experience of gifted and thoughtful practitioners, and it is my hope that in total they will enhance the reader's clinical work, whether he or she is a beginner or an experienced clinician.

I

Psychodynamic Approaches

1

Dynamic Psychotherapy and Its Frustrations

Michael Franz Basch

Resistance in therapy is opposition to change. Freud demonstrated that psychological symptoms serve a purpose that, once it is understood, explains their necessity for the patient. For psychoanalysts and psychoanalytically oriented psychotherapists, symptoms are not the indicators of what is wrong but are instead a demonstration of how the patient is trying to guard a vulnerable area of his emotional life and protect himself from further pain. Clearly, in most cases, these coping mechanisms will not readily be given up. Every one of us in his character development comes to use various compensating and protective traits meant to fend off embarrassment, guilt, self-doubt, and other threats to his sense of integrity. People do not come to see us because they are upset about the way that their personality evolved; they come because, for one reason or another, the particular adaptations that they have made to life no longer work. Whether they realize it or not, what our patients want from us is to be shown how to restore the balance that they had achieved without their having to make any fundamental changes in the way they see themselves and others. Sometimes it is possible and reasonable to take this course; when it is not, one must sooner or later work against the patient's resistance to change. To use an analogy, if a person has been walking with the aid of a crutch, no matter how much he may desire it, when it comes time to do without

Michael Franz Basch • Suite 3605, 55 East Washington Street, Chicago, Illinois 60602.

it there is a doubt as to whether or not his legs alone will really support him and there is a strong tendency to cling to the now no longer necessary support. We all understand such anxiety, can identify with it, and do not blame the patient for being afraid. In psychological matters both the patient and the therapist may be less sanguine about the anxiety generated by the need for giving up a ritual, a fear, an inhibition, or a character trait, especially when life could be ever so much better for the patient if he would only accept the help that is being offered him. Of course, unlike a broken leg, what ails our patients is not visible, its history is not evident, and furthermore the patient may never have had the experience of getting along any other way. Thus in our field we should not hope or demand that our patients will respond to our offers to help them as they might in the case of a physical disturbance—and yet we tend to do so.

Because the patient's helplessness in the face of his resistance is often forgotten, "resistance" has acquired an undeserved pejorative flavor. Resistance is a much more frustrating phenomenon if we believe on some level that the patient is willfully opposing us and could, if he were only a nicer person and less bent on making our life miserable, do something about it. However, the way Freud initially described it, resistance is not an interpersonal problem, that is, something that the patient is doing to the therapist, but instead an intrapsychic one that is bringing a struggle within the patient into the foreground of the treatment. Looked at that way resistance becomes a guide to the therapist, indicating where he can profitably concentrate his efforts. I realize that that is often easier said than done.

It is exhilarating when you can point out to a patient that he is undermining his treatment, win his cooperation, and together scale the heights of insight. However, when a patient cannot ally himself with us and is unable to step back from his own behavior sufficiently to let us look together at what he is doing to himself we find ourselves frustrated in our therapeutic efforts. In other words it is not really resistance that is the problem but, so to speak, the patient's resistance to examining his resistance to change that threatens to create a therapeutic impasse. It is the latter phenomenon that makes for the frustrating patient, and it is the focus of this essay.

In order to understand why helping some patients is a relatively straightforward matter in spite of the expected opposition to change, whereas others fight us tooth and nail, let us turn the question around. In view of the fear of change and of the unfamiliar, why would anyone cooperate with us in the therapeutic task? Obviously, the pain and unhappiness created by the patient's difficulties are an incentive. But the matter is not that simple. After all, both the patient who is able to cooperate with us and the one who is not have come to us in distress; yet one can use us and the other cannot. So there is a factor over and above the patient's suffering that is needed to motivate him to explore the nature and meaning of his problem. That factor is the therapeutic transference, the readiness to find someone with whom to reexperience the fears, wishes, and relationships of the past in the hope of restructuring the self along happier and more serviceable lines.

Transference and resistance are the two sides of one developmental coin. To use the previous analogy again, the urge to walk normally combined with the trust that the doctor knows what is good for him and will assist him if he gets into trouble outweighs the patient's fear sufficiently for him to put his crutch aside and put weight on his previously injured leg. Once past that sticking point the patient's sense of achievement and his recognition that he can look forward to walking normally again give him the incentive to tolerate whatever discomfort he must endure as he gradually regains full use of his leg. As psychotherapists we function in essentially the same way. Our job is not to tackle resistance (the patient's fear, mistrust, anxiety, and other guarding behavior) directly, for that would be unrealistic given its origin, but to create a situation in which the patient's relationship to us generates an imbalance that favors progress rather than the status quo. What makes for a so-called difficult patient is the anxiety-based resistance that opposes either the mobilization or the appropriate utilization of the therapeutic transference. I have elsewhere (Basch, 1980) documented the centrality of the transference relationship in psychotherapy and discussed its nature, theoretical justification, and practical significance. Here my focus will be on some of the obstacles the therapist encounters in his attempt to implement this concept and how these may be avoided or resolved.

To clarify what I mean I will give excerpts from interviews and treatment sessions disguised, of course, that ilustrate common forms of resistance to initiating and implementing the therapeutic relationship, and some suggestions for their resolution.

Resistance to Initiating Therapy

The patient, Mr. Adam Hoheit, is a 45-year-old investment banker. His bearing and appearance radiate success and authority. The following is a condensed account of the first interview.

THERAPIST *(Walking into the waiting room and offering his hand):* Mr. Hoheit? I am Dr. Basch.

MR. HOHEIT *(Indifferently shaking the proffered hand):* I have to be out of here by 2:00 and you are 5 minutes late, Doctor.

THERAPIST: Come in, please.

MR. HOHEIT *(Settling down in the designated chair):* Will we be done by 2:00, Doctor? I have to be at a meeting by 2:15.

THERAPIST: Will we be done with what?

MR. HOHEIT: Right. I guess you don't even know what I'm here for. Actually it shouldn't take too long. Abner Tatum was your patient and he is my client. We were talking at lunch the other day and I mentioned my problem to him. Abner said he wanted to stay out of it, but he said you had been of great help to him during his divorce, so I thought perhaps I could use some of your counsel in my circumstances too.

THERAPIST: I'd be glad to be of help if I can be.

MR. HOHEIT: It's not really for me. I need advice regarding my children. I want to know whether, in your professional opinion, my getting a divorce from my wife will hurt them. I have a boy age 6, and two daughters, 16 and 14. The two older ones will be leaving home to go to college fairly soon anyway, but the 6-year-old worries me a little.

THERAPIST: I don't think that's a question I can answer. If you'll tell me about your situation I may be able to clarify your thinking.

MR. HOHEIT: You mean if I can give you more information about him then you can tell me how my boy will be affected? I suppose it does differ with each personality.

THERAPIST: No. I would like to hear from you about your children, their personalities, and the effects you think a divorce will have on them because that will help me get a better picture of what's going on with you.

MR. HOHEIT: All this will take a long time. I have to be out of here by 2:00 you know.

THERAPIST: There is no telling how long it will take. If there is reason to meet more than once I'm prepared to do so.

MR. HOHEIT *(With a sneer on his face and a sarcastic tone):* Sounds to me like you're trying to set up something for yourself, Doctor.

THERAPIST: Please explain yourself.

MR. HOHEIT: Well, I asked you a simple question. I came to get a professional opinion from you as I would from a dentist, a lawyer, or a surgeon. I'm perfectly willing to pay what it costs to get it, but you are already making me into a client or a patient—whatever you people call it—and I'm just telling you before we go any further that I just might not care for that idea. What do you say to that?!

THERAPIST: First of all, the question you asked me is not, as you suggest, a simple one. Moreover, as I told you, it is impossible to answer it as you asked it. I am willing to believe that you didn't know that and I could understand your disappointment at being told that it was so. However, what I'd like you to explain is the tone of your voice and the look on your face when you said I was "trying to set something up" for myself. It sounded cynical and sarcastic.

As if there was something dirty going on here. It seemed to me as if your initial purpose in coming here was forgotten and your goal was now not to enlist my help but to make me feel guilty and ashamed. For some reason you felt a need to attack me.

MR. HOHEIT (*Silence*).

THERAPIST: Well?

MR. HOHEIT: You and my wife.

THERAPIST: Hmhm.

MR. HOHEIT: That's what she complains about. (*In a falsetto voice*) "You're attacking me"; "You're continually undermining me"; "I love you, but if I am going to retain my sanity I have to leave you, Adam." Silly damned nonsense!

THERAPIST: You mean it's your wife who is leaving you? I was under the impression that you were going to seek a divorce.

MR. HOHEIT: What's the difference who is leaving whom! It's the boy I'm concerned about.

THERAPIST: It sounds to me as if you are in a lot of trouble with yourself and that we have much more to talk about. It's getting close to the time you said you had to leave. I would suggest that we make at least two more appointments so that I may clarify your situation for myself and make my recommendations.

MR. HOHEIT: So you think I need therapy?

THERAPIST: There's very little doubt in my mind about that. The question is whether or not you can lend yourself to that process and, if so, what form it should take.

MR. HOHEIT: Listen, the people I'm supposed to meet with aren't that important. I can let them wait if you have the time to go on.

THERAPIST: I did have more time allotted for this first meeting, but I wouldn't feel comfortable going on knowing I was willfully inconveniencing the people waiting for you. How long will your meeting take?

MR. HOHEIT: An hour, maybe an hour and a half. Definitely no more.

THERAPIST: If you have the time I could see you later in the day.

MR. HOHEIT: I don't want to keep you.

THERAPIST: It's no problem. I have to stay down late anyway today. Would 5:30 be OK?

MR. HOHEIT: Fine, thank you Doctor.

THERAPIST: You're welcome. Good-bye till then, Mr. Hoheit.

This patient displays what Murray (1964) has called a narcissistic sense of entitlement. He feels perfectly justified in demanding that the world meet his needs to the exclusion of all other reality. Incensed that he was kept waiting a few minutes, he has no hesitation about inconveniencing others when he feels it is in his interest to do so. It would of course have been a serious mistake to indulge him in this attitude. Had I agreed to prolong the appointment then and there in order to ensure that the treatment process could get started, I would have let him make me a partner in his corruption and he would have gained in that way the control over me that he could not achieve when he initially attempted to dominate me through intimidation. As it turned out, Mr. Hoheit did come back, psychotherapy was recommended, and he was seen three times a week for a period of several months. He was able to gain sufficient insight into his behavior to ease the strain between himself and his wife considerably. As it became clear that his basic difficulties were psychoneurotic, we transformed his therapy into an analysis that was successfully concluded in approximately 4 years. As we went along I learned, and was able to help the patient see, that his need to control everyone and everything around him was rooted in his fear that if he did not do so he would be seen as weak, gullible, and easily imposed on—similar to the way in which he experienced his father. Specifically, he had witnessed his mother's unfaithfulness to his father on many different occasions. In terms of his own development he saw this unfaithfulness as a loss of control on his father's part and used his considerable intelligence to see to it that he would never be in the same position. In spite of great success in his chosen field and ample evidence that he was both respected and feared by all with whom he had dealings, Mr. Hoheit remained essentially insecure and had a compensatory compulsion to demonstrate to himself that he could dominate every encounter. It was his wife's move toward independence from his sarcastic, belittling, legalistic faultfinding with her every action that precipitated the anxiety that brought Mr. Hoheit to my office. He was quite conscious of the fact, though it took him a while to talk about it, that his wife's self-assertion generated a nightmarish situation for him in which he saw her searching for and finding other men just as his mother had done. On a much deeper level, material recovered only after several years of analysis revealed that his aggressive attitude concealed the repressed wish and fear to compensate his father for the loss of his wife by offering himself as the passive participant in anal intercourse.

None of this was of course evident or suspected when I first met Mr. Hoheit. I bring up this material to illustrate an extreme example of a not uncommon situation in which the patient's fear that the therapist will not be strong enough to withstand the onslaught of the patient's needs leads him to wrestle the therapist from the very first meeting or telephone call for control of the therapeutic situation, hoping against hope all the while that the doctor will not be intimidated. Since at that point therapy has not yet begun there is no basis for dealing with the potential patient's behavior by interpretation. Attempts to placate the patient are seen by him as weakness on the part of the therapist and may well frighten him into finding some pretext for not returning. In Mr. Hoheit's case, for example, I learned that I was not the first therapist he had consulted. A search for treatment, under one guise or another, had been going on intermittently for some years. When we reviewed what had transpired with various therapists, once the superficial reasons for not entering treatment with them had been discounted, it always turned out that Mr. Hoheit had managed in some way to intimidate the therapist-to-be with his angry contempt, his aggressive demandingness, or his overbearing intellect.

It was most instructive for me to see that after the first few encounters with this patient, in which I apparently proved to him that I had the requisite strength to deal with him, the resistance to treatment dissipated and did not present a problem in the years we subsequently worked together. There was of course the expected intrapsychic resistance to uncovering aspects of repressed and disavowed memories, feelings, and motives, but it was clear to both of us that the struggle was within him and not with me. An occasional attempt to make it an interpersonal matter was quickly countered by reminding him of our initial meeting and then investigating what it was that was really going on at the moment within him.

The point I am trying to make through this example is that resistance to establishing what would become the therapeutic transference can be present from the very first moment. Although Mr. Hoheit's conduct was an extreme example of the genre, similar problems are present in many patients. I have not always been either so prescient or successful in these situations. Especially early in my career, when I was more in doubt about my professional and economic survival, my eagerness to show that I could and would be helpful as well as my fear of alienating the patient, his family, or the referring source led me to suppress the feeling that I was being attacked, depreciated, or manipulated by such patients. The result, if the patient did not leave me, was that therapy either never got off the ground or was unnecessarily prolonged until I finally got around to facing with the patient what it was that he was doing and why.

There are many different ways in which patients who need to do so attempt to dominate the therapist. Mr. Hoheit is presented only as a dramatic illustration of what often confronts us in more subtle and disguised form. Nor am I advocating my approach to this particular patient as paradigmatic. Another therapist might have handled the situation differently but equally effectively. Indeed, the same patient, responding to the immediate, nonverbal clues that tell the sensitive patient so much about the therapist, might well have engaged him in a struggle for control dissimilar to the one he mounted against me. This particular clinical example is only given to illustrate that when a patient's resistance takes the form of acting out the question "Who is in control here?" it behooves the therapist to respond, in whatever way is congenial to his personality, "I am."

Pseudoresistance

Much of what is called resistance in psychotherapy is an artifact. It is a therapeutic stalemate generated by the therapist's attempt to introduce the model of the psychoanalytic treatment of the psychoneuroses into the psychotherapy of patients whose disturbances have a different basis. The expectation that an examination of the patient's past will lead to an understanding of the present that will, as a matter of course, carry with it a resolution of the problems that brought the patient for therapy is usually disappointed in these cases. Psychotherapy depends on the formation and examination of the therapeutic transference (Basch, 1980), and, as is the case with most of our patients, as long as their behavior in or out of the treatment situation stands in the way of the formation of that relationship it is their behavior in the here and now rather than the real or imaginary traumata of childhood that must be brought into the therapy.

The most common problem that is presented to me when I am functioning as supervisor or consultant is that of the patient who is said to resist interpretation. The therapist feels that he has insight into the genetic roots of the patient's difficulties, interprets these, that is, helps the patient link the present problem with the past; yet, though the patient may seem to understand, that insight leads to no apparent therapeutic result.

Mr. Peter Ilge was a 28-year-old doctoral candidate in business administration who was referred to me because he seemed unable to finish his thesis. He had been in psychotherapy off and on throughout his college years, usually in connection with some crisis or other in his life. His last therapist had told him that he had gone as far as he could in psychotherapy and should consider psychoanalysis. In his conversation with me the therapist suggested that perhaps a psychoanalysis would be able to resolve the passive-aggressive resistance that the patient had displayed with him. He felt that the patient had a so-called negative therapeutic reaction to his efforts since interpretation seemed to have no result other than to frustrate both of them. The patient only redoubled his complaints about his inability to function and usually managed to precipitate some catastrophe within his department that served to underline how helpless he was in the face of the demands that academic life made on him, even though neither his intelligence nor talent for his chosen profession was ever in question.

Mr. Ilge, when I first met him, seemed a pleasant and cooperative person who eagerly launched into a detailed account of his personal history. Based on his previous therapeutic experiences he expected that we would be talking about his childhood and looking to it for explanations as to why he could not finish his work. I listened to him for several sessions as he painted the background picture that he felt I should know to understand him. In essence he described himself as the only child of a father who had failed in his life's ambition and a mother who resented the restricted circumstances that the father's lack of material success had forced on them. Although both parents had come from reasonably prosperous backgrounds, the father's ineptitude had resulted in the loss of a family business and he was now employed in a minor managerial capacity in what had been a competitor's firm. The patient's paternal grandmother, aware of her son's lack of ability, had taken the precaution of selling her portion of the business that the grandfather had left the family. A shrewd investor, she had parlayed that inheritance into a comfortable sum that now left her quite well-off. She had steadfastly refused over the years to support her son, but apparently seeing promise in her grandson, had provided the money for his education and its ancillary expenses, including whatever psychiatric treatment he might need while completing his degree.

In the third interview the following exchange took place.

MR. ILGE: My past work in therapy seemed to indicate that I am afraid to surpass my father and, in a symbolic sense, compete for and take my mother away from him. A belated oedipal victory you might say. I guess that's why I have to have a psychoanalysis. Dr. G. said there must be repressed aspects of that that psychotherapy can't get at.

THERAPIST: How did you get along with Dr. G.?

MR. ILGE: Very well, I thought. He seemed very nice and I had no trouble talking to him.

THERAPIST: How do you feel about leaving him and coming to see me?

MR. ILGE: In a way I was sorry. You know, who wants to rehash the same old story over and over. But then, I have changed therapists before and I expect we'll get along all right. It's nice to have someone to talk to when you get upset, but I have to get further than that. It's not that I don't appreciate what my therapists have tried to do, but feeling good for the moment about myself doesn't solve the problem of getting over that writing block that I have. I'm afraid if I keep disappointing my adviser by never having anything to show him my department will make me drop out.

What struck me about Mr. Ilge's recital was how little evidence there was of transference feelings toward any of his previous therapists. He is a nice guy and they are nice guys and that's all very nice, but this man has not been engaged meaningfully by his treatment so far.

THERAPIST: A writing block? Did you try to write anything today?
MR. ILGE: No, not today.
THERAPIST: Well, when then?
MR. ILGE: Gee, I can't remember exactly.
THERAPIST: You can't remember!? Something so important that it threatens to undermine the goals you have set for yourself and worked toward for so many years? I would think you would know exactly not only when you last had trouble, but also the circumstances that surrounded your failed attempt, how you felt, and what you tried to do about it.
MR. ILGE (A little defensive and not quite so pleasant): I'm sorry, but no one ever asked me these questions, it just hasn't occurred to me to look at my block, if that's what it is, that way.

The patient has now given two important bits of information: (1) He responds with mild anxiety when he is challenged and is not impervious to the emotional interplay of the therapeutic relationship, and (2) furthermore, the phrase "if that's what it is" shows some recognition of and readiness for the possibility that his present treatment might be different and lead to different conclusions than he has been used to.

THERAPIST: Well, let's try to establish some of these details and see what we can learn. Next time I see you let me know where and when you tried to write, what you were trying to write, how far you got, what stopped you, if anything, and so on.
MR. ILGE (With a hint of sarcasm): Perhaps I should keep a diary.
THERAPIST (Enthusiastically, as if he had not caught the patient's tone): That's a good idea. I'd be interested to know how your day went.
MR. ILGE: What about the analysis? I thought I would be coming four times a week and free associating. Like before, only more intensive.
THERAPIST: Right now I think there is a lot more I need to learn about you before I can give you an opinion as to whether or not an analysis is necessary for you at this time. I think once a week will suffice until we can see where we are going.

MR. ILGE: I was seeing my other therapist twice a week.

THERAPIST: If you find that you get too uncomfortable between visits by all means let's meet more often. You have my phone number, just give me a call and we'll set something up before the next scheduled time. I was thinking that with a week between visits you would have plenty of opportunity to work at your papers and gather those observations that should be a great help in understanding what's going on with you.

I was in no hurry to begin psychoanalysis with Mr. Ilge after I heard what he had to say. First I wanted to see whether he might not respond well to psychotherapy, a form of treatment that, as far as I was concerned, had not been tried yet. What he had been exposed to in his various treatment situations was pseudopsychoanalysis. I knew better than to trust the so-called insights that had been obtained by using the memories available to the patient's consciousness and then superimposing psychoanalytic formulations on them. It was no surprise that his symptoms had not responded to these foredoomed though well-meant attempts at formulating what analysts call a genetic reconstruction. (It has amazed me that no one ever seems to ask those who teach that psychotherapy is to be conducted essentially as is a psychoanalysis why psychoanalysis remains necessary. If there is no difference between the results the two forms of treatment achieve and the methods they use, would it not make sense to treat everyone by the shorter, less demanding, and less expensive method? Of course it does not work that way. What happens is that students do not learn how to do psychotherapy and leave their training programs unprepared for the work that they are now certified as being able to do.)

My emphasis when I function as a psychotherapist is on activity, mine and the patient's. I will be actively searching for some answers and I expect to find them by exploring what the patient is *doing* to make himself unhappy. This attitude is quite different from the therapist's anticipatory belief that, apart from urging the patient to speak freely, he will have to wait relatively passively for the patient's associations to reveal what was *done* to him with the expectation that this discovery will prove curative.

As I encouraged Mr. Ilge to explore the manifest details of his symptom rather than jumping to the conclusion that it was symbolic of a repressed conflict in the area of infantile sexuality, I found that it was very difficult for him to do so. The reason that he had seemingly lent himself so well to the historical explorations that his former therapists had conducted was that he welcomed the order that this form of treatment imposed on his life. He found that whatever memories he had of his past were quickly and plausibly arranged by the therapists who presented him with meaningful connections between his past life and present problems. Left to his own devices to try to present a coherent picture of his daily activities he was unable to do so. Indeed on several occasions early in our meetings I had to find extra appointment times for him as he became anxious when he tried to sit down to organize his material for his thesis. Furthermore, he was truly unable to step back and look at his behavior and tell me about it. He would beg me to tell him what I wanted to know so he could comply with those wishes. His anxiety was such that I at first became extremely concrete with him and insisted he take me through his day beginning, literally, with how and when he got out of bed, the details of his toilet, what he ate for breakfast, and so on. Gradually he became able to talk about himself in an organized fashion. I encouraged him to tell me about his thesis, and, since I did not know very much about his field, continually asked him for clarification that would enable me to follow intelligently what he was saying.

It became clear to both of us that his supposed writing block was not a block to writing, for he had written some very nice papers as an undergraduate and his master's thesis was a very good review of the literature in a particular area. I knew that these papers were good because I had him bring them to me and discussed them with him after I had read them. What was troubling him now was that he was called on to do original work, in other words, to create an order for others to follow, where before he had always worked in the framework of a system created by others for him. Why this task should be so difficult was puzzling, but I encouraged him to use our sessions to talk about his work and helped him sort out limited goals that he could fulfill one at a time. Before this point he was wont to sit at his typewriter feeling the entire burden of his thesis descending on him. He would understandably panic when the sentence or two that he would write seemed to get him nowhere in terms of the total task that had to be accomplished. Through our discussions he was managing to do serviceable work, was able to prepare himself for the meetings that his adviser scheduled, and as far as his university department was concerned had overcome his scholastic difficulties. We of course realized that relieving as this situation was for him it was by no means the desired solution because his writing was still fraught with periods of anxiety and he clearly depended very much on me for the continuation of his productivity.

A turning point in the therapy came when I found myself unable to follow the patient in something he was saying about his work in one particular session. He casually mentioned a book that gave a nontechnical overview for the interested layman of the particular subject that we were discussing. Some weeks later when the topic came up again I was able to understand what he was saying, which surprised him. When I said that I had read the book he recommended and had enjoyed it, he burst out sobbing: "You really do care," he said. What came out then was an aspect of his life that he had long disavowed, that is known about intellectually but never dealt with emotionally. Throughout his youth he had been left to grow up more or less on his own. His mother's anxious concern and questioning was directed to the father whose every move was scrutinized to see what it portended for the family's future. Since these discussions usually ended in recriminations and quarrels, the patient was glad, in one way, that his activities did not come in for very much attention. It was expected that he would do well at school and somehow amuse himself when he was not in the classroom. He learned what life was like and what was expected of him by watching others and never had the opportunity to benefit from parental guidance, interest, or advice in any meaningful way. Following the experience with me he paid more attention to his relationships outside of therapy and found that the kind of interaction that we had was readily available to him in his relationships to friends and teachers. Interestingly, his relationship to his adviser became different and much more productive now that he was able to use his sessions with this professor much as he had learned to deal with me.

Mr. Ilge's treatment remained on the level of once- or twice-weekly psychotherapy, a psychoanalysis was not deemed necessary, and the patient ended treatment on his own initiative and on a positive note some 18 months after it had begun.

Forms of Psychotherapeutic Intervention

Our therapeutic efforts are guided and to a great extent determined by the theoretical outlook we bring to our practice. I have pointed out that the model of the treatment for the psychoneuroses is not universally applicable. Until recently, however, there was no dynamic theory that could guide us in the treatment of other disorders. Kohut's extension of the psychoanalytic method (1971, 1977, 1978), in which the development of a concept of self rather than instinctual discharge is central, has made possible the evolution of a theoretical framework that meets that need.

Kohut has shown how and why successful maturation depends on the opportunity and ability to interact in age-appropriate ways with parents and other mentors. Infants and children need their parent as much more than targets for their libidinal and aggressive needs. What becomes a person's self-esteem—his sense of cohesion and worthwhile-ness—is developed through empathic transactions with his parents. When parents' empathy for their child fails significantly, the result is defensive behavior with which the child seeks to protect himself from further frustration, hurt, disappointment, overstimulation, and so on. These defenses and their offshoots, if not satisfactorily resolved, later form the problematic aspects of an individual's character. If that person becomes a patient he will sooner or later reenact in some fashion with the therapist the trauma of his earlier years, usually in response to a real or imagined failure in the therapist's empathy. If the patient's sub-sequent defensive behavior is not treated as resistance but recognized for what it is, its examination can lead to an understanding of the earlier struggle that the patient is unsuccessfully trying to resolve in his present life.

Gedo and Goldberg (1973), using Kohut's concepts as a base, sug-gest a hierarchy of therapeutic interventions keyed to undoing the de-velopmental arrest evidenced by the form and content of patients' be-havior rather than to specific nosologic entities. These are: pacification, unification, optimal disillusionment, interpretation, and attainment of self-awareness.

Pacification, as the name suggests, is that situation in which the activity of the therapist is geared to protecting the patient from over-stimulation, just as an empathic mother soothes an overwrought infant. Patients will often tell us that it was the tone of our voice or the very fact that we spoke, regardless of what it was that we said, that helped them at a distressing time. Whatever may have been our intent, it was the pacifying component of our intervention that meant something to the patient. It was with that goal in mind that I took firm control of the initial interview with Mr Hoheit. His inappropriate, dictatorial pose, his nastiness and sarcasm made me think that behind the air of importance and the fine suit was a thoroughly frightened boy whose anger signaled his distress and need for outside control.

Unification, helping the patient just as a parent does a child to achieve a sense of order, helping him to see that he can function effectively to promote a sense of cohesion and reasonable self-esteem, was illustrated in the example of Mr. Ilge. As with Mr. Hoheit, the exploration and interpretation of the developmental failures that made this problem focal in the therapy could come only after the defect had been actively exposed and dealt with by the therapist.

One of the reasons that dynamic psychotherapy has proved itself generally effective is that though the therapists have operated within a theory that was too narrow, most patients managed, incidentally, to, extract pacification and unification when they were needed from the therapeutic situation and from the attentive, helpful, and supportive attitude of the therapist. It is patients like Mr. Hoheit and Mr. Ilge who cannot do so who become therapeutic failures unless the therapist can actively engage them on the level of their maturational arrest.

Optimal disillusionment consists of helping the patient face the often painful fact that the cause for his failure and unhappiness in life is to be found in his character and in his behavior patterns. This task involves exposing him to aspects of his character that he has disavowed, glossed over, or whose significance he has minimized.

Interpretation, that is, the explanation of the meaning of a patient's symptoms or difficulties, in psychotherapy fails if the patient is not suited for that type of treatment, if it is based on superficial data and therefore inaccurate, or if it is attempted prematurely. If the patient is ready to look at himself, interpretation, which links his transference experience to other events past and present, can promote insight and understanding of his behavior. Interpretation helps a patient see his life as a meaningful whole and gives him a sense of continuity. When successful, therapy leads to the patient's attainment of self-awareness, that is, the self-knowledge necessary to function effectively, without unnecessary anxiety and with some reasonable hope of attaining one's goals and enjoying that achievement.

An Example of Optimal Disillusionment

Many a therapeutic impasse stems from the need to confront a patient with his behavior rather than trying to interpret the meaning it has had for him in the past. Optimal disillusionment is an aspect of psychotherapy that is seldom taught in training programs, so it may be well to deal with it in more detail here. Unlike pacification and unification, optimal disillusionment is seldom an unplanned, serendipitous by-product of therapy and requires that the therapist recognize the need for such intervention and be prepared to act accordingly. It is preferable that one postpone such confrontation of the patient until (1) it is clear that he has committed himself to the therapy as fully as it is possible for him to do, and (2) his self-defeating behavior patterns are clearly displayed in his relationship with the therapist. If a patient has sufficient insight to recognize, though he cannot control it or necessarily identify it, that it is his behavior that is undermining his relationships, the therapist can help him in relatively straightforward fashion to face those aspects of his character that get him into difficulties. However, we run into resistance, that is, are potentially frustrated, when the patient's ability to look at himself with at least some objectivity is significantly impaired. This situation can arise with patients of all ages and with a variety of presenting symptoms. However, in my experience a certain group of adolescents shows it consistently and in dramatic form. I am thinking of a small, self-selected group of late adolescents who voluntarily present themselves for treatment by a psychotherapist. Usually they are from homes with better than average intellectual and socioeconomic credentials. Their parents are often successful members of the professional class—doctors, lawyers, academicians, or university-trained business executives—who themselves have made use of psychoanalytic or psychotherapeutic treatment at some time in their lives. In these families, at least outwardly, there is no shame about the idea of seeking help for emotional problems. The complaint of the adolescent children of such parents is also quite uniform: "I can't find myself," or some variant thereof. Their story is also a familiar and monotonous one told in a voice that is bitter and sarcastic, with overtones of self-pity. Their parents, they acknowledge, have done their best to give them a good home environment but they do not feel understood by them. They were reasonably successful in elementary and high school even though they could not get involved in their classes because they never had to study much to get good grades. They were always aware of an undercurrent of unhappiness, but no one was dissatisfied with them. College was started with no particular aim, but with the conviction that they definitely did *not* want to become whatever their fathers were. After a semester or so at a university they just didn't see the point of going on and dropped out for a year to experience "real life" in order to see if that would give them direction. Usually they show up for consultation when this sabbatical has not produced the desired results either. By this time they have apprenticed themselves serially to alcohol, marijuana, hard drugs, and various offshoots of Eastern religions. Their genital experiences have been alternately frenzied and indiscriminate or desperately monogamous, but, even if technically interesting, joyless and one might say "sexless."

Nothing has worked. As they recapitulate their life stories they remind me of nothing so much as those older patients who become depressed when they can no longer avoid facing what they believe to be the failure of their lives. And indeed the adolescents I am describing are depressed, though they are not sad. A few years ago I wrote an essay in which I argued for the idea that the common denominator of depression was not an affect but a condition of goallessness (Basch, 1975). In the case of these adolescents, unlike that of the older patients whose goals were relinquished because they seemed unattainable, goallessness represents an arrest in development.

The rebelliousness against the authority of parents and parent surrogates that one expects in early adolescence as a reaction to the implied demand that childhood is ending and that one must prepare to grow up has, for the patients I am describing, become an end in itself. Not surprisingly, their anger becomes the focus for therapy as they go to some length to detail the often admittedly difficult circumstances of their family life. Often their parents' marriage is a very unhappy one and there is no doubt that these adolescents have been burdened by the family pathology that is very evident beneath the veneer of tolerance and liberal thinking that their parents present to the outside world. If one does not make the mistake of attempting to deal interpretively with the content of the anamnesis, the material soon shifts to the beginnings of transference where opportunities for intervention arise. What is striking about these young people is their absolute conviction that their viewpoint is exemplary. That others might see things differently than they do without necessarily being incorrect is something that never occurs to them. What seems to have happened is that the cognitive transformation that takes place in adolescence and the newfound capacity for abstraction and hypothetical thought (Basch, 1977) has reinforced the infantile grandiosity of these patients thereby promoting the not unfamiliar arrogance and self-righteousness of adolescence. Naturally the therapist—if he has not aborted the transference by seeking to play either fatherly adviser or good buddy—is soon drawn into the adolescent's weltanschauung. The patient's grandiosity leads him into a mirror transference (Kohut, 1971) of a mixed sort, that is, his attitude conveys the expectation that the analyst of course shares his opinions, admires him, and is there to serve as a willing tool for whatever purpose the patient deigns to employ him. It is in this phase of the treatment that the crisis that determines the eventual outcome of the treatment occurs. The patient's sense of entitlement collides with the therapist's need to preserve his self. This collision is inevitable, because the only thing between the goalless patient and the apathy of melancholia is the pseudogoal of destruction, either self-destruction or the destruction of precisely those people who care enough about him to be hurt by him. As his parents were initially, now the therapist becomes the target of his helpless but quite painful thrashing about for some order in his universe even if it is cataclysmic. I have found that the crisis situation is usually one in which I am sufficiently in the wrong to permit the patient to self-righteously draw the sword of his grandiosity with every expectation that I am now at his mercy. (There is, by the way, nothing artificial or staged about such an episode. At the time that it happens, although by no means out of control, I really am affectively involved in maintaining my integrity vis-à-vis the patient.) It may be that I have been inattentive or given less time to his session than I ordinarily allot, or a series of such errors of omission or commission have taken place. In any event, the patient angrily and triumphantly calls me to task for my errors and it is clear that he seeks neither redress nor apology, our relationship has come to an end as far as he is concerned, but before leaving he demands the satisfaction of exposing me for a fraud, a hypocrite who does not live up to what he claims to be. At this point he clearly expects a denial from me, instead of which I acknowledge that he has been hurt by me and place the blame for the disappointment he has incurred squarely on his shoulders where it belongs. "Yes, I guess your incessant complaining has become boring and I probably don't want to listen to it anymore," I might say. Or, "Your uninformed diatribe about the inadequacies of psychotherapy is probably not something that I think is going to further your treatment," and so on, depending on what the bone of contention might be. Imposing oneself on such a patient as an individual rather than simply serving as an extension of his needs is a narcissistic blow to his grandiosity that is both necessary and salutary. The reason that the patient does not leave when he receives it is that the transference hunger is much too strong, as indicated by the fact that though right from the beginning of treatment he disparaged the adult world of which the doctor is clearly a part, his faithful attendance at sessions, his need to persuade the therapist to accept whatever point of view he was espousing, and so on, attest to his longing.

I am accustomed to seeing a fairly immediate and dramatic change in the course of the treatment following such an episode. Once he sees that he can depend on me to have a firm sense of self, his need to idealize a parental figure asserts itself and there is a corresponding diminution and maturation of his former compensatory and defensive grandiosity. It is an undeniably gratifying experience to see such a patient escape the stereotype that he fitted when he first came and become an individual, usually a very interesting one, in his own right. He passes fairly rapidly through an idealization of the therapist and then develops abstract goals of his own. It is these that give him a zest for life and mobilize resources he had not been aware of previously. Quite spontaneously the patient's capacity for empathy develops, manifested first in an ability to treat the therapist as an individual and then in the experience of understanding his parents quite differently than he had heretofore. Although he may be no less aware of what he feels are their shortcomings, he has a different relationship with them. Having ideals of his own he need not remain tied to his parents by accusations that carry the implicit unconscious wish that they change and by changing rescue him. He has changed and can let them lead their own lives. Interestingly, what frequently happens is that the patient, no longer afraid to admire what he values in his father, chooses to follow the profession of his parent. Once such a choice is made it is not uncommon to see genuine oedipal issues develop for the first time in the patient's life. The earlier failure in narcissistic development, not surprisingly, had precluded a normal oedipal period and attempts at its resolution. The whole issue of competitiveness, fear of punishment for one's temerity, and so on is now played out in fairly typical form in the treatment where it can be resolved by interpretation. (There were a few women patients that I treated who fell into this category; they too chose to follow the occupation of their fathers. No conclusion can be drawn from this fact since it so happened that in my sample these female patients' mothers were housewives who resented their position and were glad to see their daughters prepare themselves for a career outside the home. However, these patients did not reject the possibility of having and caring for a family and saw no opposition between femininity and professionalism.)

Basing themselves on the model of the treatment of psychoneurotic patients for whom a neutral, inquiring stance is sufficient to permit mobilization of the transference neurosis, therapists are often reluctant to appear critical, judgmental, or emotionally affected in their work. But there are many patients who demonstrate by their behavior that the therapist's neutrality is experienced by them as disinterest, weakness, or ineptitude. Often the product of parents who were insecure about their own life choices and, therefore, unprepared or unwilling to serve either as models for their children or as targets for their needs for idealized and idealizable objects, the patients I have been discussing seek and require a period of what Freud called *Nacherziehung*, a belated opportunity to complete their upbringing. Their self-justification, their blaming of the past for their present difficulties, even if historically accurate, becomes an evasion of the primary therapeutic issue—the need to look at what is going on today. The resistant patient in this category is usually one who has learned early in life that by ferreting out the weakness, sensitivities, and corruptions of the adults around him he can manipulate and forestall being called to account for his own behavior. This strategy gives him a sense of power and feeds his grandiosity, but leaves him isolated, unhappy, and afraid of his own impulses which no one seems able to control. Of necessity he will play the same game with the therapist and usually expertly. It is important for the therapist to acknowledge to himself and to the patient that the latter may be quite correct in some criticism of the therapist but that that does not put him in command of the relationship. It is important for patients to learn that one no more needs or is entitled to a perfect therapist than one needs or was entitled to a perfect parent. In the process the patient learns that he too need not be perfect. He finds out that one can be flawed, sometimes irremediably so, without being worthless or excluded from reasonable happiness and satisfaction.

Summary and Conclusion

Genetic interpretation appropriate for the treatment of psychoneurotic problems not unexpectedly results in therapeutic failure when applied to patients suffering from developmental disturbances. What happens then is that the patient's lack of response and/or improvement is called resistance. In this way resistance, originally an indicator of intrapsychic conflict, has become a relatively meaningless euphemism for the therapist's frustration. However, if the therapist can let the patient guide him in his exploration he will become aware of a much wider range of development and developmental problems than can be dealt with in the framework of a theory that views all pathology in terms of the oedipal conflict and the vicissitudes of infantile sexuality. The therapist's liberation from an unnecessarily narrow viewpoint regarding his role and his therapeutic goals resolves many a therapeutic impasse.

Genuine resistance is to be expected sooner or later as part of every therapeutic effort geared to examining and restructuring a patient's basic perception of himself and the world around him. When it arises, however, it should not be seen as a sign of therapeutic failure, but as a resistance to therapeutic progress that has made the possibility of change a reality and aroused anxiety. The confrontation, examination, and resolution of that anxiety, which manifests itself as a resistance to therapy, can then become the focus of treatment. In the process the patient's resistance to examining himself usually ceases to be a source of frustration for the therapist and, rather than its nemesis, becomes, as Freud originally suggested it was, a guide to therapeutic activity.

References

Basch, M. F. Toward a theory that encompasses depression: A revision of existing causal hypotheses in psychoanalysis. In E. J. Anthony & T. Benedek (Eds.), *Depression and human existence*. Boston: Little, Brown, 1975.

Basch, M. F. Developmental psychology and explanatory theory in psychoanalysis. *The Annual of Psychoanalysis*, 1977, 5, 229–263.

Basch, M. F. *Doing psychotherapy*. New York: Basic Books, 1980.

Gedo, J. E., & Goldberg, A. *Models of the mind*. Chicago: University of Chicago Press, 1973.

Kohut, H. *The analysis of the self*. New York; International Universities Press, 1971.

Kohut, H. *The restoration of the self*. New York: International Universities Press, 1977.

Kohut, H.*The search for the self: Selected writings (1950–1978)* (P. H. Ornstein, Ed.). New York: International Universities Press, 1978.

Murray, J. M. Narcissism and the ego ideal. *Journal of the American Psychoanalytic Association*, 1964, 12, 477–511.

2

Resistance as Process

Herbert J. Schlesinger

As a longtime libertarian, I find myself from time to time in the position of supporting an unpopular cause, taking up the cudgels for some concept fallen from popular esteem or misidentified among the public enemies. Thus I rose to the defense of denial and proposed that this maligned mechanism is actually one of man's best friends. I now champion the cause of all of denial's associates, its alleged partners in crime, the members of the "resistance" gang who are alleged to oppose the good works of the analytic establishment.

Why defend resistance? It is certainly not an underdog; it sometimes even seems to threaten to take over all of psychotherapy. Is it not true that if it were not for resistance psychoanalysis would take no time at all, therapists would not be so frustrated by their hard work, and third-party payers would smile on psychotherapy? In short, is not resistance to blame for all that is difficult, painful, unpleasant, and expensive about psychotherapy and psychoanalysis? Are we not entitled, even obligated, to "break through," undermine, avoid, or hypnotize away resistance? How could we treat a patient without "neutralizing" his resistances?

Perhaps I can explain my paradoxical stand in the form of a summary of my main points and at the same time offer some definitions:

1. What therapists commonly call resistance is behavior that manifestly opposes what the patient believes the therapist wants to

---

Herbert J. Schlesinger • Denver V. A. Medical Center, Department of Psychiatry, University of Colorado School of Medicine, Denver, Colorado 80262.

do or wants to happen. Obvious examples are a patient's prolonged silence, refusal to talk about what the therapist wants to
hear, coming late or not all all. But these flagrant "misbehaviors,"
though they certainly involve resistance, are not the most common forms of resistance or even the most important ones. Resistance is not a sometimes thing, not an event, but is a process
constantly operative in ways that do not usually call attention to
its presence. These more subtle forms of defending are far more
important in shaping the process of psychotherapy than the more
egregious forms.

2. What do we mean then by resistance? A comprehensive and
   nonpejorative definition is that *resistance is defense expressed in the
   transference.* This simple definition, which I owe to Gill (1981),
   has a host of important theoretical and technical implications. It
   implies that resistance as an expression of defense is a function
   of the ego, though issues of drive and fear of punishment may
   inspire defensiveness and hence resistance. The usual understanding is that when defense is expressed in the transference
   as resistance, the patient externalizes one side of an unconscious
   conflict and acts out the conflict with the therapist. He reenacts
   the unconscious fantasy rather than remembering it. At such
   times the therapist may seem to the patient to be his enemy and
   the process between them an adversary one. The situation becomes even more complicated when the therapist yields to the
   temptation to play out the role created for him by the patient.

   Defense is not always expressed in the transference in such
   noisy and flagrant ways. Nor is the only pattern of interaction
   of patient and therapist in transference an adversarial one. The
   motive of defense can be expressed quite subtly in behavior in
   such a way that it does not call attention to itself; it operates
   synergistically with other motives subsumed under adaptation.
   The therapist may be led to acquiesce in these more subtle forms
   of defense expressed in the transference as effectively as he may
   be led to aquiesce in the oppositional forms by colluding with
   the patient, unwittingly acting out some complementary, though
   not necessarily adversarial, role in the patient's unconscious
   transference fantasy such as taking an approving maternal role
   or basking in the patient's idealizing fantasy.

Much of what follows will be an exposition with illustrations of these more subtle forms of defense and resistance, but the principles apply equally to the noisier forms.

3. What then do we *do* about resistance? The question is put in a misleading way since it suggests that we *must do* something about resistance, obviously to prevent it, get it out of the way, undermine it, or in other ways confirm the transference position given us by the patient to serve as his enemy, one who threatens him. But recognizing that the patient is resisting should at the very least tell us that the patient is frightened. Something has just happened that intimates threat. Thus to the therapist resistance should be no more a nuisance or inconvenience than is pain to a physician when it occurs in the course of a physical examination. Both the resistance and the pain tell the doctor that something important is going on in that area. We are therefore interested in resistance and would like to know more about it, why the patient needs to behave in that way. Note the paradox: Although the resisting patient may be attempting to thwart us, to withhold information, to deny cooperation, or more subtly to avoid collaborating in the therapeutic task, the resisting patient is also conveying a good deal of information and in a larger sense is fully cooperating in the treatment. Since our major premise is that the patient does not fully know what the problem is, cannot remember but is forced to repeat, the behavior we call resistance is part of that repetition and is his way of communicating with the therapist through reenactment. Rather than being dismayed by resistance, the therapist might well welcome it. The technical problem is how to help the patient communicate more effectively whether through resistance or otherwise. Certainly all therapists are prepared to empathize with the patient's feeling of anxiety and hence with his need to resist. It is only a step further, but a most important one, to desist from feeling, "I suppose the patient feels it necessary to act that way, but I do wish he would stop it" to feeling instead, "Since he has to act in that way perhaps I can help him communicate with me through this odd and painful behavior so that we can come to understand it better." I shall call this stance "going along with the resistance."

In what follows I shall first discuss the idea of process as it applies to neurosis, transference, and resistance and then discuss some forms of resistance that occur in response to a therapist's intervention. I shall

illustrate some forms of resistance that are not expressed by open oppositional behavior but that operate by subtly interfering with the cognitive, the affective, or the action components of a response to a therapist's interpretation or intervention. In regard to the technical handling
of resistance, I shall discuss the problems of diagnosing the nature and
purpose of the resistance and then ways of working *with* rather than
against resistance.

Neurosis as Process

We speak of neurosis being present when a significant portion of
one's personality resources is devoted to purposes of defense against
unrealistic dangers. Like personality itself, neurosis can be thought of
as a conservative organization. Like any bureaucracy it is concerned first
with its own preservation, though long ago the neurotic patterns ceased
to serve any useful function. All bureaucracies resist change and so does
a neurosis. The prospect of change itself, of whatever kind, seems
dangerous.

Although the patient brings himself to a therapist saying he wants
help, his concept of help is generally not that of the therapist. The patient
wants relief from pain, inconvenience, the heavy expense that his neurosis entails. He does not essentially want to change or to give up the
neurosis and most often would be happy to pay off the therapist the
way he pays off his superego to let him retain the primary and secondary
gains of illness. Much of the course of any treatment can be viewed as
a patient's effort to bring the treatment into the neurosis, to force the
therapist to play a role in the "scenario" of the patient's unconscious
fantasy and thus to reduce the danger that the therapist's ability to act
independently might threaten the continuation of the patient's style of
life. It is only the uncomfortable portions of this style of life that the
patient is willing to recognize as his "illness." This process of including
the therapist and therapy in the neurosis we call transference and acting
(out) in the transference. It is also, clearly, a resistance.

The patient tries to present the neurosis as something he *has*,
whereas the therapist's objective is to try to show the patient that it is
not what he has but what he *does*. The neurosis is not an albatross that
hangs around the patient's neck but is something the patient recreates
constantly, day by day in his life, and minute by minute in the therapeutic situation as well. Paradoxically, it is this recreation of the neurosis
in the therapeutic situation, that is, in the transference, this major resistance, that gives the therapist his major leverage to help the patient

think, feel, and *do* differently. The field of the treatment is the therapeutic situation, chiefly the transference.

Although the transference is an expression of resistance, primarily resistance against change, it is also the only way in which the patient can communicate what he cannot remember. As he repeats and reenacts his conflicts and neurotic solutions of them, he provides himself and the therapist important information about the reasons why he feels it is necessary to do so. The transference repetition, motivated mostly by the patient's need to defend himself and resist change, also sets up an *in vivo* situation in which the therapist can make a difference in the patient's life because he has become part of it.

Thus neurosis is best thought of not as a static entity but as a process, a way of relating to oneself internally and, through transference, to others externally.

Neurosis is constantly being recreated and repeated. Repetition is the essence of neurosis. From this point of view the role of the therapist is to *participate* in these acts of continuous recreation and by judicious interventions to permit the patient more choice than he previously has experienced because he has achieved greater awareness of what he is doing.

Transference as Process

Like neurosis, transference is generally spoken of as if it were a state. We say or think, "this *is* transference." In what sense then should we consider it a process? The term "process" of course implies that time is a major dimension of whatever is under consideration. To refer to transference as process says at the very least that it does not stand still. In fact we do expect change in transference, change that implies development, growth, and unfolding. The term "process" implies a history, a past and a future.

All therapists agree that transference changes, but by this we usually mean that its content changes. The transference paradigm changes. It is customary, if not particularly useful, to speak for example, of "mother transference" or "father transference," or positive and negative transference. These crude labels which do imply shifts in the person's repertoire of transferences, fall under the heading of what I will call the content of transference.

More important for our present discussion is the current *function* of transference, which Freud early suggested (1912/1958) is resistance. But our awareness that the purpose of retaining or restoring the "familiar" and preventing new and potentially painful experiences is largely defensive should not lead us to ignore that these motives could serve adaptation as well. In our professional usage transference has become almost totally identified with psychopathology, by definition maladaptive. Indeed, part of the usual definition of transference is the word "inappropriate," but that cannot be the entire story.

Clinical experience, to say nothing of common sense, tells us that much of the time transference is quite adaptive. The very need to invent the psychotherapeutic and psychoanalytic situations derives from having to contrive situations in which the maladaptive and inappropriate aspects of transference can be highlighted. For most of us much of the time, transference and reality testing function synergistically. Transference plays a large part in everyday behavior. Much of the way we behave in unfamiliar situations is based on our previous experience. Our inclination to regard strangers as well intentioned or malevolent draws as much from infantile experience and unconscious fantasy as it does from current experience and logical deduction. We constantly construe the present and future in terms of our past. To do otherwise would be to abrogate memory.

It is important to consider transference as a process not only because its content shifts and its dominant affective tone shifts, but also because its mode of expression shifts from verbalization to autonomic expression to action, and its purposes shift. In fact, transference is so responsive to the state of arousal of unconscious fantasy and the opportunities and dangers of the therapeutic situation that it is fair to say that another major function of transference is to serve as a medium of communication. It is a way for the patient to tell about his fantasies, wishes, fears, and dilemmas that he cannot express in any other way than through reenactment. Thus transference, like the neurosis it expresses, is not a static condition but a constantly changing process.

Resistance as Process

If resistance is defense expressed in the transference, is there anything we can say about resistance that we could not just as easily say about transference? Indeed, a discussion of the therapeutic and technical issues involved in transference would also be a discussion of resistance.

But although there is great overlap of transference and resistance as concepts, the terms are not fully interchangeable. To maintain clarity, I prefer to use these terms not to describe kinds of behavior or categories of phenomena, but as points of view toward behavioral phenomena. Thus we could describe the behavior of a patient from the point of view of transference and from the point of view of resistance. At times the two discussions might overlap a great deal; at other times they might be different enough to be mutually illuminating. The overlap is greatest when we are considering gross transference disturbances, transference crises, episodes of acting out in the transference, flagrant examples of oppositional behavior, and the like. But recall that transference can also be adaptive and that much of the time transference and reality testing function synergistically. The self-preservative needs of the neurosis can often be accommodated without calling attention to themselves through flagrant opposition and without egregiously disrupting smooth, reality-oriented functioning. There are times when the function of defense expressed in the transference, the resisting, is accomplished without making it at all obvious what, if anything, is being transferred. If a therapist is queried at such a time he may respond that at the moment "the alliance" seems dominant and the therapy is proceeding smoothly "without resistance."

It is one of my articles of faith, or at least a heuristic assumption, that in psychotherapy defense and transference and hence resistance are *always* present. To draw an analogy from the late, late show if the "resistance" wants to prevent a train from reaching its destination, it is not necessary to blow up a bridge. It may be enough to throw a switch the wrong way, to bribe the conductor, to mislabel some cars, or to uncouple them. The most economical way for the underground to function is to achieve maximum disruption of the enemy with minimum exposure. The best resistance is the one you do not see. So it is in psychotherapy: Resistance can most effectively operate to prevent change by subtly interfering with just one of the components of change. The kind of change we mean in psychotherapy or psychoanalysis is intrapsychic change, structural change. Psychic change, which, broadly speaking, corresponds with changes in the meanings of the major events of one's life, in the significance of relationships, and in ways of solving problems, generally is the outcome of an interpretive process. The therapist will observe the patient's response in the course of the interpretive process to see if the hoped-for result is occurring: Has the nature and direction and patterning of the patient's associations changed, has his mood or affect tone changed, has his behavior inside and outside the therapeutic situation changed in other ways? Note the three expressive modalities to which the therapist must attend. A complete response by the patient must involve all three, cognition, affect, and action. The relationship among these modalities, these forms in which communication can be cast, is complex. Although classical theory favors the sequence: interpretation–insight–affect–behavioral change, in actuality any of the three may lead.

Therapists soon learn to be suspicious of a patient's reaction to interpretation that is only in words. Words without feelings are likely to imply the defenses of intellectualizing or isolation. We tend to be less suspicious of a wordless affective response, at least at first; but we soon learn that affectualizing can also be a formidable resistance. Words with appropriate affect carry greater conviction, as well they might, for they generally lead to appropriate action. My point at the moment is that the therapist's diagnostic attention following an intervention should turn to the patient's response. This assessment of the need for further intervention—for follow-up interpretation—will be determined by the completeness of the patient's response to the earlier interpretation.

Let us first consider resistance operating in the cognitive realm, since it may be harder to detect than resistance against affect or action.

In the cognitive realm, defense is most often accomplished by rather subtle acts of isolation—breaking the connection between ideas which then can remain in consciousness since their relatedness and implications are not obvious. One can demonstrate this phenomenon in clinical material to show that the work of defense and "synthesis" can go hand in hand so that the content of thought does not look as if it has been censored. There are no gross gaps to be seen; subtle shifts in emphasis and the obscuring of relationships accomplish the work of defense.

Correspondingly, the work of interpretation is to restore the sense of relatedness that has been removed by defense. The most common way for this task to be accomplished is for the therapist to summarize his understanding of what the patient has been telling him. In doing so he condenses the patient's verbiage. In the therapist's boiled-down version, the patient's major ideas are much closer together. Their interrelationships thus become more obvious and their collective impact correspondingly greater. Listening to the therapist "say the same thing" also makes the ideas seem more real and more "objective" to the patient. The fact that some time elapses between the patient first saying something and the therapist's summary may also diminish the patient's defensiveness, as what is being heard and considered is now not totally new or fresh.

The patient's acts of defensive "disjunction" are accomplished by separating the elements of a sentence with time and with indifferent material. In effect the patient has avoided making some meaning clear by removing conjunctions. Thus an interrupted series of associations can be diagramed as A_____ B_____ C_____ A_____, and so on. The blanks stand for the defensively inserted "filler" material. The work of interpretation may be accomplished by the therapist's summarizing and replacing the missing conjunctions. Thus, as he says to the patient, "It sounds as if you are telling me that you feel A *because* of B *instead of* C and *therefore* feel quite justified about A."

There are, of course, other ways for resistance to operate in the cognitive realm. The whole range of cognitive abilities can be used for purposes of defense. In general these methods deal less with the content than with the formal aspects of the patient's communication. Doubting and reasonable weighing of alternatives can easily serve resistance. As each side of a conflict is given balanced expression the net movement averages out to zero. A move in one direction is countered by a move in the opposite direction, a yes by a no, a wish by a fear, a promising idea is neutralized by a doubt. There are instances when these modes of defense seem obviously pathological as when the paralyzed obsessional or schizophrenic patient shows classic ambivalence. For most of the patients we see in psychotherapy these dramatic states of affairs do not obtain; the intrusion of defensive purposes is more subtle and the needs of defense are synthesized for the most part with the needs of adaptation and make up what Shapiro (1965) has called neurotic styles. Thus, unless the therapist is especially attuned to it, he is likely to overlook these expressions of resistance, though he may feel put off, or bored, or otherwise made to feel ineffectual.

Let us next consider resistance operating in the affective realm. Among the ways that both sides of a conflict may be expressed so as to conceal the fact that there are conflicting forces at work is by expressing the conflict in some formal way rather than through content. A common way is for a patient to express the conflict not *in* what he says but *between* what he says and the way he says it. To say something with an affective tone that does not fit the content permits one to say something and to unsay it at the same time. In the most extreme form of this kind of resistance we speak of patients showing inappropriate affect. We call milder forms irony or sarcasm. Consider the following example:

The patient is a woman in her late thirties with several children who presented for marital discord and intermittent child abuse and who also carries the clearly unwarranted diagnosis of schizophrenia for which she has been overmedicated. In the course of psychotherapy she begins to show pattern of externalizing conflict in a way that also arouses anxiety in the therapist. She speaks at a very rapid pace, seeming to require very little input from the therapist, and describes events in her life of vastly different levels of significance for herself, for others, and for her treatment as if they were all of the same importance. As the therapist listens and tries to grasp what the patient is telling him he finds himself getting irritated and anxious, feeling controlled as he hears the patient run down her laundry list of daily events interspersed with allusions to having pulled her daughter's hair or having struck her son. The affective "leveling" of these communications, telling them as if one were no more important than others serves to externalize the patient's problem and leads the therapist to have the anxiety and concern that the patient should have.

One could say here that the resistance is toward awareness on the part of the patient that she has a problem, or that she is trying more or less unconsciously to deal with it by concealing it from the therapist. We could also say that the resistance is against changing, which might come about should she allow herself to be fully aware of her feelings about what she is saying and to take responsibility for her actions. We could speak also of resistance to reinternalizing the conflict, and resistance to experiencing the pain that would surely be present if she would have to face the consequences of her actions and their effects on her self-image and self-esteem. Helping the patient express her conflict in ways less destructive to herself and to her relationships would involve first of all helping the patient slow down her rate of communication so that she could listen to herself. It would also involve the therapist's making use of the anxiety evoked in himself to help the patient see that the *way* she tells him about these things is important and seems to serve some function for her. These issues could be approached in any number of ways once the therapist senses what it is the patient is doing to herself and to him and the way she does it. The therapist must also, of course, appreciate the legitimacy of what the patient is trying to do and help her to do it. He must *go with* the resistance, that is, help her defend herself to the extent that she needs it, hopefully in less expensive and destructive ways.

It is important that the therapist carefully observe what the patient does about a new awareness (or a new affect, for that matter) to see whether he intends it to lead somewhere or intends it to be complete in itself. These antinomies are never complete; it is never totally one or the other. If the therapist is alert to these possibilities, he will sense the degree to which an interpretation leads to a complete response and continuing change or has merely forced some accommodation from the neurosis.

This issue has often been discussed in terms of a flaw in the gaining of insight. Insight may be disparaged as "pseudo-insight" if it is not accompanied by appropriate feelings or seems to serve resistance by not leading to action. The terms "pseudo-insight" or "intellectual insight" wrongly fault insight because it is *only* insight. The fault is not with the insight but in the failure to act on it.

In analyzing this state of affairs it is important that the therapist not fall into the trap of considering the insight "ungenuine" because the patient has "chosen" to do nothing about it. It is far more useful to recognize that the patient has again accomplished a neurotic solution and has managed to have his cake and eat it too by stopping his response short of action. This solution draws on a capacity that was highly useful in early childhood when good intentions or saying "I understand" were enough to put an end to a state of tension between parent and child. We should also consider that inaction may be a form of acting—a quiet way of saying no. The idea that a promise is the *beginning* of a process of performance rather than the equivalent of an apology that puts an end to an unsatisfactory state of affairs is a later developmental achievement (Schlesinger, 1978). It is a task for follow-up interpretation to help the patient see the ways in which he tries to ignore insight, to quietly sabotage the possibilities of change. The therapist must interpret the ways in which the patient tries to include the new within the old, or makes an empty concession by saying "yes, but," or makes room for the insight in the neurosis rather than seizing the implication that the neurotic system itself could change. What I am proposing also fits with the concept of interpretation as a process rather than a one-shot affair.

It is important that the therapist be ready to diagnose the patient's response to an interpretation and ready to interpret that response both in its positive and negative aspects, that is, to interpret the ways in which the patient makes use of what he has learned and the ways in which he tries to ignore what he has learned, to say in effect there is nothing new to that and I, therefore, need do nothing about it. By approaching the art of interpretation in this way, the therapist will avoid making the mistake of damning the insight as ungenuine or intellectual.

Instead he will see that the problem is one of a neurosis struggling to survive and a patient needing help to extricate himself from the old while fearful of the new.

Let us now consider resistance expressed against the action component of response. One of the general goals of all psychotherapy is to promote a patient's own activity in therapy. A major style of resisting is to avoid becoming active. A major task for interpretation and follow-up interpretation is to promote activity in this sense.

By "action" I mean first of all a conscious effort by the patient to become active in relation to the interpretation, to grapple with the new idea, to test its truth and make it his own or modify it or reject it. A very common resistance takes the form of silent refusal to act in this way masked by a willingness to "assume the truth" of the interpretation; "I suppose you're right, Doctor . . . ." The therapist must be prepared to follow up his original interpretation to include the resistances the patient erects to avoid taking account of the interpretation, to avoid having any feelings about it, to avoid acting on it, or to avoid letting it act on him.

Readers who have patients who are themselves psychotherapists may have noticed an interesting sidelight to the question of action in response to interpretation. Frequently such "professional patients" manage to put their insights into action via their own patients. One of the first signs that something is getting through to such a patient may be the report that *his* patients unaccountably are getting better. Sometimes the patient is quite aware that he is serving as a "middleman" between his analyst and his own patients, trying out the analyst's advice on a guinea pig, as it were, before using it himself. Other professional patients may treat the analyst's interpretations as "export goods," not intended for domestic consumption. Here the pattern of resistance is clear—wisdom is allowed to skip a generation and the patient's patient is nominated to be the surrogate actor. The interpretation, "You seem to be able to help your patient to do what you yourself find impossible" can have considerable impact.

I do not want to be understood as making a univocal plea for action in psychotherapy. Although I believe it is axiomatic that insight must be confirmed through action and that action is essential to test out the truth of insight, I recognize that action can also serve the purposes of resistance. A patient's flight into health is one example. Another common form is a patient's tendency to derive a suggestion to act from an interpretation and to demonstrate willingness to act on the implications of the therapist's words before they have actually been understood or evaluated to test their truth. Such behavior implies, "I do not want to understand, accept, and be responsible for that idea as my own; I would rather act on the therapist's suggestion and let him be responsible. And if it doesn't work, it will be his fault."

Since resisting implies holding back, it may seem paradoxical that leaping ahead or acting prematurely can also serve the purpose of resisting. But as a reminder, if resisting can be said to have to do with preventing change by inhibiting or exaggerating one of the three components, then perhaps it becomes clearer that by leaping ahead, by acting prematurely, the patient can prevent a full response for which he might then have to feel responsible.

Consider the following example:

> A patient responds to a therapist's interpretation with increased tension, saying, "You mean that the reason I am so cool to my wife when I get home from work is that I resent her easy life, the kind of life my mother used to have, and that it reminds me of how exploited my father used to seem—she hasn't had to suffer all day at the office, she just waits around for me to come home and take care of her needs. Well if that's the way it is, it's silly, I don't have to behave that way. When I get home this evening I will be nice to her."

This vignette could be used to illustrate resisting on several counts. (1) The patient treats the idea as still belonging to the therapist. It is not his idea but someone else's. (2) He does not reflect on it to see if it fits with his own experience, if it makes sense, and if therefore he could make it his own. (3) Instead he prefers to assume it to be true, as a kind of hypothesis, (4) yet he declares his willingness to act on the untested and unproven idea as if the idea, if true, would of its own power change things. The patient thus leaps ahead to put into action, at least in fantasy during the hour, an idea whose implications he has not stopped to examine. He has explored neither its cognitive nor affective significance though, as we noted, he seemed to become more tense. We might presume that the therapist's interpretation made him anxious and he deals with his anxiety with seeming compliance, making of the interpretation an order or suggestion to do something different out there. His rushing ahead to fantasy applying the therapist's idea thus expresses his resistance to testing the idea fully, making it his own, and acting accordingly if it suits his purpose. Premature action, or talk about it, thus serves resisting.

The therapist could intervene at this point and make use of any portion of the analysis of the event thus far laid out. I do not mean that it does not matter what the therapist does at this point but instead that there are insufficient indications in the example as given to select among interventions that could include for example, "Something about what I just said made you anxious," or, "It seems easier for you to put that idea into action than to consider it long enough to see whether it makes sense to you," among other possibilities.

The usual advice in regard to characterological defenses and styles that seem to serve the purpose of resisting is to "confront" the patient with his (mis)behavior. In recent years confrontation, although never an innocuous term, has acquired an overburden of connotations. We now have the "politics of confrontation," which in its most frightening form becomes "international chicken." Confrontation, in this usage, connotes an adversarial relationship. Unwelcome information is to be thrust on an unwilling recipient.

It is a natural desire for the therapist to want to make the patient aware of what he has just discovered, for example, that the patient is using his intellectual resources and characterological habits more or less unwittingly to "sabotage" his treatment. And so he says something like: "Have you noticed that every time I offer an idea about what might be going on, you shrug it off?", or, "Each time you consider a plausible solution to the problem, you find a reason to doubt it would work."

These "classical" confrontations of resistance not infrequently "work," in the sense that if the patient's anxiety is not too high he may be intrigued enough to stop and look at his behavior. But this description of the process conceals the problem with this approach. The confrontation stops the patient; he is now expected to attend to the therapist's observation that he was doing something he possibly was unaware of doing, with the implication that he should not have been doing it and should therefore now desist. Of course it makes a huge difference how confrontations, as all interventions, are worded and expressed and also what the state of the therapist–patient relationship is. When the manner of intervention conveys little hostility or condescension and the state of the relationship is largely trusting and cooperative, such interventions can be quite helpful. These needed conditions, however, suggest the point I am trying to make. Certain inherent tendencies in this technical approach must be overcome by therapist and/or patient for the intervention to "work."

We can derive an alternative approach by considering resistance and interpretation as processes. If we assume that the patient's behavior is serving some needed purpose, that the patient is doing "the best he can" in the conflicted circumstances in which he finds himself, then to "point out" what he is doing with the inevitable implication that he should not be doing it is contrary to this way of understanding his behavior. An alternative way can be derived from awareness that the patient's defenses are being expressed in the transference in order to control the behavior of the therapist, that is, of the transference object. Often it is the therapist's discomfort at being in this position that inspires a confrontation. The patient is reenacting an unconscious scenario in which the therapist is also assigned a role. The therapist tries to relieve the sense of impotence that results from feeling forced to play a role not of his own choosing. In confronting the patient, I believe the therapist's motive, at least in part, is to try to break out of the assigned transference position—usually an uncomfortable position of ineffectuality, though other painful positions are not uncommon.

The key concept underlying the alternative approach is the "therapeutic split" the therapist must continuously cultivate in himself. He must be able to allow the patient to communicate his problems by molding the transference object and he must allow himself to be sufficiently plastic that the patient can reenact his conflicts in the transference to a useful degree. At the same time the therapist must keep part of himself split off, uninvolved in the transference reenactment, and able to observe the interaction between patient and transference figure from various vantage points. Chiefly, the therapist views the interaction from over the patient's shoulder—viewing the transference figure as the patient sees him. From this viewpoint the therapist can empathize with the patient's fears and his need for the defenses he expresses in the resistance. Since the patient who is resisting is preoccupied with threat and defense, the therapist will want to assist him by empathizing with him in his difficulty with the transference figure, not by educating, cajoling, or scolding him out of it.

The alternative way I am proposing, to go *with* the resistance rather than oppose it, may sound paradoxical, but it is derived from the larger view of psychotherapy as a process and the general principles to begin where the patient is, to facilitate the expression of what the patient is trying to say, to work from the surface, to deal with defenses against affects and affects before everything else, and to allow the patient to be as active as possible in his treatment. Going with the resistance answers each of these requirements and permits a sympathetic exploration of the

resistance, its sources in unconscious transference fantasy, and its pre-
cipitants in the proximal events in the psychotherapy. In the course of
this process, the patient also has an opportunity to test the reality of the
unconscious fantasy and the necessity for his defensiveness. It is thus
an advantage that much of the interpretive work in this approach can
be done by the patient and much of it can be done in metaphor. Let us
compare the two approaches when defense is couched in metaphorical
communication that expresses the patient's resistance against recognizing his involvement in transference. From the point of view of the transference, the advice to "go with the resistance" could be paraphrased as
"stay in the metaphor."

> A therapist described an incident toward the beginning of the
> treatment of a young man whom he does not regard as particularly
> "psychologically minded" and who is getting progressively more
> dissatisfied with his treatment. Although the therapist believes he
> is being very active in helping the patient, the patient does not
> experience it that way and feels he is expected to "do all the work"
> while the therapist "just sits there." The therapist feels the patient
> has one foot out the door and he is afraid the patient might become
> so irritated as to quit.
>   In the course of one hour which falls well within this description,
> the patient lapsed into a disgusted silence. After a while he said that
> he had to tell the therapist a story about something that happened
> to him just the other day. At his job he has been very angry with
> his boss who pushes him and everyone else around. He feels he
> wants to speak up to his boss, but after all the guy is the boss and
> he has the right to act like one. But he sure would like to tell him
> off. The therapist told the supervisor that he tried to "interpret" the
> patient's story and had succeeded in showing him a series of cor-
> respondences that finally led the patient to agree that he probably
> was trying to say something about the therapist, although this grudg-
> ing acknowledgment had no particular effect on his mood, attitude,
> or anything else.

In presenting this case, the therapist had not noticed that the differences
between the "story" and the patient's overt feelings about the therapy
and therapist were even more impressive than the similarities. Whereas
he was complaining that the therapist was inactive and silent and made
him do all the talking, his complaint about the boss was that he was so
authoritarian that the patient was afraid to speak up at all. Although it
seems a safe assumption that the patient's story expressed and made
use of transference, direct correspondences are not all that obvious. One

might infer that the patient *would like* to make the same complaint about the therapist as he does about his boss, that he *feels* pushed around, but it seems the therapist's behavior does not sufficiently justify this complaint. Perhaps that is why the patient is so silent. Perhaps the need for this "story" is that it permits the patient to make his complaint without violating his sense of reality. To follow the advice implied in this analysis of the situation, it might have been useful for the therapist first to facilitate the patient's willingness to express his irritation verbally through metaphor and to empathize with the displaced expression of transference rather than attempting to "translate it," that is, to remove the disguise as a first step. The interchange might then have gone as follows:

THERAPIST: It must be galling not to be able to tell your boss what you think.
PATIENT: Yes, I get so mad I feel like quitting and I would if I didn't need the job. Sometimes I feel it's not worth it. A man shouldn't have to put up with that.
THERAPIST: If a man can't speak up when he wants to, he may not feel like a man.
PATIENT: That's right! I quit the last job I had when I began to feel that way. I wish I could afford to do the same thing now. *(Patient looks pensive and is silent, his thoughts seeming to be elsewhere.)*
THERAPIST: Something about what you just said makes you a bit thoughtful.
PATIENT: Yes, I was just wondering about another job that was offered to me, but I didn't take it because that boss also looked like he might be trouble.
THERAPIST: I guess each time you get into a new situation you have to wonder whether the boss will make trouble for you. *(Patient looks thoughtful again but not withdrawn.)* I guess you can hardly help but wonder if the same thing might happen here in your therapy.
PATIENT: Yes, I have—I do. I am irritated and worried. It hasn't happened yet, but I feel it is going to and I can hardly sit still expecting it. I am so jumpy.

This constructed continuation of the example demonstrates that the patient can be helped to communicate through metaphor that both defends against and expresses transference. In this instance, as is frequently the case, the communicative possibilities of the metaphor and of transference, their adaptive significance, are more impressive than their resistive implications and they are essential to the therapeutic process. As the patient is helped to communicate about his "bosses" through the metaphor, he also has the opportunity to hear himself and thus to begin to wonder about (that is, to interpret) the meaning of what he is telling the therapist. At the end of this constructed example he is much closer to being able to tell the therapist directly about his fears about what might happen in the therapy situation.

The commonest reason for a patient to lapse into metaphor is the presence of more or less unconscious transference feelings against which the patient is defending. In general, it is a sound technical stance for the therapist or analyst to stay with and attempt to facilitate the patient's communicating through metaphor, so long as it seems that the patient is able to communicate more freely in that way, so long as the metaphor seems capable of including the therapeutic situation allusively. By listening to and facilitating the expression of the metaphor, another version of going with the resistance, the therapist can also learn more about the nature of the transference that is hinted at as well as the reasons for defending against it. Thus he arrives at a much better position to help the patient understand what is going on.

To put it another way: Imagine the transference and metaphor as parallel tracks, like railroad tracks. We can then view resistance as the force that keeps the two parallel tracks apart. But so long as the tracks are only a little distance apart and continue parallel with each other, there is no great advantage in insisting that the patient uses one track if for some reason he finds it easier to use the other one. As he continues down his preferred track he is able to communicate indirectly while also maintaining the measure of defense he needs. Sooner or later the patient will notice that what he has been saying in metaphor also applies to the therapist. Thus, while speaking metaphorically the patient's tolerance for more direct communication may improve and his defensiveness may lessen.

Around the termination of psychotherapy it is common to see revivals of behavior patterns that were characteristic of the patient earlier in treatment.

> A patient had been in treatment for several months for severe anxiety states and incipient phobias which she saw as potentially crippling her life. In the course of weekly therapy she came to see the source of the anxiety, its function in her life, and its connection to previous patterns that kept her from realizing her full potential. With the relief of her major anxiety symptoms and her ability to understand their meaning, and with the growing sense of her ability to master things, she had been wondering whether she needed more treatment. Clearly there were characterological problems that she might profit from exploring, but the therapist did not feel it right to urge her to do so.
>
> During one hour she mentioned that she had been talking with her husband about her treatment and he said he believed she was doing much better, better than he had ever seen before. She felt

gratified by this endorsement and agreed with him. Then she stopped and did not seem to know what to say next. The therapist observed that she fell silent, and he felt that she seemed to want him to say something. The patient confirmed that she was eager to hear something from the therapist "but she didn't know what."

The therapist said he guessed that she and her husband had just about decided that it might be the right time for her to stop her treatment but she was concerned about what the therapist might think about such a decision.

The patient blushed and lowered her head as if guilty about a forbidden thought. With head still lowered she nodded her agreement and the therapist commented then on the pain she was apparently feeling. The patient was then able to verbalize that she indeed felt guilty.

The therapist was then able to connect her wish to stop her therapy because she was feeling and doing better with the guilt she had once felt about growing up and leaving home when she felt her presence was needed to keep the family together. Getting better and leaving the therapist was equated with disloyalty to the therapist and connected to her earlier "crime" of growing up and away as an act of disloyalty to her mother—one genetic source of the anxiety attacks that had brought her into treatment.

This example illustrates the way in which the patient's reluctance to mention her and her husband's decision that she should stop therapy expressed resistance. The conflict once experienced in connection with her mother and the guilt for failing her mother's supposed expectations were transferred to the therapist.

Is resistance just a renaming of the patient's momentary reticence? The example should make clear that the reticence was just the tip of the iceberg—only a sign of a quiet but major transference revival of an earlier setting of that same conflict. Although we could speak quite literally, if trivially, of the reluctance, reticence, or resistance as impeding the treatment at that point since the patient indeed fell silent, her behavior told much more than it concealed. It communicated a great deal to the therapist who was prepared to understand it and who was then able to tell her once again what her silent but expressive reaction seemed to say, helping her make sense of her uncomfortable and for the moment "senseless" behavior.

We can speak of this behavior as resistance to termination as a shorthand way of expressing that around the time of stopping treatment one typically encounters such revivals of transference, among whose functions is to retard change, to hold on to the relationship with the therapist and avoid separation.

In this instance, although the therapist seemed to focus on what was resisted, the telling that the patient and her husband had decided she should stop treatment, the therapist's main interest was in *why* resistance was appearing at that point. Thus the focus was not on what was withheld but on what was told, the link to the major transference paradigm and genetic conflict that had led to the patient's problems in the first place.

References

Freud, S. The dynamics of transference. *Standard edition* (Vol. 12). London: Hogarth Press, 1958. (Originally published, 1912.)

Gill, M. Analysis of the transference. In H. J. Schlesinger (Ed.), *Psychological Issues Monograph Series* (No. 53). New York: International Universities Press, 1981.

Schlesinger, H. A contribution to a theory of promising. I. Developmental and regressive aspects of the making of promises. In S. Smith (Ed.), *The human mind revisited: Essays in honor of Karl Menninger.* New York: International Universities Press, 1978.

Shapiro, D. *Neurotic styles.* New York: Basic Books, 1965.

3

Psychoanalytic Perspectives on Resistance

Paul A. Dewald

From a psychoanalytic perspective, the concept of resistance is an element of clinical theory based on repeated observations in the therapeutic situation. These clinical observations have influenced the theory and practice of psychoanalysis since Freud's (Breuer & Freud, 1893/1955) earliest attempts to formulate a therapeutic process. Initially he used hypnosis in an attempt to promote the recall and verbal expression of otherwise inaccessible memories of psychologically traumatic experiences. When hypnosis failed with many of his patients, he subsequently substituted various other forms of suggestion and other actively directive techniques, attempting to overcome the patient's difficulties in recovering unpleasant memories from the past.

The Topographical Model

The discovery that what he had believed to be traumatic memories were in fact usually intrapsychic fantasies expressing the patient's own internal drives and wishes (particularly the libidinal ones) led to the introduction of the *topographical model* of the mind (S. Freud, 1900/1953). In that formulation psychic conflict was understood as conflict between

Paul A. Dewald • Department of Psychiatry, St. Louis University School of Medicine, St. Louis, Missouri 63104.

the manifestations and expressions of the childhood sexual wishes and drives (which were unconscious) and the other components of the patient's mental processes, namely the ego instincts. The ego instincts were conceptualized as existing predominantly in the conscious-preconscious regions of the mind, and the patient's resistances were understood as mental functions in opposition to the recall of the unconscious sexual material. In this way resistances were presumed to be under the control of the patient's voluntary and conscious mind, and were thus understood as expressions of negativism and opposition to the analyst and to the treatment process. These theoretical formulations served as the basis for psychoanalytic therapeutic technique until the early 1920s.

During that era psychoanalysts reflected the attitude that resistances were getting in the way of treatment and were obstacles that had to be eliminated or overcome. In that context resistances acquired a pejorative implication as signs of negative transference to the analyst, and as expressions of the patient's refusal to cooperate in the treatment process. The analyst needed actively to persuade the patient to give them up, or find other means of bypassing them, or else wait until the resistance had run its course and the transference once again became positive so that the patient became amenable and accepting of the analyst's interventions.

The Structural Model

Increasing clinical observation, experience, and sophistication demonstrated that often the expressions and manifestations of a form of resistance occurred outside the patient's awareness and that such resistances might operate at unconscious levels of mental function. This repeated observation was one of the crucial clinical findings that led Freud (1923/1961, 1926/1959) to revise his basic theoretical conceptualizations and to introduce the *structural model* of mental functioning. From this new theoretical and clinical perspective, those components of the patient's mental functioning that were in opposition to the progress of the treatment were ascribed to preconscious and unconscious ego functioning. Their immediate motivation was the patient's attempt to avoid experience of various unpleasurable affects. And since the resistances were largely unconscious, the analyst's previous negative attitudes toward them were replaced by a greater tolerance and acceptance, as well as greater interest in them as manifestations of how the patient attempted to cope with inevitable conflicts.

At that time Freud (1926/1959) described five varieties of resistance: the ego resistances of repression, transference, and secondary gain; the id resistance of the repetition compulsion; and the superego resistance of a sense of guilt and need for punishment. Resistances were thus understood as emanating from all aspects of the mental apparatus, and were seen as unconsciously determined and continuously present manifestations of the patient's attempts to cope with intrapsychic conflicts and disturbances. This basic formulation has been expanded by many authors, including Anna Freud (1936), Fenichel (1941), Glover (1955), Greenson (1968), and Stone (1973).

The Meanings of Resistance

Basic psychoanalytic observations and theoretical formulations of psychopathology (which cannot be elaborated here) indicate that no matter how disabling or painful the presenting symptoms or complaints, they nevertheless represent an unconscious attempt by the patient to deal with an even more frightening, guilt-inducing, painful, or distressing conflict through the construction of a compromise solution to that conflict. The therapeutic task in psychoanalysis requires that the patient participate actively in a process through which there is a progressive mobilization and regressive activation in conscious awareness of those elements of internal unconscious psychic conflicts that he has sought to avoid and for which he has instead substituted (unconsciously) his various neurotic symptoms and/or character traits.

Thus every patient enters treatment with mixed motivations. On the one hand are the conscious wishes and hopes of relief of symptoms, improved functioning, psychic freedom, and psychological maturation, along with a varying degree of confidence and willingness to participate in efforts to modify his psychological and emotional organization and to resolve the pathogenic unconscious conflicts. However, the patient also has motivations to avoid recognition of what would be anxiety-, shame-, guilt-, or pain-producing awareness of unacceptable internal wishes, fears, fantasies, and drives, and the situations of "psychological danger" that they unconsciously represent for the patient. Furthermore, at a deeply unconscious level the patient's neurotic disturbances are partly maintained by a continuing attempt still to achieve fulfillment and satisfaction of infantile and early childhood forms of drive satisfactions, object choices, and modes of defense and adaptation. Although the patient wants to be rid of the limiting or pain-inducing manifestations of his conflicts, he still unconsciously seeks to satisfy the earlier forms and manifestations of his drives, fantasies, and wishes, and hence is reluctant to give up or renounce their fulfillment or his unconscious sense of their appropriateness. No matter how disabling the condition that the patient presents, it still constitutes the best he has been able to do on his own in attempting to resolve the internal conflicts; his unconscious perception is that other forms of expression or solution to these conflicts will be dangerous, anxiety or guilt producing, new and unfamiliar, and so on.

For the therapist the concept of resistance represents an interpretation of meaning ascribed to any behaviors manifested by the patient that interfere with or delay the therapeutic process of uncovering and bringing to the patient's conscious awareness the hidden nature and manifestations of his intrapsychic conflicts. Once these conflicts are consciously manifest, the concept of resistance is also applied to any behaviors that delay or oppose the renunciation of the inappropriate unconscious wishes, fantasies, and defensive operations. Also understood as resistances are the patient's hesitations to attempt new and more age-appropriate methods of adaptation and psychic organization.

From the patient's point of view, however, the same behaviors that are labeled "resistance" by the therapist serve an immediately useful and adaptive purpose. From the vantage point of the patient's unconscious neurotic processes and psychological organization, they represent his attempts at maintenance of the status quo. They protect the patient against conscious awareness of unacknowledged and unpleasurable elements within his own psychic life; and they promote and sustain the continuing search for fulfillment of inappropriate drives, fantasies, and relationships.

In that way they protect the patient from experiencing the painful affects of grief, anger, and disappointment connected with renunciation of previously sought earlier forms of satisfaction. As such, therefore, the patient may find them immediately useful and gratifying, and he may therefore understand his behavior in quite different ways than does the therapist. Even at times when the patient himself recognizes that his behavior may be in opposition to the avowed wish for psychological maturation and change, the unconscious adaptive and anxiety-reducing functions of the behavior may take precedence over the wish for maturation and growth.

As such, then, resistance occurs in all patients, although its intensity, persistence, level of conscious recognition, and disruptive impact on the therapeutic process varies greatly from patient to patient, and within the same patient at different times in the treatment process.

Classification of Resistances

From the therapist's vantage point, resistances may be grouped into two major categories. First are the *tactical* resistances, which include those psychic operations and behaviors by which the patient seeks to avoid full, personalized, and emotional awareness and detailed recognition of those aspects of himself, his past life, his fantasies, wishes, and actions of which he is guilty, ashamed, or afraid, and which he unconsciously chooses not to acknowledge or accept as parts of himself. The other group of resistances might be thought of as *strategic* and involve the patient's continuing unconscious efforts to seek fulfillment of infantile and childhood wishes or object choices and/or the fantasies by which these are experienced and expressed. These strategic resistances include the patient's reluctance to give up attempts to relive the past and to experience previously gratifying or unfulfilled satisfactions and/or relationships; and the patient's reluctance to accept in the present what is age appropriate and realistically possible, rather than the impossible, no longer appropriate, and outmoded satisfactions and relationships. This form of renunciation activates grief, mourning, and a recognition that it is "too late," all of which involve unpleasurable affects and sustained psychological work.

During the course of psychoanalysis the strategic resistances become manifest as unconscious wishes and feelings experienced toward the therapist as part of the transference relationship. The treatment process is structured and developed in such a way as to promote regression in the service of the therapeutic task and thereby to activate and intensify the experience of the archaic wishes and fantasies toward the therapist. The purpose of this approach is to produce an artificial situation between patient and therapist so that through application of more adult, rational, self-observing, integrative, and reality-testing ego functions the patient is now able to recognize and resolve the earlier forms of the wishes and the conflicts that accompany them.

Psychoanalysis versus Psychoanalytic Psychotherapy

A detailed discussion of the differences between psychoanalysis and psychoanalytic psychotherapy is beyond the scope of this discussion (see Dewald, 1978a). In summary, however, they may be differentiated on the basis that in psychoanalysis, the therapeutic goal and the task for the patient and the analyst are to uncover and resolve the basic infantile and early childhood core of the patient's unconscious wishes and fantasies and the conflicts that arise from them, as well as the attempted solution and/or improved adaptation to those conflicts. These core conflicts, although usually deeply repressed and unconscious to the patient, produce subsequent impact upon maturation and development of the personality, mediated by and through later occurring experiences, relationships, and the vicissitudes of development and maturation. Many of these later processes are closer to consciousness as the individual progresses chronologically through the life cycle.

In psychoanalytic psychotherapy the therapeutic work is usually aimed at these later occurring and evolving derivatives of the basic and core conflicts, with a limited and focused selection of certain areas to be the subject of therapeutic scrutiny and efforts. In psychoanalysis there is a steady, systematic, continuing, and extensive attempt at coping with all manifest varieties (both tactical and strategic) of resistance to the therapeutic task of full exploration of the infantile and earliest childhood components of psychic structure and conflict. In psychoanalytic psychotherapy there is a more selective, chronologically later, less extensive, or less intensive attempt to deal with resistances, and then chiefly with those maintained against awareness or renunciation of the selected derivative tactical or strategic conflicts.

The therapist's range of technical activity in handling the patient's resistances is qualitatively similar in psychoanalysis and in psychoanalytic psychotherapy. In both forms of treatment the therapist may use confrontation regarding the existence of a form of resistance; clarification as to the details of its nature and impact on the therapeutic process; interpretation of its meanings and motivations; and assistance to the patient in working through to the point where the particular resistance is reduced or abandoned. The technical differences between psychoanalysis and psychoanalytic psychotherapy are more related to quantitative factors, such as the depth to which resistances are traced, the breadth of resistances being dealt with, the degree to which frustration or interference with their function is attempted, and the degree of insight the patient achieves in regard to their operation. Another variable is the issue described above regarding the approach to primary-process core resistances in psychoanalysis, in contrast to predominantly secondary-process derivative resistances in psychoanalytic psychotherapy.

But in both forms of treatment the therapist must recognize that only the patient can modify, reduce, or eliminate a particular resistance. The therapist by himself cannot alter or dissipate the patient's resistances. He can only avoid strengthening, supporting, or evading specific resistances in keeping with the overall therapeutic strategy; increase the patient's conscious awareness of them; and by his total behavior foster and support the patient's attempts to overcome them.

In other words, the therapist's technical interventions are aimed at encouraging the patient gradually and progressively to adopt the therapist's attitude and orientation toward the meaning of the behaviors that serve the function of resistance. As the patient becomes increasingly aware of these meanings, as he recognizes their effects, and as the more rational and adult aspects of his personality identify with the therapist's therapeutic attitude and functions, the patient increasingly seeks to modify his own resistance behaviors.

Technical Handling of Resistances

In handling resistances in psychoanalysis and psychoanalytic psychotherapy, the therapist goes through a series of processes that may be schematically isolated and described in the following sequence.

Recognition

The therapist must be constantly sensitive to and vigilant for patterns of behavior and communication in the patient that may signify the existence of a tactical or strategic resistance. Manifest behavior cannot be the only cue, since the same manifest behavior may on one occasion represent a resistance and yet in another context have other meanings. The therapist must be aware that the principle of multiple function (Waelder, 1936) applies to resistances, inasmuch as a particular pattern of behavior may involve multiple resistive features. The therapist must also recognize that the resistance may involve not only unconscious patterns of ego adaptation and defense but may also contain elements of drive expression (either libidinal or aggressive) as well as reflections of the functioning of the superego and guilt or needs for punishment.

The diagnosis and recognition of a resistance must also be correlated with the overall goals of the therapy and the nature of the therapeutic process. If, for example, one of the goals of therapy is to foster the patient's capacity for independent and self-directed motivation, then various attempts by the patient to be compliant, cooperative, and to please the therapist through his treatment progress would eventually assume the characteristics of a resistance. If, on the other hand, the goal of therapy is predominantly focused on symptom relief and modification of specific behavioral patterns, then these same forms of compliance will be seen as helpful and the concept of resistance will not apply. If the therapy is of a focal variety with deliberate emphasis on some aspects of psychic function and conflict, while simultaneously avoiding other components of neurotic dysfunction, the patient's avoidance of recognition or awareness of the latter would again not be conceived of as significantly resistive since part of the plan was to allow those elements to remain unconscious.

The therapist must also recognize that countertransference forces may influence his perceptiveness in regard to the existence, manifestations, or meanings of a resistance. At times countertransference may stem from the therapist's reluctance to face the barrage of conflict or emotion in the transference if the resistance is understood; or it may reflect a parallel between the patient's conflicts and those of the therapist; or at times it may be caused by the therapist's reluctance to activate pain or distress in the patient. If the patient is already aware of a specific resistance and the therapist fails to understand it, the patient's interpretation may be that the therapist cannot tolerate the issue in question, which may lead to a further intensification of resistances.

Integration into the Therapeutic Context

Having tentatively recognized and understood the manifestations of a resistance, the therapist must then integrate this understanding into the current context of the therapeutic situation and the process. This task must include an assessment not only of the current therapeutic context that has activated the resistance in question, but also of such issues as how much the patient is aware of it, whether or not the patient can tolerate reducing the intensity of the resistance at that moment, the nature of the therapeutic alliance and overall relationship including the currently predominating transference, whether the resistance is new or has already been observed and/or dealt with, whether the patient should be allowed to struggle longer with the situation on his own, the nature of the overall therapeutic goals and strategy, and so on. In other words, when the therapist recognizes and understands the existence of a resistance, he may elect for a variety of technical reasons either to bring it to the patient's attention or to delay any therapeutic interaction regarding it.

Preparatory Interventions

If the therapist elects to begin to work with the patient in regard to the resistance in question, it may be necessary through preparatory interventions to approach the behavior in a series of tentative steps. These steps of confrontation, clarification, interpretation, and ultimately working through have been clearly described by Greenson (1968).

In the earlier phases of treatment, the therapist usually focuses first on those resistances that interfere with the establishment of an optimal therapeutic relationship and interaction. The early focus is also usually on those resistances that will be ego-alien (undesirable) to the patient himself, as well as those resistances that are not crucial keystones for the patient in terms of character structure and overall functioning. Experiences with the reduction of these relatively noncrucial resistances permit the patient to recognize the advantages for the treatment of their reduction, and thus enhance the therapeutic alliance and the patient's motivation for gradually increasing the focus of therapeutic attention on more central, ego-syntonic, and crucial resistances in regard to overall psychic organization. An approach to more crucial ego-syntonic and major characterological resistances usually requires an already well-established and solid therapeutic alliance, as well as prior experience by the patient that reduction or modification of a resistance will not result in profound disorganization or intolerable levels of anxiety.

The therapist's attitudes toward the resistance itself as well as his freedom from anxiety about the disruptive conflicts being warded off serve as important models for identification by the patient, and thus further foster the therapeutic alliance and with it the reduction of the intensity of the resistant behavior (Dewald, 1978b). The sophisticated therapist avoids any pejorative attitudes that resistances imply a lack of cooperation or participation. Instead the therapist uses the understanding from the analysis of resistance as a means of further exploration of patterns of ego defense, superego organization, and drive-derivative expression. Resistances are anticipated and are not seen as something to get out of the way, but instead are accepted as an integral part of the patient's psychic operations. Understanding them becomes part of the patient's recognition of how his own synthetic, defensive, and adaptive mental processes function.

Interpretation

Although in focusing on a particular resistance the therapist usually makes his interventions in a piecemeal fashion, ultimately the patient's understanding of the resistance will include not only the fact of its existence, but also the motivations for its use, the earlier forms and origins of the particular resistive behavior pattern in question, the nature of the conflicts against which the resistance was established, and the effects that the particular resistance has on the treatment process and on the patient's general life experience. Tactical resistances usually must be dealt with therapeutically prior to the emergence into conscious awareness of the more strategic resistances, which then are chiefly manifested in the patient's transference reactions and wishes toward the therapist. The latter are usually dealt with not only by interpretation but through the maintenance of transference abstinence by which the therapist withholds reinforcement, thereby promoting a greater motivation in the patient for the ultimate renunciation of these forms of fulfillment and satisfaction.

Therapeutic Attitude

In his various interventions regarding resistance, the therapist must maintain a therapeutically neutral and interested position that avoids any suggestion of lack of cooperation by the patient, or of a judgmental accusation that the patient "is resisting." The therapist must also be aware that a correct interpretation of a resistance may activate a substitute resistive pattern to serve the same dynamic functions as the previous one. The therapist's interest and tolerance toward the resistances and also the conflicts they defend against serve as a model for the patient in the therapeutic alliance, thereby fostering an identification with the therapist's therapeutic attitude including his comfort and freedom from anxiety in the face of the affects or conflicts that may emerge.

Repetition

The therapist also recognizes that a single interpretation of a resistance may be only partially or transiently effective and that not infrequently the same resistance must be interpreted again, often from different perspectives or in different forms. Particularly in dealing with strategic resistances, the therapist must empathically recognize the reluctance every patient experiences in renouncing neurotic wishes and fantasies as well as patterns of organization and defense, and must allow enough time and repetition for these processes to occur.

Avoidance of Strengthening Resistance

Throughout this entire process the therapist, through his understanding of the nature of the resistances, maintains behavior patterns that avoid strengthening or gratifying the patient's resistances. At a preconscious level, the therapist is constantly observing and monitoring the state and intensity of the resistances and is observing the patient's readiness to modify them as manifested in the expressed spontaneous communications and behavior patterns. The therapist must also be sensitive to the possibility that resistances may be expressed in nonverbal form as well as in various verbal forms, and must also be constantly alert to the possibility of silent resistances that may not be overtly manifest either to the patient or to the therapist.

Testing the Therapeutic Situation

Having made his interventions in regard to a particular resistance, the therapist must also observe the impact such interventions have on the patient and his capacity for further effective therapeutic work. At times the interventions may be in the nature of a test which is then followed either by a clincial decision to press further with the interventions, or by the clincial judgment that the patient is not yet ready to reduce the intensity of the resistance and a clincial decision to suspend further approach for the time being.

Therapist's Interest in Resistance

Like the young Freud himself, most beginning therapists tend to be more interested in the unconscious manifestations of drives and the nature of intrapsychic fantasy and conflict. Freud's full recognition of the importance and the unconscious nature of resistances took many years to evolve. Similarly, as therapists gain more clinical experience and sophistication, their appreciation of the importance of resistances increases. The experienced and sophisticated therapist has as much interest in the processes by which tactical or strategic resistances are manifest as he does in the contents of conflict thus being avoided.

Patient Responses

The processes described in this format may seem cumbersome and possibly stilted. However, in the actual therapeutic situation these therapeutic functions are carried out at preconscious levels in a relatively smooth, continuous fashion.

The therapist's technical interventions and attitudes represent only one side of the therapeutic process in regard to resistance. It is the patient who must then respond to the therapist's behavior and interventions in ways that ultimately reduce the intensity or persistence of the particular behavior pattern, in order that its interfering effects on therapeutic progress will be reduced or eliminated. The patient's motivations for trying to reduce the intensity of his own resistances include the relatively adult and reality-oriented wishes to overcome and resolve the neurotic disturbances. But the patient is also motivated by transference-inspired wishes to accept the therapist's implicit or explicit suggestions, and to achieve approval or acceptance by the therapist as a reward for reducing the intensity of the resistance. Another component of the patient's motivations is a pressure toward identification with the therapist and his attitudes, which may stem from a variety of internal sources.

A bright, perceptive, and introspective young man began psychotherapy for a variety of neurotic symptoms. During the first 6 months of treatment he carefully observed the therapist's behavior and responses to his material. Slowly, a sense of trust and confidence developed, to the point where he finally indicated that he felt he could reveal his most limiting and disturbing symptom, namely, an intense phobia against public toilets. The therapist had been continuously aware of the patient's mistrust, testing, and hesitancy in revealing his feelings, and that what was involved was a repetition in the therapy of a pattern of interaction begun with his parents in childhood. He had gently and repeatedly pointed out these resistances, maintained a stable and accepting therapeutic atmosphere, and stimulated the patient to understand the meanings of his behavior.

Slowly and cautiously the patient began to describe his bathroom-phobic reactions and to explore some of their intrapsychic meanings, becoming progressively more verbal and direct. But even in this phase of the work he said that "although I'm talking about this problem more directly in words, I'm keeping my feelings about it at arm's length, and in a feeling way I don't even really accept it as my problem."

This vignette illustrates the limitations in the therapist's capacity directly to influence the reduction of resistances, and the fact that this capacity ultimately rests with the patient. The therapist can only point them out, create a therapeutic environment that fosters the patient's efforts, and allow sufficient time and repetition for the process to influence the patient's behavior.

As the patient learns from his own experience that reducing the intensity of a resistance is possible, that the discomfort involved is transient, that the ultimate effects include a sense of mastery and an extension of his own awareness, and that therapeutic progress results, he becomes more willing and confident in applying the same process again. The result is a circular set of experiences, leading to the subsequent reduction of more crucial and ego-syntonic resistances. In successful cases the patient becomes increasingly responsible for his own resistances, capable of recognizing their operation, and accepting of them as functions within himself. As this process occurs the therapist may find it less necessary to intervene, and one sign of therapeutic success is the patient's capacity to recognize and overcome his own resistances.

Manifestations of Resistance

The specific forms and manifestations of resistance are protean, and no listing or cataloging of resistive behaviors is possible. Any form of behavior may at times be used in the service of resistance, even behaviors that manifestly seem to represent compliance with the therapeutic task, or "normal" behavior patterns. A few clinical examples may help clarify this concept.

A passive and compliant patient came regularly to all sessions, was always on time, faithfully tried to report all thought processes and feelings, paid his bill promptly, and seemed to be cooperating with the therapist's requests. That these behaviors were attempts to appease and please the therapist, gain approval and praise, and avoid any potential criticism (and thus served the resistive function of avoiding potential conflict and negative interaction with the therapist) became clear only after the therapist withheld the praise and approval sought by the patient. He then recognized that his characteristic passive, compliant behavior was not achieving for him the goals that he sought and was able to achieve with other people. For this particular patient, progress in treatment was manifest when he was able to be less outwardly cooperative with the therapist, and to begin to risk experience and expression of feelings and behavior that were more in keeping with his own wishes even at the risk of evoking conflict in the therapeutic relationship.

Reporting extensively on current reality situations may serve to avoid exposure of the patient's past experiences and intrapsychic mental processes. Conversely, exclusive focus on past relationships and events may protect the patient from dealing with important current problems.

Emotional isolation and avoidance of affects may serve an important resistive function. But the patient who continually experiences affective storms without occasionally observing himself from a more remote cognitive and integrating position may likewise be expressing a resistance to treatment.

Patients who "forget" their dreams are often manifesting a resistance; but so are patients who repeatedly bring more dreams than can be dealt with in a session.

These clinical examples, which could be continued indefinitely, illustrate the concept that the diagnosis of a resistance rests not on the manifest behavior itself, but instead on the context of the treatment process in which the behavior occurs, the nature of the patient's preexisting characteristic adaptive and defensive functions, and the immediate tactical and strategic situation of the treatment process.

Levels of Consciousness

There is a spectrum of the extent to which resistances may be conscious to the patient. In some instances the patient may be fully aware not only of the resistance but also of some of the motivations that activate it. At other times a patient may recognize the activation of a resistance but be unaware of its motivations or meanings. And frequently the patient is unaware of the resistance as well as of its motivations or meanings.

> During her initial history and early phase of therapy, a woman maintained that she fully enjoyed and actively participated in sex with her husband. It was only in the eighth month of therapy that she reluctantly "confessed" she was frigid, and felt disgusted by any sexual activity or interchange. She had recognized at the time that she was deliberately lying about her sexuality out of fear that the therapist would immediately focus on her sexual malfunction and would also think of her as less feminine or healthy.

> Another patient recognized spontaneously that she preferred not coming to her sessions, was reluctant to talk, and found herself frequently arriving late. She was surprised at herself since consciously she recognized considerable improvement in her symptoms since beginning therapy, and felt herself to be deeply attached to and dependent on the therapist. The meaning of the resistance became apparent to her only after eventual interpretation by the therapist of her unconscious and unacknowledged anger at him.

> A man entered a session in an intense state of emotional turmoil and spent most of his time describing in detail an argument he had had with his wife. The patient had previously been unable to deal with feelings of hostility and aggression against the wife, and in his description of his feelings about the incident he was expressing anger that previously had been impossible for him to approach. He accused his wife of caring more for someone else and of not putting his interests at a high enough priority. Until it was brought to his attention by the therapist, the patient was totally unaware of the possibility that he was in fact angry at the therapist who in the previous session had announced a future vacation separation. In that instance the patient had unconsciously displaced the unacceptable hostile and bitter feelings toward the therapist to the wife as a function of resistance, in terms of his fear of confronting the therapist directly. The apparent "progress" in terms of being able to express anger toward the wife was also serving a resistive function in terms of his fear of a fight with the therapist.

Levels of Therapist's Activity

The more the therapy is focused on psychoanalytic processes and goals, the more the therapist seeks predominantly to rely on repeated confrontation and interpretation in the handling of the patient's inevitable resistances. However, there may be instances where repeated interpretation of a resistance is ineffective and where the therapist must then use more active measures in the attempt to confront the patient's resistance or interfere with its effectiveness. Interventions of this kind, usually conceptualized as necessary parameters (Eissler, 1953), generally are not introduced unless confrontation, clarification, and interpretation over an extended period have failed to produce therapeutic progress.

A man presented an intense hand-washing compulsion. Eventually, after a long period of work without progress, the therapist found it necessary actively to suggest to the patient that he deliberately refrain from the hand washing for 5 minutes at any time when the impulse occurred and that he instead try to become aware of thoughts and feelings during the 5-minute delay. As the patient attempted to do so he became increasingly aware of the fantasies and feelings being avoided by his continued symptom.

A woman with a severe masochistic personality disturbance sought treatment because of her recognition that she characteristically established relationships with men by whom she would be humiliated, disappointed, hurt, and sometimes pathologically abused. Her termination of another such relationship had precipitated her entry into treatment. Within a few weeks the patient resumed her masochistic relationship with the same sadistic lover and spent much of her therapeutic sessions describing in detail the various hurtful and humiliating experiences she underwent at his hands. Simultaneously, her relationship to the therapist remained pleasant and cooperative and she attended the sessions regularly; yet there was very little affective investment in the therapeutic relationship and no experience of masochistic wishes or fantasies in the transference. Repeated confrontations, interpretations, and reconstructions regarding the neurotic gratifications achieved in the relationship with the lover and the avoidance of awareness of her own wishes for this kind of treatment were ineffective over the next year.

Eventually the therapist made it clear that the continuing masochistic gratification offered by the relationship to the lover was making therapy ineffective, and that if she wanted the treatment to succeed she would have to stop seeing the lover. The patient eventually complied, and although she interpreted the therapist's intervention in many distorted ways and subjected it to repeated analytic scrutiny, nevertheless the cessation of the masochistic gratification outside of the treatment enabled the patient increasingly to focus those needs into the transference relationship. As that occurred, the patient's previously unconscious guilt and need to be punished were increasingly directed and felt toward the analyst. As the analyst maintained the neutrality of the situation and did not attack or punish the patient, she became aware of how much she wanted such mistreatment and how she equated it with love and attention. Only after that step could she recognize the distortions and begin to modify her behavior.

A physician's wife in psychoanalysis "confessed" after the third year of treatment that throughout the entire process her husband had been regularly and continuously providing her with tranquilizers. She had been unwilling to acknowledge this fact to the therapist, knowing that in analysis the use of medication is discouraged and anticipating that if the analyst knew about it he would discontinue her treatment. For the next 6 months the analyst regularly provided the patient with prescriptions for the tranquilizer, thereby focusing the use of the medication into the analytic relationship. The patient could then recognize the symbolic meanings of the medication, the wishes and fears regarding oral incorporation of the analyst, the uses of the medication as defenses against anxiety caused by separation, and so on. As long as the medication was taken outside the analytic relationship, it served as a resistance against awareness and resolution of the deeper conflicts. The parameter of the analyst himself prescribing the medication was an intermediate step designed to bring these issues into focus within the analytic relationship. Eventually, as they were worked through, the patient no longer needed or wanted the medication.

Strategic Resistances

Strategic resistances are frequently manifest in the form of transference wishes and expectations throughout the therapeutic process. These forces are particularly intensified during the termination phase of the therapy. During this phase the therapeutic task involves the acceptance of the inevitability of transference frustration, the recognition of the inappropriateness of continuing the search for transference satisfaction, and ultimately the renunciation of the earlier forms and manifestations of transference-inspired wishes and fantasies in favor of reality-oriented, age-appropriate, and realistically available forms of drive satisfaction and object relatedness. Optimally these goals should be achieved without the search for a substitute relationship to take the place of the therapist, and with the patient affectively experiencing and working through the accompanying anger, grief, and mourning. Whatever the intensity of transference involvement and the degree of eventual renunciation of the transference wishes, the patient (using the therapist as the current prototype) is simultaneously relinquishing his demands on and expectations of the earlier objects and relationships.

Characteristically, however, during termination even patients who have been functioning at significantly improved levels of psychological operation and organization will manifest anger, sadness, grief, and reluctance at the renunciation of infantile and childhood wishes that is a necessary part of the treatment process. There is also a significant reluctance to experience the painful affects involved, and to carry on the necessary work of mourning. Another typical component of the termination resistance involves the uncertainty, anxiety, and difficulty in establishing and sustaining new modes of psychic organization, and in developing new forms of adaptation that to the patient may appear fumbling, unsuccessful, and less fulfilling than would be the satisfaction of the infantile and childhood fantasies. These components of the resistance (the reluctance to renounce the infantile wishes, to experience and work through the affects, and the anxiety and fear toward new and different modes of adaptation) characteristically lead to a variety of typical, tactical resistive maneuvers characteristic of the termination phase. These may include transitory recurrence of symptoms that had previously disappeared, a search for substitutes for the therapist and therapeutic relationship, a recurrence and intensification of old transference wishes, and various feelings of anger, rejection, and wishes for revenge in regard to the ultimate frustration. There is an extensive literature dealing with the termination phase and its proper conduct by the therapist, but in essence it is during this phase that the strategic resistances against change are maximally present.

> A woman in analysis exhibited an intense oedipal-phase transference neurosis. The analysis had been significantly successful with marked structural change, and she was now well into the termination phase. Increasingly she recognized the impossibility of fulfillment of her oedipal wishes by the analyst. "It's not fair! You represent everything I ever wanted as a girl, and I know I could be very good for you. When I was a girl I used to dream that when I grew up I could have my daddy for myself. I'm not neurotic anymore and so I've grown up, but I'm still not going to have what I want, and everything else that I could have seems liked mashed potatoes by comparison." These recognitions were followed by a lengthy period of regression to profound depression, the return of various neurotic inhibitions, and the experience and expression of intense and sustained rage at the analyst, accompanied by a variety of provocative, consciously chosen and understood tactical resistances against work-

ing through this final phase of her treatment. In handling this resistance the analyst maintained the analytic situation and the same levels of transference abstinence; interpreted the patient's reaction as related to the forthcoming termination; interpreted the patient's attempts to make the analyst feel guilty and that the analysis was a failure; emphasized the patient's own responsibility for her current symptoms and distress; and interpreted the patient's repeated attempts to avoid experiencing the painful affects connected with the termination of treatment. In other words, the analyst continued to analyze as usual without introducing any new or special techniques.

A man had suffered a variety of deprivations and psychic traumata at the hands of his parents from birth on. His analysis had produced significant change, and early in the termination phase he had mellowed in his feelings and attitudes toward his parents, and had recognized that his deprivations and traumata had not been deliberate but instead were a function of his parents' psychological limitations. A parallel change had occurred in his transference reaction regarding the inevitable frustrations of the analysis. When he realized that these changes meant that neither his parents nor the analyst would ever apologize, that he was in the process of forgiving them, that none of them felt guilty for his suffering, and that he had never directly expressed his bitterness to his parents, he became outraged that his parents and the analyst would "all get off scot-free." He demanded revenge, experienced an intense return of rage and negative transference, underwent a regression and return of symptoms, and fantasized that no matter how much better his life might be as a result of the analysis he would give it all up until he had first made his parents and the analyst suffer as he had done.

In the face of these types of strategic resistances the therapist must more than ever maintain the structure of the therapeutic situation, and his continuing therapeutic role in it. In spite of the patient's barrage in the transference, and the patient's genuine sense of distress and suffering, the therapist must maintain the position of transference abstinence. He must continue to interpret both tactical and strategic resistances, and confront the patient with the self-defeating and self-limiting implications of his reactions. He must be empathic to the difficulties for the patient in this process of renunciation, and must allow sufficient time for the process to occur. Anticipating that these forms of response are typical effects of the strategic resistances helps the therapist avoid being drawn into countertransference feelings of failure, changes in therapeutic technique or posture, or a change in treatment goals. Backing away from these issues or behaving in ways that support or reinforce these strategic resistances encourages the patient to avoid the necessary renunciation, and thereby reduces the ultimate benefits of the treatment.

Intractable Resistances

There are instances, however, when in spite of appropriate therapeutic techniques the patient's resistances are maintained and the therapy may involve extensive and prolonged periods where little or no progress is made, or at times even end in a stalemate.

A man in analysis for chronic depression occurring in a mixed masochistic and narcissistic personality disorder manifested a characteristic behavior pattern in which he would complain bitterly about his symptoms, his lack of progress, his feelings that the analyst was of no help, and his continuing personal and professional failures. Nevertheless he came regularly for his sessions, was deeply involved in the process, and consciously attempted to cooperate in the therapy. Again and again interventions that in most patients would reduce anxiety and symptoms caused an increase in his suffering and inhibitions. If, on occasion, an intervention was successful in reducing his symptoms and he felt better, it would invariably be followed by days or weeks of intensified suffering and disturbance, or by emotional withdrawal, canceled sessions, or a barrage of angry resentment in the transference.

This typical negative therapeutic reaction arose from a variety of intrapsychic sources, including the masochistic need to suffer and not receive anything good, the need to "prove" that the analyst was impotent and could not influence his behavior, the fear of dependence and engulfment if the analyst did succeed in helping him, and the fear that any sign of progress or relief of suffering brought him one step closer to the termination of treatment.

(This type of resistive behavior pattern evokes many difficult countertransference responses in the analyst, including a sense of discouragement and hopelessness; a tendency to forget that these resistances and their sources are unconscious; a wish to accept the patient's manifest declarations and discontinue the treatment; a sense of impotence and helplessness, with increasing doubts about the effectiveness of the method of treatment; a hesitancy to make any interventions [even if appropriate and indicated] lest they be followed by a renewed storm of suffering, accusation, and rage; a feeling of impatience and anger toward the patient; and a feeling of pressure to intervene in nonanalytic ways in hopes of short-circuiting the entire therapeutic process.)

In this case only a careful and sustained attention to the countertransference reactions (accompanied by the realization that if things were really hopeless the patient would have quit treatment) allowed the analyst to maintain an analytic position and technique, and eventually (after several years) this pattern of resistances was resolved and the patient had a satisfactory therapeutic result.

A patient in once-a-week, face-to-face analytic psychotherapy developed an intense eroticized transference toward the therapist after the first few months of treatment. She insistently proclaimed her availability and desire for a direct sexual relationship with the therapist, a behavior pattern that became increasingly insistent, demanding, and unrelenting. In spite of repeated interpretation, reconstruction, and apparent understanding of the origins of these demands, the patient persisted and manifested less and less capacity to recognize the inappropriateness and unreality of her wishes. Increasingly, she began to act these out by seeking out the therapist in nontherapeutic settings, calling his home repeatedly, refusing to leave the office when sessions were over, and so on. After 2 years of treatment it became apparent that she would be unable to resolve or renounce the transference demands, although in other areas of her life she was functioning at reasonably effective and nonpsychotic levels. The therapist eventually elected unilaterally to set an arbitrary termination date, with the recommendation that she transfer to another therapist who might then help her deal with the apparently unresolvable strategic resistance manifest in the transference psychosis.

A professional man entered analysis because of chronic feelings of emptiness and emotional isolation, depression, difficulties in the relationship with his wife and children, sexual inhibition, and social and interpersonal ineptitude. As a child he had suffered numerous deprivations, including multiple separations of his parents, several foster-home or orphange placements, lack of warmth from either parent, death of his mother during latency, and remarriage of his father a few years later. He had managed by an adaptation of fierce independence, dogged persistence, high intelligence, and careful planning to put himself through college and professional school, and to marry and establish an outwardly stable and successful life.

As expected, in spite of high conscious motivation for treatment, he repeated in the analysis the characteristic adaptive behavior patterns that had allowed him to succeed in his life thus far. He remained emotionally aloof, could not allow himself to undergo a therapeutic regression, withdrew into prolonged silences whenever he experienced any affective reactions, and maintained a careful editing and anticipatory scanning of his associations. Repeatedly he was consciously aware of his multiple resistances, summarizing his position as follows: To become emotionally involved with the analyst was to run the risk that he would be hurt if the analyst failed him, canceled a session, went on vacation, and so on; the analyst must first prove he will never disappoint the patient, and never terminate the analysis; no matter what "tests" the analyst "passed," it did not prove that at some future time he would not disappoint or hurt the patient; and his ultimate weapon in any relationship, about which the other person was helpless, was the patient's ability to withhold his own emotional investments.

Throughout the course of his treatment the patient recognized the irrationality and impossibility of his demands, but in spite of the analyst's multiple interventions he maintained his resistances without therapeutic progress. Eventually, after $3^1/_2$ years, the stalemate was broken by a mutual decision to discontinue the attempt at analysis.

The last two vignettes illustrate the concept that tactical and/or strategic resistances may at times be so intense and rigidly persistent that treatment by psychoanalysis or psychoanalytic psychotherapy is ineffective. However, as illustrated by the case of the negative therapeutic reaction, this determination usually can be made definitively only during the course of an actual therapeutic attempt. Although the therapist may recognize from the beginning that difficult resistances will occur, knowing whether or not they will prove intractable requires experience in the therapeutic situation. In such cases the therapist must continue the search for other hidden resistances, and must also accept the possibility that his own personality characteristics or countertransference factors are involved in the resistances. At such times one possible resource for the therapist is to obtain a consultation from an experienced colleague. Another is to consider referring the patient to a different therapist.

Psychoanalytic or Nonpsychoanalytic Forms of Treatment

In retrospect the question might be raised whether other types of interventions or other forms of therapy might have been more effective and successful with these patients.

In the case of the woman with the eroticized transference, it is possible that more frequent sessions might have enabled her to more comfortably tolerate the transference conflict, have a more sustained situation in which to resolve it, and thus reduce the intensity of the acting out. However, reality factors precluded this possibility. It might also be suggested that when the transference reactions first emerged, the treatment could have been changed to one less likely to promote

transference responses. However, many patients with eroticized transferences are eventually able to resolve them satisfactorily with positive
therapeutic gains.

In the case ending in a stalemate, it might be argued that given the
intensity and repetitiveness of his early psychic traumata and experiences the patient was probably not analyzable from the outset, and that
a more actively encouraging, modeling, confronting, or reinforcing form
of treatment would have been indicated. However, this patient had
undertaken a prior attempt at psychotherapy in which some of those
techniques were used, presenting himself for analysis with no significant
personality change. In spite of the poor prognosis it was felt that he
warranted a trial psychoanalysis, and given his characteristic negativism
and oppositional behavior it is unlikely that more active or directive
parameters would have influenced the outcome.

Even more intense resistances may be manifested in patients whose
presenting symptoms and neurotic behaviors provide immediate pleasure, satisfaction, or relief of tension. These include such behaviors as
the sexual perversions, sexual promiscuity, compulsive gambling, overeating, alcoholism and/or drug abuse, and so on.

Clinical experience demonstrates that there are also patients for
whom psychoanalysis or psychoanalytic psychotherapy will not be effective with any therapist. In such instances the goals of treatment must
be changed to be compatible with the patient's resistances, and either
the therapist himself can conduct the appropriate nonpsychoanalytic
treatment or the patient should be referred elsewhere to obtain it.

The most intense resistances of all are found in those patients who,
in spite of significant and prolonged suffering and disability, refuse to
enter therapy, or after beginning treatment elect to quit almost immediately.

Resistance as a Single Aspect of the Therapeutic Process

In this discussion the concept of resistance has been artificially sin-
gled out and separated from other elements of psychoanalytic process.
In the actual clinical situation, attention to resistances is only one of
many activities in which the therapist engages. But the understanding
and management of resistances is an important hallmark by which psychoanalysis and psychoanalytic psychotherapy can be separated conceptually from each other, and from the many other kinds of psychiatric
treatment.

References

Breuer, J., & Freud, S. Studies on hysteria. *Standard edition* (Vol. 2). London: Hogarth Press, 1955. (Originally published, 1893–1895.)

Dewald, P. A. The process of change in psychoanalytic psychotherapy. *Archives of General Psychiatry*, 1978, *35*, 535–542. (a)

Dewald, P. A. The psychoanalytic process in adult patients. *Psychoanalytic Study of the Child*, 1978, *33*, 323–332. (b)

Eissler, K. R. The effect of the structure of the ego on psychoanalytic technique. *Journal of the American Psychoanalytic Association*, 1953, *1*, 104–143.

Fenichel, O. *Problems of psychoanalytic technique*. New York: Psychoanalytic Quarterly, 1941.

Freud, A. *The ego and the mechanisms of defense*. New York: International Universities Press, 1936.

Freud, S. The interpretation of dreams. *Standard edition* (Vol. 5). London: Hogarth Press, 1953. (Originally published, 1900.)

Freud, S. The ego and the id. *Standard edition* (Vol. 19). London: Hogarth Press, 1961. (Originally published, 1923.)

Freud, S. Inhibitions, symptoms and anxiety. *Standard edition* (Vol. 20). London: Hogarth Press, 1959. (Originally published, 1926.)

Glover, E. *The technique of psychoanalysis*. New York: International Universities Press, 1955.

Greenson, R. R. *The technique and practice of psychoanalysis*. New York: International Universities Press, 1968.

Stone, L. On resistance to the psychoanalytic process: Some thoughts on its nature and motivations. In B. Rubenstein (Ed.), *Psychoanalysis and contemporary science*. New York: Macmillan, 1973.

Waelder, R. The Principle of multiple function: Observations on overdetermination. *Psychoanalytic Quarterly*, 1936, *5*, 45–62.

4

Levels of Resistance in the Psychotherapeutic Process

Sidney J. Blatt and H. Shmuel Erlich

Introduction

Psychotherapy, when approached and practiced from a psychodynamic point of view, often gives the impression of resting on conceptual structures that, to some degree, seem circularly defined. Most of the concepts are interlocking and involve the definition of other related concepts. That is certainly the case with such concepts as transference, repetition compulsion, defense, ego function, fixation and regression, and many more. With the possible exception of transference, however, there is hardly a concept that overlaps and partakes of so many other definitions as that of resistance. There is little doubt that without this term and the clinical phenomena it represents, the practice of psychodynamic, psychoanalytically oriented psychotherapy, as well as psychoanalysis proper, could hardly be envisioned. Indeed, it was the very discovery of this phenomenon, particularly in its transference form, that led Freud to the first dynamic reformulation of his views, and eventually to the development of such concepts as censorship, ego defense, the bound-

Sidney J. Blatt • Departments of Psychiatry and Psychology, Yale University, New Haven, Connecticut 06520. H. Shmuel Erlich • Department of Psychology, Hebrew University, Jerusalem, Israel.

aries among the Unconscious, Preconscious, and Conscious, and ultimately the entire structural point of view. One can thus rewrite the entire history of the development of psychoanalytic theory from the vantage point of the theory of resistance.

There is little doubt about the centrality of resistance in our daily psychotherapeutic work. It is a tall order to describe, define, and illustrate resistance, a task that calls for considering and reviewing the entire practice of dynamic psychotherapy. Obviously that is beyond the scope and purpose of this chapter. Instead we shall try to identify and approach resistance as it occurs in clinical practice, and to conceptualize these phenomena at the level of what George Klein called the clinical theory of psychoanalysis.

Traditionally resistance has been used almost synonymously with defense, or as "everything in the words and actions [of the patient] that obstructs his gaining access to his unconscious" (Laplanche & Pontalis, 1974, p. 394). In this view, resistance is an obstruction that interferes with the work of therapy, something that occurs within the patient and is an impediment to the treatment process. There is resistance when the patient is unable to consider certain issues and when there is a disruption of the flow of the therapeutic process. At such times one observes discontinuity, fragmentation, or disorganization in the flow of material and in the development of the therapeutic alliance. Therapy does not proceed according to expectation, and the therapist considers the possibility that to some degree the patient is consciously or unconsciously resisting.

This formulation of resistance was based on the original focus in psychoanalysis on instincts, drives, and the vicissitudes of defense. But there has been a progressive elaboration of psychoanalytic theory to include a focus on ego functions and processes of adaptation and especially on the role of object relations in psychological development. These new emphases require a reexamination and redefinition of basic concepts and observations, including the concept of resistance—one that is central to a theory of psychoanalytic technique. Resistance, in this expanded psychoanalytic model, can no longer be viewed as an occurrence exclusively within the patient—as a defense against "gaining access to his unconscious"; instead resistance must be defined in terms of the object relationship—as occurring within the therapeutic dyad, as something between the patient and the therapist that interferes with the flow of the therapeutic process. Resistance is manifested as a disruption of the work of the therapy, and yet at the same time the task of therapy is the resolution of the forces that create these disruptions. Resistance can be relatively brief and limited, or a relatively enduring and extensive impasse within the therapeutic relationship experienced by the therapist and/or the patient. Resistance is thus an expression of distortions in the patient's mode of relatedness as they impinge on a particular therapist at specific moments in treatment. It is a consequence of the transaction between a patient's modes of relating and personal distortions, and the therapeutic context established by the therapist. Conscious and unconscious reluctance, hesitation, fear, inability or unwillingness to consider certain issues may or may not become a resistance depending on the response of the therapist, the capacities of the patient, and the general context of the therapeutic alliance. Reluctances, hesitations, and fears all have an inherent potential to reach the proportion of an impasse or resistance in the therapy. Within the limitations of the patient's capacities, a therapist can transform this reluctance into a resistance, or respond in a way that enables the patient to gain increased awareness and understanding of his tendencies to limit and/or distort his experiences. Although resistances typically evolve out of a defensive reluctance or hesitation within the patient, it depends in part on the therapist's response whether the reluctances and hesitations become a resistance that disrupts the therapeutic process. Resistance is as much an experience within the therapeutic relationship contributed to in part by the style of the therapist, as it is a dynamic process within the patient. Resistance is a natural consequence of the transaction between the patient's characteristic modes of relatedness and the analyst's therapeutic style and skill. As such it constitutes an integral aspect of the evolving therapeutic process. Paradoxically, although resistances are brief or prolonged attempts that thwart the therapeutic process, the entire process of psychoanalytic psychotherapy involves an essential working out of the resistances that arise within the therapeutic process.

Resistances are expressions of fundamental distortions in the patient's modes of relatedness within a particular therapeutic relationship. The skill of the therapist in helping the patient become aware of and understand the presence and power of these resistances is an essential aspect of the therapeutic process. Thus, although resistance may be regarded as an expression of conscious and unconscious attempts to defend against recalling a particular traumatic event or acknowledging a particular drive or impulse, it has come to be seen as a basic aspect of the patient's personality organization and character style expressed in a particular therapeutic relationship. Resistance is a fundamental reaction that enables an individual to avoid frustration and anxiety, and to rely on established, repetitive modes of gaining satisfaction and re-lating to others. The therapeutic task is to create a climate in which the patient feels relatively safe and free to explore experiences, thoughts, and feelings about himself and aspects of his life. Interpretations, rather than being definitive statements of fact that seal off inquiry, should be observations that facilitate inquiry either by enabling the patient to ob-serve his reluctance, unwillingness, and fear of exploring aspects of his life or by facilitating the patient's willingness to observe facets of ex-perience of which he has been unaware. The patient must come to understand and recognize the mechanisms and processes of resistance as well as what it is that he is reluctant to recognize and explore.

Types of Resistance

Resistance, however, is not a unitary phenomenon. At least three levels or types of resistance can be articulated: episodic resistance, trans-ference resistance, and fundamental resistance to change.

Episodic Resistance

Episodic resistance is a relatively circumscribed form of resistance in which a particular defense or reluctance occurs around a specific conflictual issue within the limited context of a single or several thera-peutic sessions. The resistance is delimited and well defined in its expres-sion and effect. Although it has some relation to broader expressions of resistance and defense, the episodic resistance is usually more focused, related to a particular, immediate situational event, and, when handled effectively, has limited effect on the therapeutic process. It occurs within a limited sequence of hours, usually in consequence of an immediate environmental event and in relation to a particular conflictual issue. A patient, for example, may come to an hour after a series of experiences and be hesitant to discuss them because of embarrassment, guilt, shame, or fear. The patient may forget to discuss the event, or fail to introduce it in the therapy because it was not considered important, or the patient may be querulous and uncooperative as he consciously or unconsciously suppresses and avoids dealing with the content and the affect associated with the event. The therapist's sensitivity to the issue, his recognition and articulation of the patient's difficulty with the experience, and his tactful comments, which diminish the patient's fears about discussing the issue, facilitate the flow of the therapeutic process. Although sensitive and successful intervention around particular episodic resistance may seem to have only a limited consequence in that it appears to deal with a limited and temporary interruption of the therapeutic process, it actually may have important long-range consequences. Sensitive and tactful handling of episodic resistances facilitates the patient's feeling that he is understood and respected by the therapist. It also establishes the paradigm for dealing with the more difficult and painful issues.

Transference Resistance

The second form of resistance, expressed in the transference relationship, involves a repetitive reenactment of earlier modes of interpersonal relations. The patient is unaware of the repetitive nature of his interpersonal relationships and of the availability of alternative modes of relating within the therapeutic relationship. Transference resistances are the expression of well-established, primary modes of relatedness that have their antecedents in primary relationships in the past and that are expressed in minor and major form in many subsequent relationships. Transference in and of itself is a form of resistance because it reflects the reluctance or inability to relinquish well-established, deeply ingrained, repetitive modes of adaptation in favor of attempting new, alternative, and more mature modes. The therapist is experienced and reacted to in ways that are essentially repetitions of earlier relationships. There is little recognition of the distortions the repeated mode of relatedness creates, and the patient is unable to consider alternate forms of relatedness. This type of resistance pervades much of the therapeutic process and its eventual analysis is central to the progress of the therapy.

The same basic issues can be expressed in limited episodic resistances as well as in a more pervasive transference resistance. But the transference resistance occurs in a broader context and is expressed in a variety of specific forms throughout the analysis. Transference resistance has a continuity over time. It has continuity with the past as well as continuity in basic form, content, and structure throughout the analysis. The resistance is expressed in the establishment of repetitive modes of relating which are inappropriate for the therapeutic context because they are a transference reenactment of well-established modes of interpersonal relations established at an earlier point in development.

Fundamental Resistance to Change

The third form of resistance, although related to transference resistance, is still broader and more basic: a fundamental resistance to change and growth. This resistance has been discussed previously as a developmental resistance, that is, as an adhesion of the libido. It is an expression of the basic wish to maintain well-established modes of adaptation that, although limited and at times even painful, are at least familiar and predictable. These modes, even though somewhat maladaptive, have achieved a degree of stability that the patient is fearful of relinquishing for new and as yet unproven modes. The resistance is against change per se and the disruption of an established equilibrium. There are intense pressures to inhibit growth, a fear of the future, of change and the unknown. Thus there is a block against the natural propellant toward growth.

This level of resistance, though often well hidden and insidious, is disruptive to the entire flow of the therapeutic process. The patient is fearful of exploring new conceptions of self and of progressing to new levels of thinking, feeling, and relating. There is a fear of considering oneself in new ways, a fear of the demands and expectations of more mature modes of adaptation. The patient takes an essentially counter-developmental stance.

This fundamental resistance occurs to some extent in every psychotherapeutic undertaking, and one of the primary tasks of the therapy is to analyze the resistances that thwart the natural impetus toward growth and development. In some patients fundamental resistance to change can be extensive and profound, and can seriously limit the effects of the therapeutic process. The task of the therapist is to create a context in which the patient can begin to consider alternate ways of relating, and to recognize some of the forces that compel him to repeat prior modes of adaptation, thus initiating a natural process of unfolding with its momentum toward becoming. One of the primary tasks in analysis is to make use of episodic resistance and the repetition of former modes of relatedness to articulate some of the forces that thwart the natural movement toward growth and more mature forms of relatedness.

Resistance in Clinical Practice

Thus, resistance should be considered on three overlapping, interdependent, and interrelated levels. This view of resistance distinguishes momentary, episodic resistances from resistances that are fundamental to the entire process of change. Resistance evolves within the therapeutic relationship and occurs on any or all of these three levels. Differentiating the levels of resistance can help the therapist determine his reactions to instances of resistance. The meaning and purpose of episodic resistance, for example, can be differentiated from the more pervasive forms of resistance. Episodic resistances may be dealt with more directly because they are limited in expression and are of less long-range consequence. One must consider their situational context, their meaning, purpose, and intensity, and when during the analytic process they occur. This form of resistance is common in therapy; its management depends on the skills and tact of the therapist. It is often relatively easy, for example, to facilitate a woman's consideration of her envy of the social power and prerogatives of men, including penis envy, by pointing out that men are often equally envious of the biological creative potentiality of women. Although episodic resistance is important in intensive psychotherapy and psychoanalysis, the transference resistances and the fundamental resistances are much more pernicious and must be more fully understood because they can seriously limit and even disrupt the therapeutic process.

It is important to stress that all three types of resistance always occur in an interpersonal field within the therapeutic dyad. But the three vary in terms of the degree to which they are influenced by unconscious forces within the patient, the patient's current life situation, and factors within the therapeutic context. Episodic resistances seem primarily to be an expression of aspects of the therapeutic context that have meaning for the patient, such as personal aspects of the therapist, changes in the physical properties of the office, the general experience of being in therapy itself, and so on. They may also stem from particular thoughts and feelings and the apprehensions and defenses associated with them, for example, shame about mentioning frankly oral, anal, or sexual impulses and fantasies. Although this form of resistance may contain elements that are congruent with more extensive forms, in the episodic resistance they have a circumscribed and relatively transient character. These resistances usually do not pose serious blocks to the therapeutic process. To manage them the therapist must be clinically sensitive in identifying the nature of the resistance, in understanding its meaning for the patient, its possible relation to the patient's current life situation, and the role the therapeutic context may have played in its emergence. The therapist must have interpersonal tact in helping the patient recognize some of the personal and situational factors that have contributed to the formation and expression of the resistance. Clinical skill and interpersonal tact are needed to help patients discuss their experiences freely, so that their hesitations do not reach the level of becoming an impasse to treatment. It often suffices simply to wait a brief while until the patient gathers the courage to begin dealing with the issue, or simply to comment on the fact that the patient seems hesitant about discussing something.

Other types of resistances, however, are determined much more by powerful, internal, unconscious forces within the patient than by immediate or situational factors. These types of resistances are also expressed in the therapeutic dyad, but they seem to occur relatively independently of the therapist or the therapeutic context. The transference resistance and the fundamental resistance to change seem to be more expressive of the patient's major difficulties, and their resolution is much more central to the therapeutic process.

It should be noted that every resistance is in some way connected to an object relation, present and/or past. The difference between transference resistance and resistance to growth primarily lies in the degree to which the object relation and the issue it represents are both more central and apparent. The therapist's task with fundamental resistance to change is, paradoxically, to use all his tact and skill in order to turn it, as it were, back on itself and into an object-related issue. In this sense the analyst transforms a third-level resistance into a transference resistance. Another way of stating it is that every resistance in psychotherapy can and should be conceptualized as taking place within the therapeutic dyad.

One of the implications of this conceptualization of resistance is that there are also three levels of therapeutic gain or avenues to change. Analysis of the resistance has yield to the patient at three possible levels. At the episodic level, it enhances awareness of specific states and events and their related, underlying meaning. At the second, or transference level, it broadens awareness of the genetic or historic base underlying the repetition of numerous episodic events. Finally, at the third level, once that resistance is overcome, it creates self-awareness, and that involves to some extent personality reorganization and even characterological change. Thus there is a direct link between the analysis of the various levels of resistance and the occurrence of different types of change in the process of psychotherapy.

Another important implication of our model is for the understanding of countertransference. Resistance occurs in the therapeutic dyad, and is heavily influenced by the therapist's capacities and limitations, sensitivities and insensitivities, astuteness and blind spots. The therapist's countertransferential difficulties may also occur at any of the three levels discussed. He may, for example, be oblivious or unresponsive to specific issues brought up directly or indirectly by the patient, thus contributing to their becoming episodic resistances that are, at least for the time being, difficult to resolve. In this or other ways he may contribute to their becoming transference resistances, especially when the patient begins to sense the shortcoming in the therapist. The therapist may also be blinded by broader, object-related issues from his past, and this problem will interfere with the patient's ability to resolve his transference resistances. Usually these are the issues around which horns are locked and analyses and psychotherapies come to a standstill or stalemate. A final and not unrelated factor is the therapist's capacity to overcome his own resistance to growth. It is the therapist's own capacity as well as openness to personal growth that provide the leverage for analyzing and resolving difficult transference–countertransference resistances and stalemates. In the final analysis, it is the therapist's capacity courageously to face his own resistance to growth and to realize his own strengths and limitations that provides the upper limit for the success of any therapeutic undertaking.

Case History

To illustrate the more pervasive forms of resistance we shall present a detailed summary of an analysis of a single patient. The patient entered psychoanalysis because of his concerns about homosexuality and made progress in analysis. Eventually he was more comfortable with his sexual orientation, less vulnerable to intense feelings of depression, and able to develop appropriate career plans and establish more meaningful interpersonal relationships. The treatment was unsuccessful, however, in terms of the patient's original goal in entering analysis, which was to become heterosexual. Homosexual patients are generally considered to have poor prognosis in all forms of psychotherapy, including psychoanalysis, because of their fundamental resistance to change. This case is presented in the hope of illustrating the nature of transference resistance and the fundamental resistance to change—the more pervasive forms of resistance and the real challenge in intensive psychotherapy and in psychoanalysis.[1]

Mr. K., a 23-year-old social work student at a local university, was seen in psychoanalysis five times weekly for 2½ years. He sought analysis primarily because of his concerns about homosexuality. He had been involved in homosexual relationships since early adolescence (age 12 or 13) and throughout his attendance at college. He felt increasingly uncomfortable about his homosexuality and was apprehensive that it would "destroy his life." His new part-time job involved working with adolescent youth groups and especially with young adolescent boys, and he was concerned because he was sexually attracted to some of them. He was also frightened that he would become an "old queer" who would start picking up young boys in railroad stations and public toilets, and would eventually be caught and held up to public ridicule. He felt relatively comfortable with other aspects of his life, and his concerns focused almost exclusively on his homosexuality. He was a bright, physically attractive, engaging young man who made superficial friendships easily, was liked by his contemporaries, and functioned reasonably well in his academic work.

Mr. K. described his mother as a domineering, manipulative, harsh, and controlling woman who made the major decisions in the family. His father was described as a passive, introverted man who often refused to accompany the family on vacation trips. The father was a merchant and spent a great deal of time puttering in the garden, cleaning and dusting the house, and continually straightening up and emptying ashtrays. Mr. K. felt no relationship with his father and little in common with him.

Mother's control and manipulation were exemplified in early memories of her excessive concerns about Mr. K.'s inguinal hernia. When he was a child she would often interrupt his play and press her finger into his groin to check if the hernia had popped out, and would push the hernia back in place. Later on she often gave him lectures with stern prohibitions about aspects of dating, and discussed at length her censure of "sexually loose" girls. He recalled an incident in seventh grade when he was walking downtown with his mother. As they approached a group of girls, his mother told him to walk along, past the girls, mother following somewhat behind. Mother then reported that she overheard the girls comment about what a "queer" guy he was. Mr. K. could not understand her

---

[1] In presenting this case we do not mean to suggest that all individuals with a homosexual orientation should be seen in psychotherapy or psychoanalysis. Instead, therapy should be available to them, as with all individuals, if and when aspects of their lives create personal distress and/or functional inefficiencies they find unacceptable or intolerable.

reasons for mentioning this comment to him other than her hope that he would change and improve.

Mr. K. had one sibling, a brother 10 years his senior. His mother also had a daughter who died at 6 months in a "crib death," and Mr. K. often had the fantasy that his mother viewed him as a replacement for the dead baby sister. His brother was unmarried, and shortly after he began analysis Mr. K. learned definitely that his brother was homosexual. Mr. K. had many painful early memories of his brother's leaving home for vacations, class trips, to go to the military, and subsequently to college and law school.

Mr. K.'s primary psychological organization was obsessive-compulsive and he was greatly concerned about maintaining control. Intellectualization and isolation were his major defenses; they were rigidly held and only late in analysis did they yield somewhat. When he began to associate or elaborate some aspect of his fantasy life, he would suddenly stop because he felt he was losing control. Analysis was difficult for him; he often felt he was losing control and talked about being able to press a button in his mind and change the scene. He was interested in possessing "weapons": that is, information about someone that he could use in order to maintain the upper hand. In his homosexual relationships he was concerned about who would make the first overture, and he gained a sense of control when people approached him. He became depressed and anxious when he felt he lacked this sense of control. He wanted to be sought after, desired, and he became tense and uncomfortable if he had to initiate contact. This issue of having weapons and being in control expressed itself continually in the transference.

He tried to maintain control over the analysis by remaining distant and aloof. Whereas he continually protested that the analyst was cold and distant like his father, he also wanted to keep the relationship distant and safe. He spoke with fondness of one of his homosexual partners prior to starting the analysis who had a receding hairline like his brother. As he discussed this relationship, he realized that the hairline was also similar to the analyst's and he became angry about the implication that he might have homosexual wishes toward him. If he acknowledged these homosexual wishes the analyst would have something on him that could be used to control him and hurt him; and he wanted something on the analyst. He wanted the analyst to avow affection and attraction toward him so that he would be the one to have power. He feared rejection, and fought for control and distance so as not to feel vulnerable and risk being rejected. He was frightened of any close emotional contact, and wanted no "entangling alliances." He did not want to become dependent on analysis and he protested at length that he was certainly not interested in the analyst. He reacted strongly, however, to the analyst's vacations and absences; he became depressed and had suicidal thoughts, which he defended against by seeking homo-sexual contacts. He was concerned about showing his frailty, weak-ness, and affection and instead tried to maintain an isolated, intel-lectualized, narcissistic posture in which he was powerful and in control. Being dependent was "like being on a fishhook," to be a follower was "like putting your head in a lion's mouth, you leave yourself open." He was unable to accept and express passive long-ings and feelings of depression, and he dealt with these feelings by seeking homosexual contacts. When they approached him sexually, people showed that they needed him and sought him out. He strug-gled to "be above people," to have them need him; he wanted to be a leader, God-like, independent of everyone.

He became increasingly uncomfortable about his losing control in analysis, and feared that his weakness and inadequacies were being exposed. He resented the fact that the analyst was "in the driver's seat." If the analyst remained silent, Mr. K. experienced him as aloof. If the analyst attempted to comment on aspects of Mr. K.'s feelings, he felt the analyst was in control and had the upper hand. In the ninth month of the analysis, he made a dramatic gesture to leave analysis by abruptly getting up from the couch and announcing that he was leaving because it was clear to him that the analyst did not care about him. In a somewhat authoritative manner the analyst abruptly told him to return to the couch and continue his associa-tions. Although he could have experienced the analyst's reaction as an expression of power and control, he instead experienced it as an indication that the analyst cared about him. He needed to have this experience in concrete terms and the usual general supportive tone of the analytic relationship seemed insufficient to assure him of acceptance and respect. The analyst's abrupt, somewhat authorita-tive command to return to the couch dealt with the episodic resist-ance, but the basic issues of feeling vulnerable and unloved were to reappear throughout the analytic work.

After this episodic expression of resistance he resumed the anal-ysis; in subsequent hours he reported several dreams about the analyst that had homosexual content. Throughout the analysis he continued to deny what he considered the "obvious implications" of his dreams, associations, and slips that revealed affectionate feel-ings or homosexual fantasies about the analyst. He felt he could not acknowledge these feelings because there was no possibility of their being reciprocated. Acknowledging such feelings would only give the analyst the upper hand. Late in the analysis, when these homo-sexual transference feelings became most apparent and intense, he began to miss hours. Much of the transference was associated more with his brother than his father. As the analysis unfolded there were suggestions of a homosexual seduction by his brother during the patient's childhood. When this material began to emerge in the third year of the analysis, the patient abruptly interrupted the analysis.

The fact that his homosexuality was focused around his brother initially became apparent in his first homosexual contact after starting analysis. When he began analysis he had not had homosexual relations for over a year. He went to visit his brother for winter vacation; his mother and father were to join him there. It was during this visit that Mr. K.'s brother revealed to him that he was homosexual. In addition, the brother introduced Mr. K. to his homosexual friends and it was at this time that Mr. K. began the first of a long series of homosexual affairs. Mr. K. also spoke of his discomfort when his brother would sit beside him on the couch or bed and place his hand on Mr. K.'s thigh while they talked. The homosexual involvement with the brother during Mr. K.'s childhood emerged in fuller form only late in the analysis, shortly before the analysis was interrupted. The patient had a dream that the analyst had changed offices, and he would now see the analyst in a new office that had oak-paneled walls. His associations to this dream extended over several weeks and he finally recalled that until the age of 5 he and his brother shared a bedroom, but at that time the family built an addition to their house that included a new bedroom for the brother paneled in oak. Mr. K. recalled, in a dramatic moment, how on entering this bedroom he was always impressed by the paneling. It was the most outstanding feature of the room. Mr. K. became very upset by this memory because it occurred at a time when he had been "accusing" one of his friends of being introduced into homosexuality by the friend's older brother, and he was aware that it had implications for how he was introduced to homosexuality. It was at this point that he felt he had "gone far enough in the analysis," that he was "comfortable with being a homosexual," and that he should terminate his analysis.

Mr. K.'s intense castration concerns, which involved both the fear and the wish to be castrated, were another major issue in his homosexuality. Since childhood he felt that there was something wrong with his penis. He was concerned about the "hole" in his penis, and had the thought that it was really a vagina. His early homosexual play during early adolescence was in part motivated by the desire to see if his genitalia were similar to other boys' and if "they were in the same place." He was very troubled in adolescence by his erections, and spoke to his mother about it. When he was 11 to 12 years old both his mother and his brother teased him about his interest in girls. His mother continually admonished him "never to touch girls," but "she never said that touching boys was bad." During the time he was discussing his childhood concerns that his penis was defective, he reported a dream in which a painter came into his dormitory room in order to paint it. When the painter opened his mouth to speak he had seven sets of teeth, arranged in tierlike fashion. He found this dream dirty and obscene and was upset by it. When the painter opened his mouth he was also upset by the

man's halitosis. His association to this feeling was that vaginas are
smelly and dangerous because one can get syphilis from them. He
recalled that one of his childhood fantasies of female genitalia was
that the vagina was full of sores. He also spoke of his concerns that
he too had halitosis and that he might lose his friends because of
it. It was at this point that he first mentioned mutual fellatio as one
of his early adolescent homosexual experiences. At this time in analysis he became upset because thoughts were emerging too rapidly
and he was being overwhelmed by them. He felt as if someone were
pressing against his penis and testicles and pushing them back into
his body. His next association was of his mother pushing her fingers
into his hernia and his thought that she was trying to make him into
a girl. He felt unable to express anger at her at that time because
she was "simply too strong and emasculating," and so the feeling
of unexpressed rage persisted. Not only was she preoccupied with
his hernia, but each day she inquired about his bowel movements
and insisted on giving him an enema if he had not had a bowel
movement. He believed that his mother wanted him to be a replacement for his dead sister, and he was glad his sister was not named
Phyllis because it reminded him of syphilis. As a child he often
thought of himself as a girl. He spoke of envying women because
they were able to give men satisfaction in ways he never could. In
his homosexuality he sought to be close in a "fatherly or brotherly
love" where he was accepted and could express tender feelings.

Mr. K.'s homosexual activity became more intense during times
when he was trying to deal with separation, such as the end of the
academic year, when his friends would leave for holidays, or during
vacations from analysis. He would react strongly to people leaving,
often being unable to say good-bye. Interpretations of the recourse
to homosexual experiences to cope with feelings of loss and depression led to memories of when, as a young boy, he would imagine
himself with his brother who was in the military. He recalled that
at age 7 he would lie in bed and press an immaginary button that
would transport him to being back with his brother, lying together
in bed. He recalled how upset and depressed he became when his
brother left home to go on various trips. He also remembered being
particularly depressed at age 12 to 13 when his brother left home to
go to law school. It was during this time that he "lost his interest
in girls."

He became increasingly aware that heterosexuality meant disappointing his mother's wish to have a daughter to replace the child
she lost. Heterosexuality also meant rejecting his father and brother.
It was during this hour that he commented on a photograph on the
wall of the analyst's office in which there was a cloud formation. He
interpreted, with considerable delight, the cloud as looking like a
"rubber beach toy, a hobbyhorse without feet, sort of a Donald Duck
rubber beach horse." The cloud underneath the hobbyhorse looked

like an "Arabic dagger." The forms were well perceived, but the content clearly expressed his castration wishes and fears. In subsequent hours he reported several dreams of knives and razors that belonged to his father or brother. Based on his associations, the analyst interpreted his concern about being castrated as his apprehension that his penis would be broken or damaged during intercourse. It was impressive that during the several months Mr. K. worked on these dreams there was a marked decline in his homosexual activity. He explored his fears of castration as well as his wish to be castrated. He became very upset by an explicit oedipal dream in which he attempted to seduce his mother in a motel room. In the dream the mother was naked and he touched her thigh. On awakening, he felt uncertain if the person in the dream was really his mother or one of his homosexual partners. It seemed clear that his homosexuality was, in part, a regressive defense against unresolved oedipal impulses. He recalled playing "horsie" with mother on Sunday mornings and that on one morning he saw a spot of blood on the bedsheet; and he thought that she refused to let him play horsie (get on her stomach and bounce on her) ever again because he had an erection. He was unwilling to consider the relationship of his homosexuality to these incestuous wishes, and again missed several analytic hours. After missing these hours he returned to comment that the one time he was on a class trip his grandfather had died. He expressed concern about the analyst's forthcoming vacation, and he commented that several of his friends were also leaving and once again he had begun to seek homosexual partners to cope with feelings of loneliness. During these hours he discussed his fondness for the analyst despite the "impersonal situation of psychoanalysis." He then had a dream in which the analyst told him he was leaving for another city so he "could continue his surgery and psychoanalysis there." He was sad and unhappy during the dream, and embarrassed about reporting it. For the first time he began exploring feelings of depression and loneliness when abandoned and his need to do something to cope with these feelings. He began to talk about homosexuality as now being accepted in society, that it was not an illness, and that there was nothing wrong with being a homosexual. He expressed concern that he might make an "asshole" of himself but at the same time he began wrapping his legs around the bolster of the analytic couch. The movement of the bolster back and forth between his legs seemed to indicate his wish to become an "asshole" for the analyst to penetrate. The sequence of the material over these months of analysis made it clear that a significant part of his motivation for homosexuality was the danger of the incestuous wish for a castrating and intrusive woman. In these incestuous wishes he felt in danger and depreciated. He experienced loneliness and depression around feelings of being abandoned and unloved, and he turned to men for love, tenderness, and affection. But the men he unconsciously sought were also often incestuous objects, fraught with both excitement and danger. He wanted to be certain of their acceptance and love, but at the same time was frightened by the incestuous homosexual impulses. Although he actively sought the analyst's love he also had to keep him at a distance—as unavailable. The more aware he became of the incestuous aspects of his longings for the analyst's love, the more he had to seek other homosexual relationships and run away.

He became increasingly upset and angered by the analyst's lack of responsiveness, and by the belief that in his feelings toward the analyst he was "compromising his dignity." His homosexual contacts increased markedly and he became infatuated with a man he picked up in a bar, began going to gay parties, and decided to share an apartment with one of his previous homosexual partners. He would often meet his homosexual dates after dinner, and he described himself as "their dessert." He had the mistaken impression one afternoon that he saw the analyst waiting for a bus, and that the analyst turned away on seeing him because he was jealous and did not want to see his homosexual partner who was riding behind him on a motorcycle. He saw this jealousy as the analyst's problem and claimed it did not represent any of his own feelings toward the analyst. He claimed that he had no feelings whatsoever about the analyst, and certainly no homosexual feelings. He had only wanted the analyst to see his partner because he was so proud of him. The analyst commented on how Mr. K. seemed to be trying to make him jealous of his homosexual partners. For the first time he commented that he always checked his trouser zipper each time before entering the analyst's office. He did not know why he did so, and he did not want to consider any implications because he had found renewed vitality in his homosexual relationship. He began to feel analysis was taking too much time and that it was difficult because the analyst remained aloof and unresponsive to him. He became involved in decorating and cleaning his apartment. He talked about inventing "spray dirt" to give things an old, used look. He thought of a new type of plastic container for the refrigerator, one on which a person could write the name of the contents of the container. He had received a set of silver candlesticks as a gift and had the impulse to cut them in half and throw them in the river. He said that the candlesticks represented both a penis and a vagina because of the opening at the top. He took increasing delight in caring for his apartment and cooking. He and his roommate began to have anal intercourse and he enjoyed being penetrated. Much of this increased homosexual activity also occurred shortly before summer vacation. Although he was aware of the relationship between his increased homosexual activity and his feelings of loss, he was unable to curtail the homosexuality. On returning from vacation he canceled 2 weeks of appointments and came in with the announcement that he had decided to terminate analysis. At the analyst's suggestion he remained in analysis several more weeks, but he remained resolute to terminate and early in October he came in to say good-bye. He felt that becoming heterosexual was an impossible dream, that he was now comfortable with his homosexuality. He had learned some "tricks," he enjoyed anal intercourse, he had made a major decision about a change in his career plans and, "most important," society was now changing its attitudes toward homosexuality so he saw no reason to continue his analysis.

The analysis of Mr. K. illustrated the complex convergence of a number of factors that can lead to the formation of homosexuality. First there was the biological factor of the inguinal hernia, which in itself probably played little direct role in his homosexuality. The mother's reaction and intense preoccupation with the hernia, however, seemed much more important than the hernia itself or its surgical correction at age 5 or 6. The surgery was rarely mentioned directly in the analysis and the associations to it primarily focused on castration themes and the abandonment in the hospital. A second factor was the death of the sister. Mr. K. clearly had the image that he was the replacement for the dead sister and that his mother wished that he were a girl. A third factor in the development of Mr. K.'s homosexuality was his mother's aggressive, "emasculating" ways, and his father's passivity, docility, and unavailability. A fourth factor, not independent of the others, was the homosexuality of the brother. The role reversal of the parents in a rather conventional, middle-class family and the death of the sister probably distorted the sexual identity formation of the brother. And the brother's homosexuality must have contributed in significant ways to Mr. K.'s confused sexual identification. There were suggestions of a homosexual seduction by the brother. In addition, the brother seemed to function as a father for Mr. K. As a second figure for identification he did not offer a constructive alternative to the passive, ineffective father.

In many ways Mr. K. worked effectively in analysis and gained considerable insight into the motivations for his homosexuality, and into his serious vulnerability to intense feelings of depression precipitated by abandonment and rejection. Although he interrupted the analysis, he seemed to have gained fuller control of his homosexual impulses and he became more comfortable with his homosexuality. This increased comfort with his homosexuality was in part attributable to his progress in the analysis and in part of his feeling that "homosexuality was now more accepted socially." Although it was possible to analyze and work through Mr. K.'s extensive use of intellectualization and isolation and other aspects of his obsessive defenses, as well as aspects of his defensive avoidance of "entangling alliances" that left him vulnerable to criticism, rejection, abandonment, and depression, the more regressive elements of the transference, particularly his intensely conflictual wish to seek his brother's and father's love through his homosexuality, seemed inaccessible to analysis.

In terms of resistance, Mr. K. illustrated both the intensity of transference resistances and a profound and fundamental resistance to change. Earlier episodic resistances, such as his impulse to abruptly interrupt an hour because he felt the analyst did not care about him, were foreshadowings of the more intense transference resistances that were to develop in the analysis. Although it was often possible to deal effectively with the various episodic resistances in the course of the analysis, it was difficult for Mr. K. to allow himself to consider the analytic relationship in terms other than those he had experienced with his parents—a battle for power and control with a manipulative, intrusive, emasculating mother, a disinterested, apathetic father, and a homosexually seductive older brother. Mr. K. alternately experienced the analyst as the intrusive, destructive mother, the disinterested, apathetic father, and, probably most importantly, an incestuous homosexual object like his brother. There seemed to be no alternative object relationship in Mr. K.'s early life that could serve as a template for him to establish a constructive working alliance. The only alternative available to Mr. K. other than a transference based on the destructive relationships within his family was to attempt to make the analyst a narcissistic extension of himself. These repetitive transference relationships and the analyst's inability to help Mr. K. find alternative models for their relationship were the basis for his major resistance to treatment.

Equally important was Mr. K.'s resistance to change. He had to maintain careful control of his thoughts and of the analytic relationship. He was frightened of the unknown, the unfamiliar, and the uncontrollable. He was unable to relinquish repetitive models of relating and to consider himself and the analyst in new and different ways. In the course of treatment Mr. K. had achieved a degree of consolidation and psychological equilibrium, and he was functioning reasonably well without undue distress and anxiety. He was reluctant to relinquish this level of equilibrium even though there were aspects of his inability to form and sustain enduring relationships that still troubled him. The exploration of the nature and the intensity of his homosexual attachment to his brother was experienced as a basic threat to his self-definition and to a newfound level of equilibrium that he had achieved in the analysis. It was this homosexual attachment to the brother, which could not be successfully addressed in the analysis, that placed an upper limit on the eventual gains Mr. K. could achieve. Mr. K. had gained considerable insight into the underlying meaning and the genetic or historic basis for much of his current behavior and functioning, but he was unable to risk entering into a level of self-reflective awareness that could have led to more basic personality reorganization and characterological change.

In some respects Mr. K.'s struggles in analysis represent important gains in beginning to understand his vulnerability to depression in response to abandonment and rejection, and the role of his homosexual object-seeking as a way of coping with this intense dysphoria. He also made gains in feeling less conflictual about his homosexuality, and was able to develop realistic plans for an alternative career in which he had less direct contact with young adolescent boys. But Mr. K.'s erotization of the transference relationship was so pervasive that it limited the gains that could be achieved in the analysis. It served as a resistance against allowing him to consider himself in ways other than as a homosexual and the analyst other than as a homosexual object. The inability of the analyst and Mr. K. to resolve this transference resistance represents a failure in the treatment process. The analyst may also have focused too much on the homosexuality per se and failed to address sufficiently the underlying anaclitic depressive issues (Blatt, 1974), the fears of abandonment, and how the intense homosexual involvements served as a defense against these depressive concerns. In part, however, Mr. K. maintained this transference resistance because of a basic fear of change and growth. To allow himself to venture into other forms of relatedness might create the "entangling alliances" that he so desperately feared because they could result in a vulnerability to profound feelings of loneliness and abandonment. But it was these alternate forms of relatedness, particularly within the therapeutic context, that were essential if Mr. K. was to achieve some degree of psychological development and growth in the analysis. The analyst, for example, remained for Mr. K. an erotized, unavailable, incestuous homosexual object rather than someone he cared about or someone with whom he could constructively identify. The only way he could resolve the dilemma of his fear of becoming "too dependent" was to denigrate the analyst and the analysis, and this attitude eventually provided the rationalization for his interruption of the analysis.

Conclusions

The analysis of Mr. K., its gains and its shortcomings, and the particular nature of Mr. K.'s resistances highlight a number of important issues about the process of therapeutic change. Progress in therapy involves the development of a greater capacity for reflective self-awareness and the renunciation of infantile object choices and infantile modes of relatedness. The goal of therapy, however, is not just an increased capacity for self-awareness, but the utilization of that awareness to establish a freedom to explore and relate, to change and to grow—a freedom to be able to make choices about how to live one's life. The understanding and handling of resistances—the interpretation of what is defended against and how therapy is resisted—is central to the entire psychotherapeutic process. Resistances are understood as they unfold in the therapeutic process as the therapist and the patient seek to identify and resolve these impasses to exploration and understanding. Resistances occur in the therapeutic relationship and are the forces that thwart active inquiry and exploration, and eventual change and growth. In its basic form, resistance is a conscious and unconscious opposition to the continuity and progress of treatment, an opposition to active inquiry, exploration, and growth within the therapeutic dyad. There are also resistances against the natural and innate tendency to move toward higher levels of organization and more mature modes of interpersonal relations. Patients resist recognizing the repetitive modes of interaction and considering new modes of relatedness. The manifest and apparent inequality and inequity of the therapeutic relationship facilitates the emergence of distorted modes of interpersonal relations. Therapeutic abstinence and neutrality encourage the expression of distorted, repetitive modes of interaction, but also provide the opportunity for recognizing and identifying these distortions and establishing new modes of relatedness. The emergence of these distorted modes of interaction is essential if the patient and therapist are to learn about these distortions and gain the insight and experiences that help the patient relinquish them. The therapeutic relationship creates an environment that gives the patient the opportunity to observe these distorted modes of relating and to develop increasingly mature object relationships. In a caring, understanding, empathic relationship, which is not directly need gratifying for the patient or the therapist, the patient is provided with empathic and insightful interpretations. These interpretations enable the patient to feel that his experiences are understandable, that there is a logic and order to his reactions, and that he can eventually gain fuller understanding of himself. Effective interpretations are not a simple uncovering or labeling of a particular impulse, defense, conflict, or traumatic event. Instead, effective interpretations facilitate internal dialogue, and broaden and deepen exploration and inquiry. Interpretations should be invitations to further exploration. They are not authoritative statements of fact, but observations of subtleties and nuances of experience that implicitly or explicitly open up a new series of observations and questions. Thus the effectiveness of an interpretation should not be judged by the degree to which a patient agrees or disagrees with it, nor by some abstract ideal of a good interpretation; but by the criterion of whether the interpretation facilitates the patient's capacity to continue exploration and inquiry within himself and within the therapeutic relationship. In this sense, an effective interpretation is reciprocally related to resistance. Incorrect, poorly stated, or ill-timed interpretations are at best of little consequence in facilitating this exploration, and at worst they provoke an increased resistance. Effective interpretations do not provide answers that seal off exploration and inquiry. Rather, effective interpretations raise further questions, open new avenues and leads for exploration, and facilitate the patient's increased participation in this exploration.

Ideally, therapy is terminated when the patient is able to conduct this inquiry and exploration for himself without fear and reluctance, without doubt and distortion, and without apprehension about discovering new, unacceptable, and dangerous facets of himself and his experiences—in brief, when resistance at all three levels is diminished or minimal.

Psychoanalysis and dynamic psychotherapy are basically processes of coming to know oneself in new ways, with new knowledge and new levels of awareness, providing the basis for new modes of relatedness. Intensive, dynamically oriented psychotherapy offers the potential to develop enriched, expanded, and more accurate knowledge about oneself, and to establish more mutually satisfying interpersonal relationships with others. The eventual establishment of an effective relationship in therapy, based on mutual respect as well as an acceptance of each other's capacities and limitations, can provide the basis for the development of more appropriate and mature relationships. There are, of course, inherent limitations to the expression of affection and respect in the therapeutic context. But as in the parent–child relationship, although these limitations are disappointing, they also provide important motivation for the development of more appropriate and mature relationships outside of the initial primary relationship. The respect, affection, and interpersonal relatedness experienced in the therapeutic relationship are internalized and provide the basis for developing more accurate conceptions of oneself and more appropriate and satisfying interpersonal relationships. As therapy progresses, the initial asymmetrical relationship ideally begins to change to a more symmetrical, collaborative relationship in which each member of the dyad contributes in his unique way to the joint endeavor. The patient recognizes that he possesses the expertise of the primacy of the data about his experience, whereas the therapist possesses objectivity and knowledge. As the patient gains more meaningful conceptions of himself and as he begins to establish a more symmetrical relationship in the therapeutic alliance, these gains begin to be expressesed in relationships outside of therapy. With successful working through of the transference resistances and the fundamental resistance to growth, the patient can relinquish infantile modes of relatedness, internalize aspects of the therapeutic relationship and use these internalizations as the basis for establishing more mature forms of relatedness first within the therapy and eventually in full and more general form in their lives. The patient internalizes the constructive aspects of the therapeutic relationship and the therapeutic process. As the patient understands some of the experiences which have forced him to seek repeatedly limited, untoward, or destructive relationships, he can begin to consider alternative concepts of himself and of relationships with others.

The constructive aspects of the therapeutic relationship provide some of the experiences through which the patient can begin to construct more accurate, differentiated, and integrated conceptions of himself and of others. Thus, the primary goals in pyschotherapy are to reduce the intensity of the resistances to inner experiences and more mature forms of interrelatedness within the therapeutic relationship, to enable the individual to become free of the need to repeat limited and untoward interactions, and to reduce the patient's fears about change and growth. These goals are accomplished by providing a climate in which the individual can come to recognize the limited forms of interaction and the forces that motivate their repetition. Therapy also provides opportunities for the individual to achieve new and developmentally more advanced levels of internalization and more accurate and appropriate concepts of himself and of others. Progress in therapy is characterized by the establishment of a more differentiated self-concept, increased self-reflectiveness, and more mature interpersonal relationships. A reduction in the intensity of resistances in analysis results in greater access to inner experiences, an openness to more mature forms of interpersonal relatedness first within the therapeutic alliance and eventually in daily life, and greater freedom and flexibility to change and grow.

ACKNOWLEDGMENT

We are indebted to Dr. Rebecca Smith Cooley for her comments on this chapter.

References

Blatt, S. J. Levels of object representation in anaclitic and introjective depression. *The Psychoanalytic Study of the Child*, 1974, 29, 107–157.
Laplanche, J., & Pontalis, J.-B. *The language of psycho-analysis* (D. Micholson-Smith, Trans.). New York: W. W. Norton, 1974.

II

Behavioral Approaches

5

Resistance and Clinical Behavior Therapy

Marvin R. Goldfried

The concept of resistance rarely if ever arose in the early literature on behavior therapy. Most of the original descriptions of behavior therapy conveyed an underlying assumption that, apart from their presenting problems, clients were totally "rational" beings who readily complied with the intervention procedures set forth. As behavior therapists began applying their procedures to unselected cases and were confronted with a wide variety of complex clinical problems, it became strikingly evident that the simple application of the appropriate technique was not always successful. Although the therapist might have been clear about the determinants associated with any problem behaviors, and may also have felt confident that certain therapeutic techniques had a good chance of bringing about the needed change, the clarity of the clinician's thinking was not always matched by the client's desire or ability to comply with the intervention procedures. It has been in the face of such instances of therapeutic noncompliance that the topic of resistance has come to the fore in behavior therapy.

Take, for example, the typical child case, where the behavior therapist attempts to enlist the assistance of parents or teachers as thera-

Work on this chapter was supported in part by Grant #MH 24327 from the National Institute of Mental Health.

Marvin R. Goldfried • Department of Psychology, State University of New York, Stony Brook, New York 11794.

peutic aides in implementing a behavioral treatment program. It is often assumed in such instances—especially by beginning therapists whose therapeutic interventions have not yet been seasoned by clinical experience—that the parent or teacher will readily comply with the instructions to use certain behavioral techniques. Would that it were so easy! Some of the causes of resistance one is likely to encounter within the clinical context are often more fully appreciated when behavior therapists attempt to use these very same techniques in dealing with their own children.

Resistance has also been encountered by behavior therapists as they have begun to develop clinical procedures for working with couples. In a most insightful chapter, Gurman (1978) has pointed out that behavior therapists engaged in marital therapy often decide on the treatment plan as if both members of the couple are comparably motivated to change. Unfortunately, the clinical fact of the matter is that one member of the pair—usually the husband—is often quite resistant to change. Even when one is fortunate enough to get the reluctant husband to enter marital therapy, he often brings with him the expectation that the therapist will help his spouse clear up *her* difficulties.

Although a great deal has been written about specific behavioral techniques that may be used in face-to-face interaction between therapist and client—relaxation training, systematic desensitization, behavior rehearsal, and the like—these procedures should be construed as preparatory aids to enable clients to react differently in their current life situation. From a behavioral approach to therapy, much of the actual change takes place *between* consultation sessions. Within this broader context, the therapist's role is to instigate the client to try out new ways of acting, and to support and reinforce such attempts when they occur. In many respects, such novel actions may be seen as providing individuals with certain needed "corrective emotional experiences" (Alexander & French, 1946). When noncompliance occurs, then, it most often manifests itself by the client not following through on some predetermined between-session homework assignment. And although much of the behavior therapy literature has tended to focus on the specific technology, it would be incorrect to assume that behavior therapists have been unconcerned with the issue of resistance. Not only some of the behavioral writings dealing with such questions as commitment to change, noncompliance, and behavioral contracts (e.g., Cameron, 1978; Davison, 1973; Goldfried & Davison, 1976; Kanfer & Karoly, 1972; Marston & Feldman, 1972; Stuart, 1971; Weiss, 1979), but also a casual conversation with any practicing behavior therapist will immediately reveal that this aspect of the behavior change process is of central concern.

As a way of providing a context for discussing resistance, it will be helpful to consider more specifically the client's role in behavior therapy. We can then turn to the actual clinical management of resistance, which consists of both generally useful and more circumscribed strategies.

The Client's Role in Behavior Therapy

When I speak of the role behaviors of the "optimal" client seen in behavior therapy, I am referring to the ideal client we often read about but all too infrequently encounter. Although there clearly are wide divergences from case to case, there nevertheless are certain attitudes and behavior patterns that can be associated with the prototypical client role.

To begin with, there are optimal *attitudes* on the part of the client that can help to facilitate the change process. At the very minimum, clients must believe that change is possible. Although one would assume that the very fact they are in therapy implies that they indeed hold this attitude, it is not at all uncommon to find clients suggesting indirectly or behaviorally that nothing could possibly be done to help them change. It is also important for clients to accept the reality that the change process will be a gradual one, and will involve a learning process entailing sustained effort on their part. Furthermore, they must accept the fact that the therapist will not be doing anything *to* or *for* them, but instead will be helping them to learn how to cope more effectively with their own lives. A client must also be favorably disposed toward the particular therapeutic strategy outlined by the therapist, holding at least a moderate amount of optimism that it will prove effective.

The ideal clients' *behavior during the sessions* reflects their willingness to discuss some of the issues that are related to their problems, their ability to follow through on specific therapeutic procedures deemed appropriate (e.g., relaxation training, desensitization, role playing), and a receptivity to the therapist's corrective feedback on their behaviors, feelings, and thinking patterns. Actual clients vary in the amount of specific direction and training they require during the consultation sessions; some are capable of making great strides on their own, whereas others require more extensive practice and guidance during the therapeutic hour. In virtually all cases, however, clients will be asked to bring in accounts of their self-observations—often in written form—summarizing their reactions to certain events that have occurred during the week. This practice enables the therapist to discuss and support their successes and to examine their difficulties in such a way as to shed light on how they may be overcome in the future (cf. Goldfried & Robins, in press).

As noted earlier, a central aspect of the therapeutic change process as viewed from a behavioral vantage point involves the *between-session activities* of the client. Consistent with the philosophy that change involves a relearning accomplished by the client's sustained efforts, most intervention programs involve some sort of "homework." At the very least, clients are expected to monitor what they do, think, and feel in various life situations. Depending on the particular problem and therapeutic procedure, homework may also entail such diverse activities as recording anxiety-producing situations, practicing relaxation exercises, trying out new assertive responses, making social contacts, restricting the physical location in which one eats or using relaxation to cope with tension.

Clinical Management of Resistance

Because the guidelines for behavioral intervention are relatively straightforward, resistance often comes as somewhat of a shock to beginning behavior therapists. For the most part, there is nothing intrinsic to the behavioral model of change—at least in principle—to suggest that difficulties in implementing the therapeutic procedure are to be anticipated. If, on the other hand, we recognize that behavior therapy is conducted by fallible human beings who have varying levels of experience and expertise and who employ methods that do not work in all cases, then obstacles to therapeutic progress should come as less of a surprise. As we have noted elsewhere:

> When progress in therapy for any given client does not proceed smoothly, we frequently accuse the client of either not being motivated enough or perhaps "not being ready for" behavior therapy. We would like to suggest, however, that *the client is never wrong.* If one truly accepts the assumption that behavior is lawful—whether it be deviant or nondeviant—then *any* difficulties occurring during the course of therapy should more appropriately be traced to the therapist's inadequate or incomplete evaluation of the case. We are not implying that this always means the behavior therapist has been incompetent in the way in which he has conceptualized or handled the case. It may very well be that our knowledge of certain problems, or the unavailability of certain concepts, principles, or techniques at this point in the

development of the field simply does not provide us with the ability to meet certain types of challenges. (Goldfried & Davison, 1976, p. 17)

In discussing how a behavior therapist can go about dealing with the client's resistance, I would like to begin by noting some therapeutic strategies that may be useful in most cases, and then move on to procedures that would be applicable under particular conditions.

Strategies for General Use

There are certain strategies that the behavior therapist would be wise to adopt in most clinical instances, either to prevent or to remedy client resistance. Among these are creating a positive context for change; structuring the treatment procedure so that it is understandable and acceptable to the client; emphasizing the gradual nature of the change process; and clearly specifying the between-session homework assignments.

Creating a Positive Context for Change. The importance of establishing a good therapist–client relationship cannot be overstated. Although much has been written about the efficacy of various behavioral techniques, these procedures do not occur in an interpersonal vacuum. Goldfried and Davison (1976) have gone so far as to suggest: "Any behavior therapist who maintains that principles of learning and social influence are all one needs to know in order to bring about behavior change is out of contact with clinical reality" (p. 55). Indeed, the importance of a caring therapist who can be trusted by his or her client may very well be a common denominator underlying most approaches to therapy (Brady, Davison, Dewald, Egan, Fadiman, Frank, Gill, Hoffman, Kempler, Lazarus, Raimy, Rotter, & Strupp, 1980).

The therapeutic relationship is particularly crucial in facilitating clients' attempts to behave differently in various life situations that occur between consultation sessions. Although such novel behavior patterns are discussed and perhaps practiced during the therapy sessions, clients ultimately need to go out and do things differently. Consequently, the therapist must often rely on a 1-hour consultation session to encourage and support clients' efforts at change during the more than 100 waking hours that comprise the rest of their week.

In attempting to establish a positive relationship with one's client, the behavior therapist would probably benefit most by drawing on common clinical lore, being perceptive of the client's thoughts, feelings, and behavior, and being capable of empathically reflecting back what is observed. Showing concern for details of the client's current life situation (e.g., remembering names of significant others, specific events, etc.) and anticipating the client's thoughts and feelings all contribute to the therapist's trustworthiness and credibility. To use Weiss's (1979) succinct description of the task requirements of the effective behavior therapist, one should "be brilliant."

The work of Erickson (1959) and Haley (1963) is particularly relevant to the question of how to enhance the therapist's credibility. They suggest that in the attempt to induce a hypnotic trance, particularly when working with a resistant subject, the hypnotist should make every effort to *utilize* whatever the subject may be doing and incorporate it into the induction. If the hypnotist is suggesting that the subject's outstretched arm has a helium balloon attached to it and is in the process of rising, but notices that the subject's arm continues to remain rigid, the suggestion may then be made that the arm is weighted down with lead, and consequently cannot rise. The underlying principle here is to have the subject construe that *anything* he or she is doing is in accordance with the hypnotist's direction. There are several ways in which this utilization technique can be employed within behavior therapy. At a specific level, it may be used in the process of relaxation training, where any extraneous movements on the part of the client are incorporated into the relaxation instructions. For the restless client, the therapist might suggest: "That's right, just move around and get yourself comfortable so you can get into a deeper state of relaxation." In the process of encouraging clients to place themselves in a somewhat anxiety-producing situation, the therapist can acknowledge that the client is *supposed to* feel somewhat apprehensive at first; if the client did not, the situation would not be very therapeutically relevant.

Although it is possible to suggest a number of procedures for establishing a positive therapeutic context and enhancing the credibility of the therapist, such suggestions are not intended as disembodied techniques that can be mechanically applied. Instead, they should be seen as guidelines that can be used to enhance the effectiveness of the already concerned and interpersonally sensitive clinician.

Structuring the Treatment Procedure. Behavior therapists have typically paid a fair amount of attention to the importance of structuring—providing clients with an underlying rationale for the use of certain therapeutic procedures and a description of what the intervention will entail. It should go without saying that, unless therapist and client are working toward the same set of goals and can agree on the means for achieving these goals, therapy has little chance of succeeding. Nevertheless, on the basis of failure experiences in the clinical practice of behavior therapy—both my own as well as those I have observed—this point needs to be emphasized. It is toward the facilitation of such agreement that careful structuring is aimed.

Inasmuch as behavior therapy tends to deal with very specific events and makes use of fairly structured procedures, there is the danger of clients not fully appreciating the relevance all this has to their more general concerns. Instead of having clients accept the relevance on the basis of blind faith, it makes considerably more sense to have them view the specifics of the therapeutic intervention within a broader context. That may best be accomplished by *not* presenting the specifics of the treatment plan until the more general framework and rationale are discussed and agreed on. As clients are able to accept the appropriateness of a general set of goals or procedures, the therapist can then become increasingly more specific, stopping at each step along the way for client feedback and reaction. Whenever possible, clients should be involved in determining the specifics of the intervention procedure, as they are more knowledgeable about their own life style and environment, and consequently are more likely to follow through under such circumstances.

This strategy of successive structuring may be illustrated in the case of clients who are depressed and would like to reduce the feeling of helplessness in their current life situation. After agreeing that this general goal is worth pursuing, the therapist can then discuss areas of the client's life in which he or she would like to have better control (e.g., social life). This phase may be followed by a more detailed consideration of specific situations and responses that would afford the client a greater sense of self-efficacy and autonomy (e.g., calling an acquaintance for a lunch date). Similarly, successive structuring may be used in delineating treatment procedures, such as behavior rehearsal. The therapist might discuss the importance of using the consultation sessions to review potential responses to various problematic life situations. Rather than suggesting that the client go out and attempt to behave differently, specific behavior patterns are then dealt with in greater detail. Finally, within the context of providing the client with a safe situation in which he or she can have a dry run, the use of role playing for rehearsal purposes may then be introduced.

What is being suggested, in essence, is that therapists take care to be "with" the client, so that goals or procedures are not pursued in the absence of the client's acknowledgment of their relevance.

Emphasizing Gradualness of Change. To increase the likelihood that clients will maintain a given level of motivation throughout the change process, it is important to convey the idea that change will occur gradually. It is not at all uncommon for clients to become discouraged on comparing where they are at a given time to where they eventually want to be. Clients should be encouraged to focus in on moving one step at a time along a given path, especially since successful compliance with a small task increases the likelihood of compliance with a more demanding one later (see Freedman & Fraser, 1966).

At the very least, clients need to recognize that therapeutic change entails a learning process, and that even their repeated and sustained efforts will result in uneven progress. Consequently, "setbacks" should be construed as temporary variations in a learning curve that in the long run reflects progress (compare the utilization technique). To the extent that the focus is on a specific behavior (e.g., number of cigarettes smoked), an actual graphing of therapeutic progress can vividly illustrate this phenomenon. Even when the particular goals of therapy cannot readily be plotted on a graph, clients may more readily see their progress by keeping written records of how they are responding to various life situations. During the therapy sessions such records can be discussed, comparing the way the clients are currently handling the situations with the way they may have responded to similar ones in the past. Such a procedure not only can encourage clients to continue their efforts to change, but also can help them gain a better appreciation of the ways they have indeed changed. Stated somewhat differently, such periodic reviews of progress can assist them in updating their self-image (cf. Goldfried & Robins, in press).

Specifying Between-Session Assignments. The behavior therapist is likely to encounter wide individual differences among clients with regard to the completion of their between-session homework assignments. Some individuals are most conscientious in following through on the therapist's suggestions, whereas others need extensive encouragement and guidance. Inasmuch as one cannot always know in advance how any given client may react, it is perhaps safest to structure the homework assignment so as to increase the likelihood of the client's compliance. Thus some discussion may be in order about the specific time and place in which the client is to engage in the activity in question.

Whenever possible, the homework should be fit into some aspect of the client's regular routine. Instead of merely encouraging clients to make attempts to cope with tension by means of relaxing, or to assert themselves, it instead might be suggested that they relax themselves each time they get behind the wheel of their car, or assert themselves while shopping in the supermarket. The use of a notebook or specifically designed record form can also help make clients more accountable to both themselves and the therapist. Each therapy session should begin with a discussion of the client's homework, so that it is very clear that this aspect of the change process is an essential part of the therapy.

As a particularly powerful method of increasing the accountability of clients for their agreed-on homework assignments, the therapist might request a telephone call on completion of the assignment. This somewhat extraordinary measure is not recommended for routine use, but for cases where clients have repeatedly had difficulty following through on a certain activity, or where there is some reason to believe they may have some difficulty doing so in a given instance. Such requests for a telephone call should not be made in a coercive context, but should be seen as coming from a concerned therapist who is sincerely interested in the client's progress. I have used this particular procedure in a wide variety of cases, and have usually found it successful.

> A 47-year-old man was seen in sex therapy with his wife because of his erectile failure during attempts at intercourse. Although sensate focus was successful in sexually arousing him, he would lose his erection as he attempted intercourse. After several instances of noncompliance in the attempt to use the "stuffing" procedure, in which the flaccid penis is inserted in the partner's vagina (Annon, 1976), the therapist got the couple to agree to attempt this method once again, but this time to follow it up with a telephone call. The telephone call proved effective in overcoming the couple's resistance.

> A 35-year-old mathematician was in danger of losing his job because of procrastination problems. Although we worked on setting up an appropriate work environment that was conducive to concentration and dealt with his inhibiting perfectionistic standards, the client was still unable to mobilize his work efforts. The telephone call made by the client after spending two hours working on a certain project proved successful well beyond my anticipation, affording him a "corrective emotional experience" that was built on in subsequent weeks.

As any experienced clinician might anticipate, however, the telephone method does not always work. In the case of a 42-year-old social
work supervisor who procrastinated over getting in his reports, the
postassignment telephone calls had only a temporary impact, and no
lasting effect. In hindsight, it might very well have been the client's self-
criticalness that was interfering with the maintenance of his efforts. In
another case, this one involving a 55-year-old clothing manufacturer
with a long history of obesity, there was a similar failure in the use of
telephone calls to the therapist following the client's attempts at controlling his eating. The most likely reason for this particular failure
seemed to be an unsatisfactory marital situation that was not readily
amenable to change. To be effective, then, this method for enhancing
accountability for between-session assignments needs to be part of a
more comprehensive treatment strategy.

Strategies for Particular Conditions

As is certainly true of clinicians from other orientations, behavior
therapists operate on the assumption that all of the client's behavior is
determined. That is held to be the case not only for the presenting
problem that may originally have brought the client into therapy, but
for any client behaviors, thoughts, or feelings that divert the course of
therapy. Although the determinants associated with resistance may be
the very same ones that maintain the presenting problem, they may also
include other characteristics of the client, factors associated with the
therapist's behavior, or aspects of the client's current environmental
situation. As is the case in attempting to gain a better understanding of
the cause of any clinical problem, simple knowledge of the *form* that the
resistance takes may provide little information as to the *reason* for this
resistance. Topographically similar actions across clients (e.g., failure to
practice relaxation homework) may be a function of one or more different
determinants (e.g., pessimism about changing, the interference of other
problems, low motivation). Thus, when encountering resistance, it is up
to the therapist to reassess the client's level of commitment, and to
explore and deal with the seemingly relevant determinants. Clinical
experience with behavior therapy suggests that resistance may reflect
any one or more of the following: a direct sampling of the client's presenting problem itself; the client's other problems; pessimism about
changing; fear of changing; minimal motivation to change; psychological
reactance; overburdening the client with too many homework assign-

ments; and interfering contingencies in the client's environment. These determinants are discussed below, together with suggestions for preventing or remedying them.

Resistance as a Sample of Client's Presenting Problem. Perhaps among the most difficult forms of resistance to deal with are those behavior patterns that are direct manifestations of the client's main reasons for entering therapy. Among the many instances of this clinical phenomenon are overly critical clients who are impatient with their therapeutic progress, uncommitted and apathetic individuals who take little initiative in following through on between-session activities, socially anxious or withdrawn clients who are minimally communicative during the therapy sessions, and procrastinating clients who never seem to get around to doing their homework assignments.

Such forms of resistance are indeed a mixed blessing in that they interfere with the course of therapy but at the same time provide the therapist with a firsthand sample of the client's problem. The situation is further complicated to the extent that such forms of resistance leave the therapist with a sense of frustration, annoyance, and at times anger. When that happens, it is particularly crucial that the clinician observe his or her own behavior and emotional reactions, and use such observation as a turning point to refocus on what the client is doing to create such feelings. On the assumption that the therapist is in relatively good contact with interpersonal reality—an issue that in itself has received insufficient attention in the behavioral literature—he or she may gain a better understanding of how other significant individuals in the client's current life may be reacting to such behavior patterns. There should follow efforts to provide the client with direct feedback on this behavior and its consequences, pointing out how it reflects the very problem that originally prompted the request for therapy. The noncompliant behavior patterns then become the particular focus of the intervention, and the goal is that any change in the therapy session will eventually generalize the other aspects of the client's life.

Resistance Resulting from Client's Other Problems. There are also instances of resistance that are primarily the consequence of client problems other than those that have been the focus of therapy. Thus if clients experience anxiety when engaging in those actions needed in following through on a homework assignment, or if they lack the necessary skills to do so, resistance is likely to occur. If the therapist is aware of these interfering sources at the outset of the intervention procedure, they can be focused on in a preventive way. Inasmuch as most practicing clinicians, however skilled, are fallible human beings, these sources of interference often must be dealt with remedially following instances of noncompliance.

Some illustrations may be helpful.

> A 40-year-old female client was anxious about being at home alone, and it became evident that she was unable to follow through with an aspect of the treatment procedure that involved spending progressively longer periods of time at home by herself. Her phobia was long-standing, and she had managed to develop a support system of well-meaning friends and relatives who had been "helping" her with their frequent visits and telephone calls. The client was extremely unassertive, and consequently was unable to do very much to discourage these attempts at assistance. Thus assertion training was required, so that the client could bring herself to rearrange her current life situation in such a way as to allow for the implementation of *in-vivo* desensitization.

> A 17-year-old male student was having difficulty adjusting to college. He had never lived away from home before, and his history of excessive dependence on parental support and guidance had resulted in extraordinary difficulty in coping with the numerous situations associated with college life. Toward the goal of fostering greater independence, training in problem solving (D'Zurilla & Goldfried, 1971) was initiated. Although the client was eventually able to decide on reasonable courses of action in response to various situations, it soon became apparent that his difficulties in actually following through with some of these activities were the result of interfering anxiety. For example, he could not bring himself to work in the library in the evening, as he was afraid to walk alone on campus at night. A treatment strategy directed at the reduction of such fears had to be adopted before the primary goal of therapy could be pursued.

When questioning clients as to the reasons for not following through on agreed-on homework assignments, the actual determinants for the noncompliance may not immediately be apparent. Clients typically give vague excuses, such as "not being able to get around to it." Although such claims may at times be true, they often are not. As a general rule of thumb, one should follow up in greater detail in an attempt to obtain more information about the sources of interference. By inquiring about the thoughts, feelings, and behaviors that preceded the client's unsuccessful attempt at following through on the homework assignment, it is often possible to uncover those determinants that then need to be the focus of change.

Pessimism about Changing. Some clients, particularly those with a long history of a given problem and/or unsuccessful therapy, enter the therapeutic situation with varying degrees jf pessimism about the *likelihood of their changing*. Given the fact that they may never have experienced another way of functioning, their pessimistic expectations should not be viewed as all that unreasonable. Although the therapist may be able to alter this set of expectations somewhat by alluding to the successful treatment of similar problems, or by pointing out how the current therapeutic intervention differs from past attempts that were less successful, attitude change is more likely to occur if clients can be helped to recall any changes they may have experienced in the past that were preceded by an initial period of pessimism. Although it is preferable to focus on changes of a personal nature, other changes may be used for this purpose as well. For example, the therapist may explore with clients any previous attempts they may have made to learn some complicated skill (e.g., driving a car), and how their initial skepticism or frustration was eventually overcome by persistence and repeated practice. The strategy of relating clients' past experiences to the current situation is illustrated in the following case.

> A 37-year-old man, on learning in the initial session that the therapy would not involve much discussion of his early childhood experiences, expressed doubt as to its likely effectiveness. The client happened to be a therapist himself, whose particular theoretical orientation was based on the premise that change could only occur as a result of insight into one's past. Instead of trying to become engaged in a theoretical debate, we began to explore other aspects of his current life situation. He proceeded to describe a relationship with a woman he had met within the past few years, indicating that the intimate nature of their friendship had made some very profound personal effects on him. After discussing the various ways in which the client had changed, the therapist smiled and asked: "Do you mean that all of this happened without any insight into the past?" This comment had its intended effect, as the client became more willing to proceed with the therapy.

A client's pessimism about change may be more specific, focused on the particular *therapeutic procedures* that are to be used. Inasmuch as some of the behavioral techniques are relatively simple, it may be difficult for some clients to accept that the intervention can be helpful in dealing with their long-term and particularly debilitating problem. In addition to conveying one's own feelings of confidence, indicating how the method helped others in the past, the therapist should also attempt to make use of the client's own experiences to foster attitude change. Consistent with the utilization technique (Erickson, 1959; Haley, 1963), the therapist may communicate to clients that he or she understands their viewpoint, adding that such skepticism is not at all unusual and, in fact, *is to be expected*. Furthermore, the therapist and client may be able to specify some short-term, readily attainable goal so that the client can experience—even in a small way—the efficacy of the procedure in question.

Fear of Changing. There is often a certain amount of apprehension associated with the change process, particularly if clients have never experienced another way of functioning in a given area of their life. For example, shy and unassertive individuals may rarely, if ever, have expressed their preferences or needs to others. To do so would cause them to have an experience that was "strange" or "different," which in turn would make them apprehensive. A delightful story by the comedian Buddy Hackett illustrates this phenomenon quite well. He reports that the first time he had ever lived away from home was when he joined the army. Since it was also the first time he had eaten other than his mother's cooking, he found that the heartburn he had all his life disappeared. This novel experience led to a sense of panic, however, as he was afraid "the flame had gone out."

When reluctance to change is mediated by a fear of the new experience, the therapist can utilize such concerns to demonstrate the *significance* of such change. Thus, after acknowledging the reasonableness of clients' fears, it can be pointed out that their concern about having certain novel experiences *is to be expected*. These new experiences should demonstrate to them that they are indeed in the process of becoming different—presumably a motivation that originally brought them to therapy. After all, if they continued to experience things as they had before, it is likely that their changes would be unimportant or superficial. In addition to emphasizing that therapy will focus only on those areas in which they want to be different, the change procedure itself should be presented in graduated steps, with every effort made to encourage clients to maintain their sense of trust in the therapist's concern and expertise.

Minimal Motivation to Change. The unmotivated client, most frequently seen in cases that are not self-referred, or when one member of a couple reluctantly brings the other to marital therapy, presents a particularly difficult problem for the behavior therapist. The problem of minimal motivation may also occur during the course of ongoing therapy when just enough change has occurred to make the client's presenting problems less pressing, though not yet eliminated. The dilemma facing the therapist, then, is that although the client may want to change, the amount of effort required to bring about such change may be more than the current motivational level will support.

In instances of low motivation the behavior therapist is presented with an ethical dilemma, namely, whether to pursue change in light of the client's minimal desire to do so. If one feels that it is very definitely to the client's disadvantage to continue to remain resistant because of lack of motivation, some steps should be taken to motivate the client. In addition to reevaluating the original reasons for entering therapy, therapists should express their concerns and explore the various possible negative consequences associated with *not* changing. In some instances the use of "emotional role playing" may be in order (Janis & Mann, 1965), where some of these negative consequences are enacted or imagined during the therapeutic session. Although these and other techniques (e.g., the use of written contracts, or forfeitable monetary deposits that go to the client's most hated charity) may at times succeed, the problem of low motivation needs far more attention than it has received in the behavior therapy literature.

Psychological Reactance. The theory of psychological reactance, as originally described by J. W. Brehm (1966) and later related to the clinical situation by S. S. Brehm (1976), maintains that under certain circumstances individuals will actively resist attempts by others to change them. Such reactance has been found to occur whenever individuals believe that their sense of freedom has been threatened, restricted, or eliminated by some external source. Given the highly directive nature of behavior therapy, it is reasonable to assume that reactance will at times occur within the therapeutic situation.

Drawing on the work of social psychology, Kiesler (1971) has made the following suggestion for anyone interested in applied work:

> If you want someone not only to behave in a particular way, but also to believe accordingly, then induce the behavior under conditions of very little apparent external pressure. Give the person the feeling that he was free to do otherwise if he wished. Make him think that he was responsible for his own behavior. (pp. 164–165)

A particularly creative way of implementing this suggestion is to use paradoxical intention (Fay, 1978; Frankl, 1960; Haley, 1976), in which the therapist actively directs clients to engage in the resistant behavior itself.

It would be inaccurate to assume that psychological reactance will occur in every attempt at direct influence. Central to the theory of psychological reactance is whether or not individuals *perceive themselves* as capable of exercising a choice in a situation, or as having sole control over a given aspect of their lives. Whereas there are clients who perceive themselves as having a fair amount of choice, there are others who would much prefer direction and guidance from the therapist. The variable of internal versus external control has received considerable attention in the literature (e.g., Phares, 1976; Rotter, 1966), and appears most relevant to the issue of psychological reactance in the clinical situation. A study by Abramowitz, Abramowitz, Roback, and Jackson (1974) offers some support for the hypothesis that an interaction exists between internality and the optimal amount of direction provided in group therapy. They found that whereas "internal" clients preferred a nondirective approach, "external" clients responded to more directive intervention. Similarly, Friedman and Dies (1974) found that "external" clients who received systematic desensitization felt that not enough direction was given by the therapist, whereas "internals" felt the amount was optimal. In general, the available theory and research, as well as actual clinical experience, indicate that psychological reactance is more likely to occur among clients who perceive themselves as having more internal control over their lives. Under such circumstances, the behavior therapist should take extra care to present the therapeutic procedures in such a way as to actively enlist the initiative and autonomy of such clients, tailor-making the intervention to the client's needs and preferences.

Overburdening of Client. Contrary to a stereotype that at times appears in the literature, clients usually enter behavior therapy with a number of different problems that are simultaneously creating difficulties in their lives. After conducting an assessment of the relevant determinants of the several problems and discussing various therapeutic goals, the therapist and client typically agree on those areas that will be the focus of therapy. To the extent, however, that clients are burdened with too many homework assignments, resistance may be anticipated with one or more of them. This resistance may be a function of an overly enthusiastic therapist and/or a client who has difficulty focusing on more than one area at a time. Unfortunately, it is not always possible to determine in advance precisely how much is too much for any given client. Nevertheless, when confronted with therapeutic noncompliance the therapist should explore the possibility of "overload."

Environmental Factors. In addition to looking at characteristics of the client or therapist as causes of resistance, it is also important to look into the nature of the client's current environmental situation for possible determinants. Thus resistance may be a function of the fact that the client's environment is *reinforcing* problem behaviors, that the client's current life situation provides *punishment* for the more adaptive behavior patterns he or she is striving to attain, or some *combination* of the two. The first instance may be illustrated with a 19-year-old boy who was reluctant to improve his academic performance or social life, as his difficulties in both these areas were being reinforced by the upset they produced in his father, whom he detested. The punishment of positive behavior patterns is exemplified in cases where attempts to increase assertiveness in some female clients are undermined by negative reactions of others toward their new independent and self-reliant posture. And the combination of environmental reinforcement and punishment is seen in certain kinds of institutional settings that may unwittingly encourage dependence while at the same time stifling initiative (Goffman, 1961; Rosenhan, 1973).

In cases where environmental determinants undermine therapeutic progress, it is clear that such variables must be the target of change. Although the therapist's influence may at times outweigh interfering external contingencies, other courses of action are often needed. Whenever feasible and appropriate, an actual shift in environmental setting may be called for (e.g., change of job). It is often wise to encourage clients to become involved with a different support system that is likely to reinforce the kinds of changes that will bring them closer to achieving the goals of therapy. Finally, the therapist may need to use a systems approach to intervention (e.g., Bowen, 1976; Minuchin, 1974; Watzlawick, Weakland, & Fisch, 1974), toward the goal of altering the problematic contingencies in the client's particular life space.

Summary

In describing a behavioral approach to the concept of resistance, consideration was given to the optimal set of attitudes, in-session behaviors, and between-session activities that constitute the client role.

Certain strategies that might be generally helpful for preventing or remedying client resistance were discussed, including creating a positive context for change, structuring the treatment procedures, emphasizing the gradualness of the change process, and clearly specifying therapeutic homework assignments. Therapeutic strategies were also presented as being relevant under specific clinical conditions. Among the various possible determinants of noncompliance in any given clinical case, it was suggested that resistance may reflect any one or more of the following: a direct sampling of the client's problem itself; the client's other problems; pessimism about changing; fear of changing; minimal motivation to change; psychological reactance; overburdening the client with too many homework assignments; and interfering contingencies in the client's environment. Therapeutic strategies were described for dealing with instances of resistance under these various conditions.

ACKNOWLEDGMENTS

I would like to thank David Martindale and David M. Pomeranz for their comments on an earlier draft. I would also like to acknowledge the role played by my clients and supervisees in providing me with the invaluable experience not readily available in the behavioral literature.

References

Abramowitz, C. V., Abramowitz, S. I., Roback, H. B., & Jackson, C. Differential effectiveness of directive and nondirective group therapies as a function of client internal-external control. *Journal of Consulting and Clinical Psychology*, 1974, 6, 849–853.

Alexander, F., & French, T. M. *Psychoanalytic therapy*. New York: Ronald Press, 1946.

Annon, J. S. *Behavioral treatment of sexual problems*. New York: Harper & Row, 1976.

Bowen, M. Theory in the practice of psychotherapy. In P. J. Guerin (Ed.), *Family therapy: Theory and practice*. New York: Gardner Press, 1976.

Brady, J. P., Davison, G. C., Dewald, P. A., Egan, G., Fadiman, J., Frank, J. D., Gill, M. M., Hoffman, I., Kempler, W., Lazarus, A. A., Raimy, V., Rotter, J. B., & Strupp, H. H. Some views on effective principles of psychotherapy. *Cognitive Therapy and Research*, 1980, 4, 269–306.

Brehm, J. W. *A theory of psychological reactance*. New York: Academic Press, 1966.

Brehm, S. S. *The application of social psychology to clinical practice*. Washington, D.C.: Hemisphere, 1976.

Cameron, R. The clinical implementation of behavior change techniques: A cognitively oriented conceptualization of therapeutic "compliance" and "resistance." In J. P. Foreyt & D. Rathjen (Eds.), *Cognitive behavior therapy*. New York: Plenum Press, 1978.

Davison, G. C. Counter control in behavior modification. In L. A. Hamerlynck, L. C. Handy, & E. J. Mash (Eds.), *Behavior change: Methodology, concepts and practice*. Champaign, Ill.: Research Press, 1973.

D'Zurilla, T. J., & Goldfried, M. R. Problem solving and behavior modification. *Journal of Abnormal Psychology*, 1971, *78*, 107–126.

Erickson, M. H. Further clinical techniques of hypnosis: Utilization techniques. *American Journal of Clinical Hypnosis*, 1959, *2*, 3–21.

Fay, A. *Making things better by making them worse*. New York: Hawthorn Books, 1978.

Frankl, V. E. Paradoxical intention: A logotherapeutic technique. *American Journal of Psychotherapy*, 1960, *14*, 520–535.

Freedman, J. L., & Fraser, S. Compliance without pressure: The foot-in-the-door technique. *Journal of Personality and Social Psychology*, 1966, *4*, 195–202.

Friedman, M. L., & Dies, R. R. Reactions of internal and external test-anxious students to counseling and behavior therapies. *Journal of Consulting and Clinical Psychology*, 1974, *42*, 921.

Goffman, E. *Asylums*. Garden City, N.Y.: Doubleday, 1961.

Goldfried, M. R., & Davison, G. C. *Clinical behavior therapy*. New York: Holt, Rinehart & Winston, 1976.

Goldfried, M. R., & Robins, C. On the facilitation of self-efficacy. *Cognitive Therapy and Research*, in press.

Gurman, A. S. Contemporary marital therapies: A critique and comparative analysis of psychoanalytic, behavioral, and systems theory approaches. In T. J. Paolino, Jr. & B. S. McCrady (Eds.), *Marriage and marital therapy*. New York: Brunner/Mazel, 1978.

Haley, J. *Strategies of psychotherapy*. New York: Grune & Stratton, 1963.

Haley, J. *Problem-solving therapy*. San Francisco: Jossey-Bass, 1976.

Janis, I. L., & Mann, L. Effectiveness of emotional role-playing in modifying smoking habits and attitudes. *Journal of Experimental Research in Personality*, 1965, *1*, 84–90.

Kanfer, F. H., & Karoly, P. Self-control: A behavioristic excursion into the lion's den. *Behavior Therapy*, 1972, *3*, 398–416.

Kiesler, C. A. *The psychology of commitment*. New York: Academic Press, 1971.

Marston, A. R., & Feldman, S. E. Toward the use of self-control in behavior modification. *Journal of Clinical and Consulting Psychology*, 1972, *39*, 429–433.

Minuchin, S. *Families and family therapy*. Cambridge: Harvard University Press, 1974.

Phares, E. J. *Locus of control in personality*. Morristown, N.J.: General Learning Press, 1976.

Rosenhan, D. L. On being sane in insane places. *Science*, 1973, *179*, 250–258.

Rotter, J. B. Generalized expectancies for internal versus external control of reinforcement. *Psychological Monographs*, 1966, *80* (1, Whole No. 609).

Stuart, R. B. Behavioral contracting within the families of delinquents. *Journal of Behavior Therapy and Experimental Psychiatry*, 1971, *2*, 1–11.

Watzlawick, P., Weakland, J., & Fisch, R. *Change: Principles of problem formation and problem resolution*. New York: W. W. Norton, 1974.

Weiss, R. L. Resistance in behavioral marriage therapy. *American Journal of Family Therapy*, 1979, *7*, 3–6.

6

Resistance or Rationalization?

A COGNITIVE-BEHAVIORAL PERSPECTIVE

Arnold A. Lazarus and Allen Fay

The concept of "resistance" is probably the most elaborate rationalization that therapists employ to explain their treatment failures. When their efforts are frustrated they frequently postulate the existence of internal forces or make causal assignment to a "frustrator," thus reducing dissonance at the patient's expense. Spoken or unspoken, the sentiment is: "It is not my own inadequate assessment or faulty diagnosis, nor the limitations of my theories or methods, but instead the patient's stubbornness, unwillingness, or inability to cooperate that accounts for his or her lack of progress." At the outset, we would like to underline our view that "resistance" is generally a function of the limitations of our knowledge and methods and the constraints of our personalities. These are the major factors that create difficulty in dealing successfully with the special therapeutic problems individuals bring to our attention.

All therapists in the course of their professional activities encounter remarkably recalcitrant problems in patients who *appear* to have vested interests in some form of "stasis." Indeed, the course of therapy seldom follows a smooth, monotonic progression; setbacks and reversals often impede progress. Nevertheless, the notion that some internal process (resistance) is responsible for most or many treatment failures or setbacks

Arnold A. Lazarus • Graduate School of Applied and Professional Psychology, Rutgers—The State University, New Brunswick, New Jersey 08903. Allen Fay • Department of Psychiatry, Mount Sinai School of Medicine, City University of New York, New York, New York 10029.

is simply an unfortunate though convenient evasion of one's clinical responsibilities.

A patient disagrees with the therapist's interpretations, refuses to comply with his or her suggestions, comes late or misses appointments, fails to carry out homework assignments, "forgets" to take prescribed medication, withholds important information, becomes evasive when asked pertinent questions, tells deliberate lies, or displays oppositional tendencies in other ways. What prevailing forces can account for these "resistant" behaviors? Is resistance inevitable? Is it intrapsychically determined, interpersonally specific, a manifestation of the therapist's incompetence, an indication of incompatibility or poor matching between patient and therapist, or evidence of secondary gain? Sometimes patients may ardently *resist* all the therapist's suggestions, interpretations, and ministrations and yet achieve rapid and lasting improvement. Would such patients' cognitive nonacceptance and behavioral noncompliance still be viewed as "resistance"? If a therapist gives poor advice, the patient does not comply, and a favorable outcome ensues, must we then assume that the patient improved in order to show up or demean the therapist? Surely we would have to elaborate some kind of procrustean explanation to get us off the hook!

It is necessary to separate resistance as a postulated mechanism explaining a clinical phenomenon (negative outcomes) from resistance as a clinical phenomenon itself. Clearly, it begs the question to speak of resistance whenever positive outcomes are not achieved. Furthermore, labeling all noncompliant behavior "resistance" obscures the essential importance of teasing out specific antecedent and maintaining factors that generate uncooperative behaviors in specific contexts.

Another relevant issue concerns the distinction between the *patient* being resistant and the *problem* being resistant. We frequently talk about certain patterns and symptoms being notoriously refractory (e.g., severe obsessive-compulsive states), regardless of who the patient is or who the therapist is.

Is resistance ubiquitous? Does every therapist's attempt to produce change lead to resistance in some form and to some degree? Or does resistance exist in specific relationships and only in particular contexts? Many clinicians contend that a certain degree of resistance is inevitable because all clients or patients are ambivalent. On the one hand patients wish to acquire more productive and adaptive attitudes and behaviors, but on the other hand they cling to the protection and security of their current styles, despite the negative consequences.

As a psychodynamic mechanism, resistance is inevitable. The analytic model of personality relies heavily on the unconscious and its repressive barriers, and one of its intrinsic ideas about human functioning is that there *must* be opposition to anyone or anything that attempts to expose unconscious processes. Its avowed purpose is to prevent the discharge of energy associated with unconscious material. From this point of view, resistance represents an active force within the patient that prevents him or her from understanding the true but threatening significance of specific symptoms. "Everything that prevents the patient from producing material derived from the unconscious is resistance" (Fenichel, 1945, p. 27).

Empirically, it is obvious that people may tend to shy away from painful revelations about themselves and that they can disown or deny unacceptable impulses, feelings, or cognitions. To avoid facing these disagreeable things, they may come late for their appointments or miss them entirely, they may overintellectualize, rationalize, refuse to carry out prescriptions, and display other negative attitudes toward therapy and the therapist. The danger lies in concluding that these behaviors are, ipso facto, evidence of "resistance" instead of searching for the *actual* reasons behind them. Thus, some chronic latecomers may have a very poor ability for scheduling time—a problem in its own right, not based on the avoidance of painful material or on antagonism toward the therapy.

By insisting on an unconscious locus for resistance, some therapists compound the difficulty of understanding and resolving intricate clinical problems. A patient may intentionally withhold information and otherwise refuse to participate in treatment because of fear, shame, or distrust of the therapist. Unfortunately, those who maintain that unconscious resistance invariably lies behind these deliberate factors deflect responsibility back onto the patient's intrapsychic forces instead of examining situational events (e.g., the therapist's failure to create a climate of trustworthiness for a particular confidence to be shared).

One of the dangers inherent in the notion of the inevitability of resistance is that it leads clinicians to be suspicious of rapid inprovement in patients who have not manifested "resistance." As a consequence, ad-hoc concepts such as "flight into health" and "transference cure" emerge that may lead a therapist to withhold positive reinforcement for rapid clinical change. We are not suggesting that all rapid remission is durable, but we would not automatically be suspicious of such a felicitous event.

Is the *locus* of resistance always within the patient? Not if one looks at the problem in terms of *systems*, in which case the process will be seen as a function of the patient-therapist-family network as a whole. (We will discuss some of the "game" aspects of therapist—patient transactions where "resistance" seems to be a problem.)

Failure to Carry Out Homework Assignments

From our perspective, one of the most significant signs of "resistance" is the patient's failure to complete homework assignments: "I forgot"; "I didn't have the time"; "I wasn't sure exactly what you wanted me to do"; "I didn't feel up to it"; "The opportunity didn't present itself." Many other excuses may be offered, but whenever *in-vivo* assignments are entirely bypassed or attempted half heartedly, progress is generally slow or nonexistent. There is persuasive evidence that in most instances, therapeutic progress follows methods that are performance based, whereas purely cognitive or verbal methods are usually less effective. We therefore dwell most heavily on *action*, on *doing*. We typically ask our patients: "What have you *done* differently this week?" If the answer is "Nothing" we assume an absence of progress. In some instances, the answer "I've been doing a lot of thinking" may signify some positive shift, but we prefer to hear such answers as, "I applied to seven colleges, " or "I stood up to my husband," or "I took the risk and went out on three dates," or "I stopped eating candy and ice cream." Similarly, therapists' preoccupation with how the patient felt or what the patient thought can impede progress.

Homework assignments are geared to enhance positive shifts in patients' main areas of concern. The timid, reticent, inhibited individual will not acquire a repertoire of assertive skills merely by talking about it, any more than someone will learn to speak a foreign language or play a musical instrument without practice. Homework assignments are dispensed along a graduated hierarchy. "Over the next week how about making sure that you simply say 'thank you' to any compliment you receive, instead of diminishing yourself as you usually do? And will you make a note of how many compliments you receive and exactly how many times you say 'thank you' instead of lapsing into your self-downing behaviors?" These instructions were given to an intelligent, attractive, well-groomed, stylishly attired 20-year-old woman who invariably responded to the frequent compliments she received with overly modest, self-deprecatory statements. At a subsequent session she reported no opportunity to carry out her homework assignment because she had received no compliments during that week. Likewise, a 32-year-old man stated that he had had no opportunity to ask his employer for a raise. A 15-year-old boy "forgot" to ask his father if he would attend a few family therapy sessions.

Before leaping to the conclusion that some unspecified "resistance" lies behind most instances of noncompliance, we find it profitable to examine a variety of more concrete possibilities.

- Was the homework assignment incorrect or irrelevant?
- Was it too threatening?
- Was it too time-consuming in terms of its "cost effectiveness"?
- Does the patient not appreciate the value of and rationale behind homework exercises? (Is the patient opposed to or unaware of the educational, self-help thrust of our ministrations?)
- Is the therapeutic relationship at fault? (If so, the patient may display passive-aggressive behaviors toward the therapist.)
- Is someone in the patient's social network undermining or sabotaging the therapy?
- Is the patient receiving far too many secondary gains to relinquish his or her maladaptive behavior?

It must be understood that homework assignments are not delivered in an authoritarian manner. The therapist suggests what appears to be a reasonable course of action. Patient and therapist discuss the advisability and feasibility of the assignment, so that the final prescribed tasks appear mutually meaningful. Nevertheless, after leaving the consulting room, the patient may have second thoughts about the advisability of the modus operandi. And some of these objections may rest on solid facts that emerged only after the patient seriously contemplated engaging in a specific behavior. By exploring the possibilities raised by each of these alternatives, it is often possible to reframe the assignments, reeducate the patient, and, if necessary, reexamine the therapeutic relationship and reevaluate the patient's family system or social network.

Control and Countercontrol

When treatment does not proceed apace, falters, or fails to get off the ground, several specific and clearly delineated reasons may be discerned. When a treatment impasse is reached, we assume that one or more of the following factors is operative:

1. Inappropriate matching or absence of rapport. (In this instance, instead of insisting that this problem can and must be worked through, it is often advisable to effect referral to a more compatible resource.)
2. Therapist's failure to identify relevant antecedents and/or maintaining factors. (A thorough and accurate assessment is often a sine qua non for effective therapy.)
3. Therapist's failure to deal with the social network. (All too often therapy is undermined within the patient's system or social network. To dwell only on intraindividual factors leaves ample room for interpersonal saboteurs.)
4. Therapist's use of incorrect techniques. (Includes all errors and blunders that the therapist may commit.)
5. Therapist's faulty or incorrect use of appropriate techniques. (Insufficient training or experience is reflected by this factor.)
6. Extreme excesses or deficits in the patient's biological or psychological functioning. (There are some people who, for numerous reasons, manifest what appears to be irreversible dysfunction.)
7. The desired outcome is not valued highly enough by the patient. (Thus there is an unwillingness to expend the necessary effort to effect change.)

We believe that these seven factors cover the range of explanations for most treatment impasses. It will be noted that in our view much of the variance rests with the therapist. In regard to the seventh factor, we have deliberately avoided the term "motivation"; but there is clearly a wide range of individual differences that patients bring to their therapy in terms of their willingness or ability to invest the necessary time and effort to effect change. It is *largely* the therapist's responsibility to inspire the patient to take the necessary steps, but it is unrealistic to place the *entire* onus on the clinician.

Undoubtedly we have all encountered patients who simply withdrew from therapy when basic issues were about to be confronted or when substantial changes were in the offing. There are people who seek therapy solely to find an ally who will support their dysfunctional styles. If one attempts to "normalize" them, they leave. Similarly, others may enter therapy not in order to change but to form an alliance against a significant other (e.g., a husband tries to team up with a therapist against his wife). There are, in short, people who do not want help, or for whom there may be too many competing factors. Whether or not we should or could devise methods to change their minds remains debatable. Salter (1949) was quite clear about these cases:

> But what shall be done with the persons who do not let you turn the wheels? Often they should be chased from the office with a broomstick, although they are not to be blamed for their personalities.
>
> I explain to them that my appointment book is like a life raft. There is room for only a limited number of people, and I do not intend to waste my time trying to convince any of the bobbing heads around me to get on board. There are others drowning who are only too happy to cooperate in their rescue.

One might be inclined to add: And beware especially of those who not only refuse one's helping hand but try to drag one off the raft in order to drown along with them. It needs to be underlined that some people who come to therapists for help are not seeking any change in their own behavior, but instead are looking for comfort and reassurance. Indeed, such support is the essence of their concept of therapy.

The most puzzling cases are not the outright resisters or deliberate saboteurs. What about those people who never miss appointments, are always punctual, and who avidly attend to our ministrations, follow our logic, carry out our assignments, but fail to change, and keep coming back? Some of these cases may be highly accomplished "passive-resisters" who derive an enormous sense of power and gratification from the therapist's frustration. In these instances, paradoxical procedures such as "symptom prescription" and "reframing" often prove effective (Haley, 1976; Watzlawick, Weakland, & Fisch, 1974).

Generally, our successful clients come regularly to their sessions, are willing to be as "transparent" as possible during these sessions (i.e., they do not deliberately lie, distort, or withhold information), and are amenable to trying a variety of procedures on for size (e.g., they will role play when appropriate, practice relaxation, meditation, confrontation, study prescribed books and other reading materials, take medication when recommended, keep activity charts, and share their reactions, thoughts, and feelings with the therapist). Our model is essentially *educational* and we liken ourselves to a music teacher or an athletic coach—we supply guidance, offer specific training exercises, correct misconceptions, try to modify faulty styles, provide up-to-date information, display caring, support, and encouragement; still, most of the responsibility rests with the "trainee" to practice between training sessions. We spend an average of an hour per week with each patient and emphasize that actions performed during the other 167 hours will determine the success or failure of the therapy.

It is quite obvious that many patients display oppositional behaviors. Indeed, most people are inclined to resist efforts by others, be they overt or covert, to modify their behavior. The tendency to counteract attempts to influence or control us makes it incumbent on therapists to establish a *cooperative* climate wherein change is predicated on mutual goals and shared objectives. The field of social psychology has shown that cooperative behaviors are more likely to occur when someone is requested, rather than directed, to perform (or refrain from) specific acts. *Telling* a client to relax, imagine scenes, act more assertively, self-monitor specific behaviors, or agree on contingency management is likely to foster some degree of opposition or countercontrol (Davison, 1973; Wilson & Evans, 1977). *Asking* for the same performance-based responses is less likely to evoke opposition. Thus resistance or countercontrol may be a direct function of the therapist's manner and style. In our experience, at least 80% of patients follow our *requests* or suggestions without travail.

Still, it is important to emphasize that no matter how tactful, supportive, or cooperative the climate of therapy may become, in the final analysis, during the helping process, the therapist will attempt to *influence* the client. As Johnson and Matross (1977) point out, "persons who are interacting are constantly influencing and being influenced by each other." Yet many feel there is a fine line between constructive and destructive influence. For example, coercion readily truncates one's freedom, and so does exploitation (i.e., the use of unfair, dishonest, or insidious means for one's own purposes or advantages). Thus there is a widespread tendency to beware of "influence"—no matter how benignly or constructively intended. Therapists are therefore required to build and maintain trust throughout the course of therapy.

Who Is the Patient?

All too frequently, individuals present themselves for therapy who are not positively disposed toward change. In our experience, it is often useful to view the patient as the person who wants change and is willing to work for it. The patient is *not* necessarily (as in the medical model) the individual with the identifiable symptom, although even in medicine there is room for a systems perspective. In clinical practice one commonly

sees a family containing a "nonfunctioning" grown offspring living with
parents.

> A young man lived a life of idleness at his parents' expense. In
> response to their pressuring, he made abortive attempts to find work
> but usually slept late, ate enormous quantities of food, and intimi-
> dated his parents into buying him a car, subsidizing expensive va-
> cations ("From what?" we inquired), and in general tolerating sloth,
> slovenliness, and abusiveness. The parents were somewhat puzzled
> when therapy was made conditional on the whole family being seen
> together. They were told, "Billy is not the patient—you are the
> patient. You are the ones who desire the change. Why should he
> work? He could not begin to support himself in the style you have
> made possible. When *you* change, he will change." Although this
> point may seem hackneyed to therapists schooled in learning prin-
> ciples, systems theory, and behavior modification techniques, the
> young man over a 12-year period had seen four therapists and had
> even been given a course of ECT. Twelve visits later (mainly by the
> parents, because Billy did not attend half the sessions), striking
> changes were evident in the parents' demeanor and approach, ac-
> companied by corresponding increases in the young man's adaptive
> behaviors.

Value Differences and the Definition of Normalcy

> A 24-year-old man received enough support from a small trust
> to live in a shabby residential hotel without having to work. Therapy
> was also paid for. Whereas initially the patient had phobic com-
> plaints, he was now improved and felt therapy was no longer
> needed. He was encouraged to get a job, but he clearly had no
> interest in working. "I've tried a couple of jobs and find them boring
> and not terribly rewarding financially. I'm really enjoying life. I can
> eat for about a dollar fifty a day [stale bread, canned soup, etc.] and
> spend my time taking long walks, going to museums and libraries,
> and socializing with friends. I date women who enjoy what I enjoy.
> When I need a few bucks I baby-sit." We asked if it would not be
> better to get some kind of training for work that might be more
> satisfying, and we suggested the long-range adaptive value of a
> different living pattern. He replied that he would take his chances
> on the future and insisted that he was perfectly content, despite the
> family's view that his life-style was grossly pathological. We were
> inclined to view this individual as a *nonpatient* rather than a "resistant
> patient."

The Varieties of Resistance

As we have indicated, four different factors can lead to "resistance" in therapy: (1) resistance as a function of the patient's individual characteristics; (2) resistance as a product of the patient's interpersonal relationships (systems or family processes); (3) resistance as a function of the therapist (or the relationship); and (4) resistance as a function of the state of the art (and science).

We will now briefly discuss each of these factors.

Individual Characteristics

A clear distinction must be drawn between unresponsive cases and resistant individuals. Let us take a person with low intelligence who fails to comply with a therapist's interventions simply because of an inability to comprehend specific recommendations. This noncompliance is not a function of "resistance," since the term implies some deliberate or unconscious *opposition*. (The dictionary meaning involves some exertion aimed at counteracting or defeating a force.) In addition to individuals with poor cognitive ability, there are patients whose genetic endowment and cultural heritage have rendered them so arid, with such a paucity of coping responses, that therapy at best amounts to a caretaking and supportive function.

As Goldstein, Heller, and Sechrest (1966) have said, it is incumbent on therapists to investigate their lack of success with certain classes of patients, "working toward the goal of developing new techniques and improving old ones to expand [their] usefulness beyond its present narrow range" (p. 152).

Clinically, some simple tactics often succeed with seemingly "unmotivated" or "resistant" clients: "As far as I'm concerned, psychology and psychiatry is worth nothing. You guys are the real nuts who should be locked away. I'm here to get my goddamn parents off by back. So cure me!" How does one "motivate" or overcome the "resistance" of a 16-year-old boy who snarls these words the moment his mother and father step into the waiting room so that the therapist and he can have a private, heart-to-heart meeting? It is easier to say how one can *fail* to overcome such resistance. Failure is almost guaranteed if one remains passive, reflective, or becomes interpretive "You seem to be an angry and frightened young man who has problems with authority"). Of course, there is no way to be sure that a particular response from the therapist will prove facilitative, neutral, or negative. The therapist may sit quietly, sagaciously nodding his or her head, and thereby trigger a positive capitulation simply because an angry outburst from the patient met with not an iota of condemnation. Conversely, stepping out of an expected role and saying something like, "Shut up you little jerk! I'm interested only in getting paid. I couldn't care less about you or your goddamn parents!" might prove enormously helpful in other instances. Such situations highlight the importance of the therapist's ability to assume different roles—in short, to be a convincing actor in his or her own consulting room. A broad array of techniques and a capacity for style change are essential if a therapist is to be successful with a variety of problems and personalities (Lazarus, 1976, 1981).

Our own clinical rule of thumb is generally to start with a logical, supportive, empathic approach. "Most people get angry when forced into things they don't want to do." This statement has a reasonable chance of eliciting a positive reaction from the patient. "Well, Doctor, how would you feel if you were always put down by your parents?" But what if the hostility merely escalates? "Quit that phony 'I understand you' act!" That was the exact response from an actual case in point. The following rejoinder broke the impasse: "Look fellow. I have very little time for this bullshit myself. But I do have a few tricks up my sleeve that might help get your parents off your back—if that is what you really want."

Openly defiant patients are generally easier to manage than those seemingly cooperative individuals who employ subtle or facile tactics that undermine one's efforts. An 18-year-old girl referred by a Pretrial Intervention Community System for shoplifting said: "I don't need a shrink. I need somebody to teach me how not to get caught." She was startled when the therapist said: "Nobody has ever caught me and I've been ripping things off much longer than you. Perhaps I can be your teacher." This approach is a variant of a well-known method commonly called "siding with the resistance" (Sherman, 1968). The girl soon dropped her facade and said: "I know you're kidding. Maybe I could use some help with my hangups."

Along similar lines, the following dialogue ensued when a 37-year-old woman arrived for her second visit:

PATIENT: I've decided to drop out of therapy.
THERAPIST: Good-bye. I hope all goes well with you.
PATIENT: Just like that?

THERAPIST: Pardon?
PATIENT: Aren't you supposed to try and talk me into being in treatment?
THERAPIST: I'm not a secondhand car salesman. I only work with people who want to receive help from me.
PATIENT: Well what makes you think I don't want to be helped?

Fay (1978) describes the successful application of paradoxical procedures to an extremely resistant 37-year-old man who had frustrated all rationally based attempts to overcome his general inertia and withdrawal.

PATIENT: I should really be getting up every morning like everyone else and going to work.
THERAPIST: Why should you?
PATIENT: Any normal person would do that and I want to be normal.
THERAPIST: Is it so normal to drag yourself out of bed every morning and do some boring work all day with all the pressures and hassles and the miserable commuting?
PATIENT: But other people do it.
THERAPIST: Is it necessary for you to do something simply because other people do it?
PATIENT: Well, I want to be good at something.
THERAPIST: You *are* good at something. You are superb at eating and sleeping.
PATIENT: I don't think that's right. I should get a job and function like other people.
THERAPIST: I think you should do what you enjoy and what you do best and that is eating, sleeping, and watching television.
PATIENT: But what I'm doing is sick.
THERAPIST: What's sick about doing the things you want to do? I think you're doing just fine. I don't see any sickness, and if you *were* sick, I would certainly be the one to know it.

Within 2 weeks the patient had a job, and in spite of early misunderstandings with his employers, he was still working 6 months later.

Patients can undermine therapy at various points. For example, when using systematic desensitization, therapists open themselves to patients' noncompliance at several stages (Rhoades & Feather, 1972). When faced with a patient who is resisting and not responding to desensitization methods, the therapist has several alternatives. The reasons behind the resistance can be explored; a collaborative set may be invoked by asking the patient to design a modified desensitization procedure that would be tailored to his or her specific needs and expectancies (for example, one seemingly resistant patient, when asked to modify the procedure, suggested bringing along a cassette recording of some of his favorite music in the hope that "music plus relaxation" would offset the anxieties generated by the specific hierarchical scenes—a tactic that proved most effective); and the therapist with a broad array of techniques at his or her disposal can always introduce a different procedure when one is not working, just as a skilled hypnotist slips effortlessly and gracefully from one trance-induction method to another.

Interpersonal, Systems, or Family Processes

From a cognitive-behavioral standpoint an important question is, Who or what is maintaining the behavior? Many patients receive intermittent reinforcement for their aberrant behaviors from significant others who deliberately or inadvertently foster the problematic styles and symptoms. It is common to find several "emotional saboteurs" within the patient's social network, but it is not necessary to become embroiled in some of the convoluted explanations and theories that certain systems and family analysts have offered. Nevertheless, it is well documented that family members often undermine a therapist's endeavors when they fear that a change in an individual will threaten their own security. Hence couples therapy and family therapy have become an important medium to offset such sources of resistance. By seeing all the principals together, "resistance" can more easily be detected and overcome.

Resistance often lies in the dyadic transactions.

> We were treating an anxious, unassertive, and somewhat depressed woman, age 35, who was married and had two children. Although she came for sessions regularly and punctually, we were unable to make therapeutic headway. She was seemingly compliant, yet managed to frustrate all our attempts to effect change. After 2 months of weekly sessions she was a little less anxious and a trifle more assertive, but no significant gains had accrued. A thorough interpersonal analysis revealed that she was extremely reluctant to achieve a nonanxious, assertive, and optimistic life-style for fear of destroying her marriage and thereby damaging her children. It appeared that her reticence, self-downing utterances, and fears tended to bolster her husband, who seemed to enjoy the role of her comforter and protector. She felt (and on meeting her husband, we concurred) that she could easily outstrip him. Developing her potential and abandoning her anxious and dependent games would

probably destabilize her marital relationship to the point of rupture. "I would rather sacrifice myself than risk my marriage and the happiness of my children." It also became apparent that her marital interactions were an exact copy of her parents' style. They had always voiced strong opposition to divorce on religious grounds.

The foregoing is a typical example of what we consider resistance. The patient's reluctance to change had little to do with resistance as traditionally conceived, but was integrally tied to her own values and those of her social milieu. This case poses several treatment dilemmas. Can a way be found wherein this woman would become self-fulfilled without damaging her marital relationship? If not, is it best to teach her to accept her lot in life? Can some of her problems be mitigated by upgrading the marital relationship so that at least partial fulfillment and some degree of independence are achieved? Should therapy aim to actualize and emancipate this woman regardless of family repercussions? Regardless of the answers to these questions, one basic objective would be to eliminate needless guilt so that decisions are based on rational choice rather than neurotic constraints.

For us the essence of the systems approach to therapy is that individuals influence and are influenced by the people with whom they come in contact (especially relatives and friends), and hence a change in one person is likely to have repercussions on significant others. If a positive change in an individual is inclined to have a negative impact on someone else in his or her network, some form of reluctance or resistance to change may be foreseen. If the individual himself or herself does not actively resist the change process, some member of the family or social network will probably find a way of preserving the status quo. Being alert to these interactive processes is often a sine qua non for therapeutic success.

The Therapist (or the Relationship)

It is always important to realize that a seemingly resistant patient may in fact simply be avoiding a particular suggestion of a particular therapist at a particular time. The patient may be very selective about accepting ideas, suggestions, or recommendations. In that case, we would prefer to call the patient *selective* rather than *resistant*.

If we say to a client: "John, since you are attracted to Mary, why not ask for her a date?", is he manifesting resistance if he does not do it? Perhaps he lacks the requisite social skills to accept our advice; or perhaps he has not been desensitized to the rejection he anticipates.

The point is that different therapists obviously vary in their interpersonal skills, their knowledge, perceptiveness, and other facilitative attributes. When a patient is "resistant" it often means that he or she is being treated incorrectly or is seeing the wrong therapist.

> A psychiatric resident was making no headway with a female patient whom he was treating along traditional psychodynamic lines. She was constantly asking him personal questions—whether or not he was married, his taste in music and art, his favorite books, and other likes and dislikes. He invariably sidestepped the questions and reflected the presumed motives behind them. His analytic supervisor encouraged him to continue in the same manner, but at a general meeting where we were present, the resident expressed the fear that his patient was about to stop seeing him. "Answer her questions like a human being," we advised him. "Play it straight, and while you are at it, offer her an apology for having behaved toward her like a computer." Subsequently, we were told that he followed our advice, the treatment impasse was overcome, close rapport was established, and therapeutic progress ensued.

> A number of years ago, a female patient who was terrified of sexual penetration had failed to respond to a panoply of cognitive-behavioral techniques. We decided to provide a "modeling experience" in the form of one of the early sex therapy films. The objective was to enable her to become more comfortable with her body and with masturbation. Unfortunately, the particular film, which showed a very experienced, creative, and free-spirited woman masturbating, did not produce the desired result but had the effect of intimidating the patient. It was only after she had left therapy, having achieved only modest gains, that we fully appreciated the importance of using coping models rather than mastery models (a film of a somewhat inept couple achieving a desired result, albeit through some fumbling and imperfect maneuvers, is likely to encourage and motivate certain patients far more than the depiction of bedroom athletes who enact a sexual encounter of interminable ecstasy).

Thus, the more a therapist knows, the fewer "resistant" patients he or she will have. Perhaps ignorant therapists or therapists who restrict themselves to the methods and techniques learned during their formal training, regardless of the requirements of the clinical situation, are the ones who are resistant.

The theme of this chapter is that what appears to be "resistance" may often have its locus within the therapist. Did the therapist fail to introduce an essential ingredient into the therapy? Again we would ask; Was the client's social network excluded and hence some powerful maintaining factors overlooked? Was exhortation relied on without first administering the necessary modeling experiences? Was instruction offered without first applying behavior rehearsal or other preparatory methods, such as coping imagery or stress inoculation?

We have alluded to the fact that there is a difference in the content and quality of "resistance" when a client deliberately countermands a therapist's endeavors because of disrespect, anger, fear, or mistrust as opposed to an inadvertent failure to comply with a therapist's ministrations. To lump a myriad of different behaviors under the heading "resistance" or "countercontrol" misses the fact that specific messages have specific meanings and call for specific (different) interventions.

If a client's noncompliance stems from his or her perception of the therapist as a parent figure and reflects the network of parent–child expectations and implications, successful therapy will hinge on a resolution of these symbolic impediments. On the other hand, different therapeutic tactics are required where the client's struggles with the therapist rest on the interpersonal ramifications inherent in the specific therapy situation with the particular therapist. "I dislike Dr. A. because he reminds me of my father" is quite different from "I dislike Dr. A. because he betrayed my confidence." Concerning the former point, Franks and Wilson (1973) state:

> If a person as a child has been able to maintain his identity only by resisting or fighting parental authority, there is no reason why we should not suspect that he will attempt to treat his behavior therapist with similar defensive tokens. These may never interpose themselves in outright defiance; rather they may take the more subtle form of an inability to respond to remedial promptings.

Therapists may unwittingly reinforce particular maladaptive behaviors and then claim that the patient is resistant. For example, a patient who consistently threatens suicide and receives a great deal of attention from the therapist for these dysfunctional utterances may continue to be "resistant" until the therapist stops responding to the suicidal threats and instead dispenses positive reinforcement for more rational pronouncements.

When therapeutic impasses arise because of incompatibilities between patient and therapist, we strongly recommend a judicious referral to a colleague whose personality and methodology seem better suited to the needs of the patient.

The State of the Art (and Science)

Obviously, there are people who cannot be helped by the methods currently at our disposal. Only with reluctance have we learned to concede that some people are beyond help, at least for the present. Yet we hang on. Even when consulted by people with malignant self-hate, intent on self-destruction, incapacitated by encrusted obsessive-compulsive rituals, with a pervasive sense of helplessness and hopelessness, we ply our balms and are intermittently rewarded for our ardent efforts. But when we fail to help these individuals, or when less floridly disturbed people (whose psychological ground is nevertheless a marsh of anhedonia and self-denunciation) fail to change, we need to parcel out the patient's *inability* versus his or her *refusal* to derive benefit.

We treated an extremely unhappy woman in her midthirties who had been a battered child. We had no methods in our repertoire that were capable of removing her numerous "psychic scars." Similarly, the best individual and combined efforts we could muster were unable to shatter the web of misery that pervaded a woman in her late forties. After failing to respond to several traditional therapies and one inpatient treatment regimen, she consulted us. We exhausted the range of our combined armamentaria, which included everything from drug treatment to biofeedback, and the patient eventually committed suicide.

On the positive side, we (like all therapists) have succeeded with seemingly intractable cases who had been declared untreatable and unreachable by several experts and authorities. To be able to articulate the exact ingredients that lead to failure or success is a worthy but lofty goal that our present knowledge does not even approach.

Although we have acknowledged that the concept of resistance has a measure of legitimacy, we nevertheless feel that its general usage is more likely to obfuscate than illuminate the course of therapeutic endeavors. In conclusion, we can only urge our colleagues to avoid confusing resistance with rationalized failure.

References

Davison, G. C. Counter control in behavior modification. In L. A. Hamerlynck, L. C. Handy, & E. J. Mash (Eds.), *Behavior change: Methodology, concepts and practice.* Champaign, Ill.: Research Press, 1973.

Fay, A. *Making things better by making them worse.* New York: Hawthorn Books, 1978.

Fenichel, O. *The psychoanalytic theory of neurosis.* New York: W. W. Norton, 1945.

Franks, C. M., & Wilson, G. T. *Annual review of behavior therapy: Theory and practice* (Vol. 1). New York: Brunner/Mazel, 1973.

Goldstein, A. P., Heller, K., & Sechrest, L. B. *Psychotherapy and the psychology of behavior change.* New York: Wiley, 1966.

Haley, J. *Problem-solving therapy.* San Francisco: Jossey-Bass, 1976.

Johnson, D. W., & Matross, R. P. Interpersonal influence in psychotherapy: A social psychological view. In A. S Gurman & A. M. Razin (Eds.), *Effective psychotherapy: A handbook of research.* New York: Pergamon Press, 1977.

Lazarus, A. A. *Multimodal behavior therapy.* New York: Springer, 1976.

Lazarus, A. A. *The practice of multimodal therapy.* New York: McGraw-Hill, 1981.

Rhoades, J. M., & Feather, B. W. Transference and resistance observed in behaviour therapy. *British Journal of Medical Psychology,* 1972, *45,* 99–103.

Salter, A. *Conditioned reflex therapy.* New York: Farrar, Straus, 1949.

Sherman, M. H. Siding with the resistance versus interpretation: Role implications. In M. C. Nelson, B. Nelson, M. H. Sherman, & H. S. Strean (Eds.), *Roles and paradigms in psychotherapy.* New York: Grune & Stratton, 1968.

Watzlawick, P., Weakland, J., & Fisch, R. *Change: Principles of problem formation and problem resolution.* New York: W. W. Norton, 1974.

Wilson, G. T., & Evans, I. M. The therapist-client relationship in behavior therapy. In A. S. Gurman & A. M. Razin (Eds.), *Effective psychotherapy: A handbook of research.* New York: Pergamon Press, 1977.

7

Resistance from a Cognitive-Behavioral Perspective

Donald Meichenbaum and J. Barnard Gilmore

This chapter is a two-sided enterprise. On the one hand it is a beginning attempt to clarify the "problem" of resistance, employing the new perspectives of the cognitive-behavioral therapies. On the other hand, this chapter is also an attempt to clarify the art and science of cognitive-behavioral therapies by reflecting on their typical responses to resistance.

Resistance can certainly be many things. It is a motivational construct and it is a behavioral construct. It can carry information that is conscious, preconscious, or unconscious. We shall emphasize behavior and information processing and preconscious thinking. And we shall emphasize a hypothesis-testing metaphor for clarifying many aspects of psychotherapy.

Every therapist knows those frustrations and worries that a creatively resistant client can release. The least and the most gifted therapists have each felt the irresistible resistances of the most dedicated clients. By way of an introduction to this topic, we would like to share a particularly prototypical example of client creativity. The senior author recently was asked to interview a rather special patient (a 30-year-old male, diagnosed as a schizophrenic) for a special consulting occasion. The patient, seriously doing his therapeutic part, participated in the dialogue as follows:

Donald Meichenbaum ● Department of Psychology, University of Waterloo, Waterloo, Ontario N2L 3G1, Canada. **J. Barnard Gilmore** ● Department of Psychology, University of Toronto, Toronto, Ontario M5S 1A1, Canada.

CONSULTANT: Could you tell me what brought you to the hospital?
PATIENT: *(After a lengthy silence)*: The number three bus.
CONSULTANT: I am wondering what are some of the problems that brought you to the hospital?
PATIENT: There was no problem. The bus stops right on the corner of my street.

We shall emphasize that the way to cope with such creativity is to invoke a parallel creativity, one that eventually helps the client to rely primarily on his or her own abilities to find and to counter new forms of resistive distress. Cognitive-behavioral therapies offer some new models for generating creative interventions. We shall explore these models in some detail.

Cognitive-Behavioral Therapy

Cognitive-behavioral interventions are active, time-limited, structured forms of treatment. Cognitive-behavioral therapy is based on the underlying theoretical rationale that an individual's affect and behavior are largely determined by the way he or she construes his or her world. Cognitive-behavioral therapy is designed to help the client identify, reality-test, and correct maladaptive, distorted conceptualizations and dysfunctional beliefs. By having the client become aware of and monitor the role negative and involuntary thoughts play in the maintenance of maladaptive behavior, by recognizing the connections among cognition, affect, and behavior together with their joint consequences, the client is encouraged to test out the effects of these cognitions and beliefs with selected homework assignments. The cognitive-behavioral therapist is concerned not only with the role the client's cognitions play in contributing to the disorder, but, equally importantly, the therapist is concerned about the nature and adequacy of the client's behavioral repertoire as it affects the resultant intrapersonal and interpersonal situation. True to the tenets of this hyphenated approach (cognition-behavior-affect-consequences), cognitive-behavioral therapies have adopted a reciprocal determinist view of change, as described by Bandura (1977) and by Meichenbaum (1976a, 1977). This view holds that behavioral change is a reflection of the intimate interrelationships among the client's cognitive structures (schemata, beliefs), conscious cognitive processes (automatic thoughts, internal dialogue, images), interpersonal behaviors, and resulting intrapersonal and interpersonal consequences.

For example, in the cognitive-behavioral therapy of Beck, Rush,

Shaw, and Emery (1979) a depressed client is asked, challenged, and cajoled to engage in graded behavioral acts that will have consequences that are incompatible with his or her prior expectations. The client is taught to view cognitions as hypotheses, the validity of which is to be repeatedly assessed by means of personal experiments. The therapist will then have the client examine the nature of those beliefs, assumptions, schemata, and current concerns (or what are here being referred to in general as cognitive structures) that give rise to expectations, appraisals, attributions, and automatic thoughts and images (here referred to in general as cognitive processes). This cognitive-behavioral therapy process is in fact distinctly similar to the processes that we as scientists engage in.

The Scientist Model: An Analogy

The scientist model, as described by Kuhn (1962), Mahoney (1976), and Polanyi (1958), provides a very useful framework for discussing the nature of change and resistance. A personal-scientist model has been advocated by many cognitive-behavioral therapists (Beck *et al.*, 1979; Mahoney, 1974; Meichenbaum, 1977). In fact, as we learn more about the passions of scientists and how they create, fudge, and selectively attend to data (or what they will consider as evidence), the closer would seem to be the fit between ourselves as scientists and our clients. (See Brush [1974], Hebb [1975], and Mitroff [1974] for descriptions of the influences of scientists' passions and resulting resistances to change.)

Exactly how do we as scientists change? What is the nature of the forms of resistance that we as scientists exhibit? What scientists can question or modify, or what they can invent or change, may be severely constrained by their "paradigms" (Kuhn, 1962), and by the structures of their "tacit knowledge" (Polanyi, 1958), which permit their understandings and beliefs. Cognitive structures guide and influence the types of experiments (behavioral acts) that a scientist conducts, which in their turn yield results (consequences). But as scientists we are quite selective (as indeed we should be) about admitting whether or not these results are to be considered "anomalous." Our paradigms and our behavior are quite as resistant to change as is the behavior of our clients.

This scientist analogy is no idle comparison. As we will see, it has very important implications for how we conceptualize and deal with our clients' resistance. Much of our work in therapy will attempt (1) to have our clients come to view their cognitions as hypotheses that are to be subjected to reality testing and evaluation; (2) to help our clients become open to anomalous "data"; and (3) to have them examine the nature of those beliefs or "paradigms" that give rise to their maladaptive behavior, so that they may learn to employ incompatible thoughts as strategies that can promote adaptive coping.

Role of Conceptualization

A key goal of cognitive-behavioral treatment is to facilitate the emergence of a new conceptualization over the course of therapy, thereby permitting the client's symptoms to be translated into difficulties that can be pinpointed and viewed as specific, solvable problems rather than as problems that are vague, undifferentiated, and overwhelming. A good deal of emphasis is placed on laying the groundwork for the emergence of this therapeutic reconceptualization. In the same way that a lawyer carefully lays the groundwork for a brief to be presented to the jury, the therapist collects the data to present to the client. Moreover, the therapist does not present the conceptualization with certainty, but offers it as reflecting his or her current view of what is going on. The therapist carefully checks with the client to see if this view will indeed make sense and will not seem highly unlikely to the client. The therapist may report to the client as follows: "What I hear you saying is . . ." "You seem to be telling me . . ." "Am I correct in assuming that . . .?" "I get the feeling that . . ., correct me if I'm wrong." "We have covered a lot of territory so far in this interview. Is there anything I said that troubled you? . . . Do you think we left anything out?" Such queries provide the basis for involving the client in the process of collaboration and reconceptualization.

The reconceptualization process gets a good deal of attention from cognitive-behavioral theorists because treatment intervention procedures will follow directly from the particular reconceptualization that has emerged over the course of the initial phases of therapy. It is not as if the client must sign an explicit contract in therapy saying that "my problem now fits this reconceptualization," but instead a conceptualization or a working framework is created and refined over the entire course of therapy. The initial, educational phase of therapy is seen as a key time for the prevention of unnecessary client resistance.

In order to consolidate initial conceptualizations, a number of cognitive-behavioral therapists (e.g., Beck *et al.*, 1979; Novaco, 1978; Turk, Meichenbaum, & Genest, in press) have also employed forms of bibliotherapy, which may augment a cognitive-behavioral view of the client's disorder and of therapy. One does not introduce such a bibliotherapy until the groundwork has been laid. The "mental set" given to the client is to read the bibliotherapy material and to see if any of it may fit his or her particular problem. This provides the basis for a mutual decision about the nature of future interventions. Thus the reconceptualization process and the early phases of treatment prepare the patient for these therapeutic interventions, in a way designed to anticipate and to minimize the interference from resistances to homework assignments and to the sequelae of change.

Affect

Because of its name, the cognitive-behavioral approach has often been seen as relatively unconcerned with affect. However, because resistance is so closely bound up with affects, it is especially important to correct this misunderstanding in the present context. Affect is heavily invested in the client's expectancies and "hidden agendas" in life. The cognitive-behavioral therapist does not disregard affect; instead he or she focuses with the client on the intimate links among thinking, behaving, and affect. Nowhere is this fact clearer than in the work of Beck and his colleagues, who treat the ultimate "resistance": severe depression. Affect invariably *is* the presenting problem from the client's point of view. It is a shift in affect that has allowed, or pushed, the client to seek therapy. And it is by his or her "improved" affects that the client will judge the success of all his or her efforts.

Cognitive-behavioral therapies stress that affect (like belief) is not under direct voluntary control. To modify affect one must change thought and behavior patterns. And to change thought and behavior patterns it is not sufficient just to reason with or "persuade" one's clients. It is in this respect that cognitive-behavioral techniques are not merely the "talking" therapies or persuasion techniques that some have supposed (cf. Berenson & Carkhuff, 1967; Ledwidge, 1979). Affect depends in part on what the client believes about affect, and these important beliefs, these personal theories of affect, can helpfully be modified by careful work that first explicates, then looks at the evidence concerning the truth value and the psychological utility of the beliefs in question. Affect is not controlled in the way the client generally imagines. It is not a given, over which he or she can have no control. Much more than psychology has hitherto stressed, affect is largely controlled by previous affects through the mediating links of cognition. It is what our last affective experience *means* to us that helps determine our next affective experience. And this key cognitive mediator is the focus of our therapeutic efforts. Where traditional psychodynamic therapies eventually point toward a correction of the unconscious origins of neurotic affects, cognitive-behavioral therapies initially focus on the interruption of such affects, after these first arise and well before they have expanded into dysfunctional complexes. In turn, as the client acquires the cognitive and behavioral skills to cope with such affective disturbances, the cognitive basis for such dysfunctional affects is explored and changed.

How is such cognitive interruption possible? We have already suggested the basic technique, and we will shortly present some examples of it. For our own part, we see the basic key of cognitive-behavioral therapy as training the client to use the scientific model: Identify the working hypothesis, test it empirically, modify it as necessary, and invent new behaviors that will solve problems in a world that works according to the model we hold. We try to help the client become more scientifically active by modeling a cognitive style that the client learns to practice with our help, a style that includes such new cognitions as: "What are the data?" "What is the evidence for my conclusions?" "Are there other explanations?" "What is the degree of harm to me if . . .?" "How serious . . .?" and so on.

In this context the client's resistance represents a new occasion for the client and therapist to do a cognitive-behavioral analysis. If the set adopted by the therapist and client is one of a personal scientist, then failures and client resistance, like anomalous data for the scientist, provide additional occasions for examining the nature of the client's cognitions, affects, behavior, and so on. At the outset it should be made clear to the client that "progress" will almost certainly not be linear, that disappointment need not spread, that resistance itself can be informative. If the affect experienced by the client in therapy can come to be nonthreatening, then affect in general can be successfully coped with and used constructively. Every client is different and it is likely that every client knows that. Coping strategies must be individually tailored. For all these reasons, it is well to anticipate resistant affects with repeated emphasis on the resilience of our therapeutic armory and, by implication, on the resilience of our clients as well. Beck *et al.*, accomplish this by saying words to this effect:

> We have a number of approaches that have been shown to be successful for various problems. We may have to try out several before we find the one that fits you. Thus, if one method is not particularly helpful, it will provide us with valuable information regarding which method is likely to succeed. (1979, p. 132)

Resistance and the Initial Phases of Therapy

There is a sense in which every resistance signals a new beginning phase of therapy, and every beginning in therapy signals a change in the vicissitudes of existing resistances. Thus the initial phases of treatment are crucial for any concentrated look at resistance. It is in the beginning phases of therapy that most clients drop out. And with the first contact, or even before, cognitive-behavioral therapies attempt to concentrate on the sources of misunderstandings that spawn resistances.

Make no mistake: As we shall argue at the conclusion of this chapter, "resistance" has its appropriate and healthy places in anyone's psychodynamics. Not every client belongs in treatment under these circumstances, at this time, with this therapist. Thus cognitive-behavioral therapy often begins even *before* the initial contact with the client. Therapists can intervene before treatment is even started by influencing the way referrals are made: who is referred, what they understand, and so on. For example, Turk *et al.* (in press) illustrate, for the case of general medical practitioners referring pain patients, how this early intervention may be done. The content and style of referrals markedly affect the nature of initial resistance. There is nothing new in this idea, as anyone who has ever tried to help a court-referred "offender" well knows. But the cognitive-behavioral emphasis on coping, on active experimentation, applies equally well to our attempts at modifying the referring agencies, including the courts. It is as likely that therapists can modify their referrals as it is that our clients can modify their symptoms, however discouraging the outlook may appear at first.

Thus cognitive-behavioral therapies do not begin only with a referral, nor does their attention to resistance begin with an initial-assessment phase of treatment. Cognitive-behavioral therapies make no significant distinction between the work of assessment and that of therapy. The types of questions the therapist asks, the types of tests and behavioral assignments given, the rationale offered all contribute to the therapy process. Within the cognitive-behavioral framework there are no "nonspecific" factors to the therapy process; nothing is "beyond" the treatment regimen. At present we may not be able to specify all of the mechanisms mediating change, but they are potentially specifiable and they play a significant role in affecting treatment adherence and resistance. The client's internal "dialogues" (expectations, attributions) concerning both his or her presenting problems and the accompanying expectations about treatment are the immediate concern of the therapist. Clients often enter therapy with a sense of helplessness, hopelessness, and a feeling of demoralization concerning their presenting problems. They often feel like victims of their maladaptive behaviors, whether these are thoughts, feelings, and/or the reactions of others. Such feelings have been ably described by Frank (1974) and Strupp (1970). Moreover, clients often have a fear that Raimy (1975) has called "phrenophobia," that is, a fear that the client's problem means that he or she may be going crazy. Those feelings and thoughts can further contribute to a client's resistance. The initial phase of therapy (and it is being suggested that this applies to all therapies, including cognitive-behavioral interventions) is designed to begin to change the client's internal dialogue concerning his or her problems, and to promote the accompanying sense that change is possible. The variety of clinical techniques we describe below are designed to convey a sense of both hopefulness and learned resourcefulness to replace the sense of helplessness.

Assessment

We begin by assessing the phenomenal world of the client, in order to understand how he or she construes reality. Insofar as the therapist can accurately and empathically perceive and share the client's expectancies, the therapist is more likely to be able to make sense out of the client's unproductive, resistant behavior. As Beck *et al.* (1979) indicate, such accurate empathy may help the therapist realize that a resistant or negative client is actually a person who regards himself or herself as so incompetent and hopeless that he or she does not feel that change is possible. The therapist tries to understand the nature of the cognitive distortions that contribute to this "paralysis of will."

The waiting room experience is invariably a focus for thoughts relating to resistance. Thus it is a sound policy to begin the assessment of the client's phenomenological experience by asking what the client thought and felt in the waiting room. Parenthetically, recent research on adherence to medical treatment revealed significantly worse adherence the longer the waiting time in the waiting room before consultation (Davidson, 1976). It is easy to imagine how prolonged waiting can result in rich, counterproductive, distressed thinking.

There are many questions that can facilitate the initial assessment of the client's world view, of the strengths and vulnerabilities in the client's thinking. One can ask why the client desires therapeutic assistance at the current time. What does the client think may happen? On what will the outcome of treatment depend, and how so? From such questioning the therapist can begin to see potential or actual forms of resistance. More importantly, the therapist can then have greater insight into whether a given form of resistance reflects an attempt at coping, or misinformation, or misexpectations, and so on.

For example, Davis (1967) reports that farm workers suffering from cardiac disease hold some of the following beliefs, which contributed to treatment noncompliance: "If you wait long enough you can get over any illness"; "Illness and trouble is one way God shows displeasure"; "Some of the old-fashioned remedies are still better than things you get at the drugstore"; "You need to give your body some rest from medicine once in a while—otherwise your body becomes dependent on it or immune to it."

What then are the expectancies with which our clients enter psychotherapy, and how do such expectancies contribute to resistance and lack of adherence? Observations such as those reported by Davis led Kasl (1975) to highlight the significance of (1) the nature of the expectations client and therapist have about their respective roles, (2) the congruence and mutuality of their role expectations, and (3) their potential for exploring and revising those expectations.

Another example of initial resistance, this time in psychotherapy, is given by a client who held the expectation that sharing thoughts and feelings would lead to possible hospitalization and electric shock treatment. Not uncommonly a pain patient is referred for therapy with the set (often shared by the referring physician) that there is "real" pain as compared to "psychogenic" pain, and that seeing a psychologist means that the validity of one's pain will be challenged ("You think it's only in my head," "You think I'm making it up"). Such beliefs contribute to resistance to psychological intervention. For if the client complies with such psychological treatment, it will only confirm his or her prior expectancy that "the pain was not real." Thus an important aspect of therapy is to assess such expectancies, and to have the client provide the evidence that can prove that such expectations or conceptualizations of the problem are incorrect.

Before one begins any intervention, whether training in problem solving, training in interpersonal communication skills, or some other kind, it is also imperative that the therapist conduct an adequate task analysis of the client's problems and goals. (See Meichenbaum [1976b] and Schwartz & Gottman [1976] for a description of such task analysis.)

Task analyses help determine whether the client is having problems because he or she has a deficit in knowledge of what is appropriate, or whether the client has the knowledge but does not have adequate interpersonal (or intrapersonal) skills to implement the appropriate coping behaviors, or whether the client has both the knowledge and a sufficient repertoire but is inhibited from acting by doubt and fear. This latter deficit is seen when the client engages in an internal dialogue of conflict that interferes with the implementation of already existing skills. Thus, as Wilson and Evans (1976) indicate, what the therapist considers client resistance may reflect the client's inability to respond to problems having that level of difficulty. The proper task analysis confirms the importance of individually tailoring the treatment to the particular needs of the client. By matching the form of the intervention to the level of the client's competences and to the nature of the deficit, one can avoid or minimize client resistance. By graduating the change process into manageable steps and by structuring therapeutic interventions in a way that maximizes the likelihood of success at each stage, the therapist will further reduce the likelihood of client resistance.

As assessment progresses, then, the working hypotheses and cognitive limits that control the affect and the behavior of the client come into clearer focus. And, in turn, a clearer picture emerges of the nature of the client's resistances to change. These resistances may be neutralized by well-chosen interventions.

Homework Interventions in Cognitive-Behavioral Therapies

Cognitive-behavioral therapies make considerable use of homework done out in the real world, where the client must function after therapy is finished. The homework is a key ingredient for dismantling problem-causing ideas, for strengthening problem-solving ideas, and for assessing the sources of new problems and of resistances to solving these problems that will occur after therapy has ended. Resistance to doing the homework assignments is a first priority for treatment under cognitive-behavioral therapy. From the very beginning, the client is shown that he or she will be a full collaborator in the therapy process.

Thus, often by employing the personal-scientist analogy, the client is made aware that he or she can contribute very helpful and sometimes very surprising data from the homework experiments that are undertaken. Levy and Carter (1976) have contrasted various ways that homework assignments can be made. The cognitive-behavioral therapist is particularly concerned that the client realizes his or her own efficacy in planning and evaluating experiments and life changes. Therefore the way that homework is seen by the client is a particularly significant datum in cognitive-behavioral therapy.

Consider the client's probable set when he or she has done a homework assignment following each of these three different kinds of directions:

1. "What you are to do is . . .," "Do the following . . .," "Do this . . ."
2. "I would like you to . . .," "I want you to . . .," "This is what I am asking you to do . . ."
3. "So what you have agreed to try is . . .," "As I understand it, you will . . .," "So you will take responsibility for . . ."

The client's attributions concerning the change process and therapy are likely to be very different under each of these three message styles, and only the third kind can facilitate looking at the resistance to homework that may be experienced while it is being attempted.

The therapist must ensure that the client understands the rationale and goal of each homework assignment. A useful way to assess such understanding is to use a role reversal procedure where the client must, in his or her own words, explain the nature of the homework assignments to the therapist. Such an explanation is followed by a discussion of the nature of the problems. The client may be asked, "How do you feel about this assignment? Do you feel it is something useful to tackle? Can you foresee some of the possible problems you could have doing it?" and so on.

Ideally, the therapist would like the client to suggest the same homework assignments that the therapist has in mind. Our style in achieving this goal is not to lecture the client in a didactic fashion, but instead to use a nondirective, Socratic-dialogue approach. The following excerpt illustrates this style.

CLIENT: I suppose I should find out if I can study somewhere else besides at my parents' house.
THERAPIST: That sounds important. How could you find out?
CLIENT: I could arrange to study at the library tomorrow.
THERAPIST: Would that help answer your question?
CLIENT: Well, yes and no. See, if it went well, it might just be because tomorrow I only need to work on an easy assignment in geography. And if it went badly, I guess that would tell me something.
THERAPIST: What would it tell you?
CLIENT *(Pauses):* I was just thinking, I might do better to try different places in the library. To see where it went best.
THERAPIST: And wouldn't you also need to know where it went worst? There could be a lot of helpful clues there.
CLIENT: I see what you mean. I wonder if I should write down my thoughts or worries again if I find I can't study in certain places.
THERAPIST: You've got a fine suggestion there. Do you want to try it? I think it would help us see what we can do next.
CLIENT: Sure. That's good.

There are some treatment situations—for example, in work with pain patients (Turk *et al.*, in press)—where the spouse or others may profitably join in deciding and/or carrying out their own allied homework assignments to support the work of the client. It is naturally important as well to graduate the homework so as to maximize the likelihood of effective adherence. Where appropriate, the effectiveness of what the client has actually accomplished in homework must be clarified until the client is fully aware of it.

The impact the client's "hidden agendas" have on treatment adherence, as well as the impact of the corresponding "agendas" held by others who are significant in the client's life must be ascertained. The client or the client's spouse may be concerned that complying with homework and treatment plans will result in the loss of welfare payments or that it may influence pending litigation, or that improvement may result in behaviors that the client or spouse finds disconcerting. For example, a spouse may sabotage treatment fearing that the client's improvement or change may threaten their relationship. Thus both the client's and the spouse's cognitions, expectations, images, fantasies, and meanings vis à vis the treatment changes receive a good deal of attention from cognitive-behavioral therapists. Gurman and Knudson (1978) have used a systems-analysis approach to argue that it is a property of any ongoing social system to resist change from within or from without (clearly, the various schools of psychotherapy demonstrate this point well). In the context of marriage therapy Gurman and Knudson highlight the roles played by multileveled aspects of a relationship as these contribute to resistance. The therapist must be sensitive to the fact that interventions and contracts established at one level of exchange (conscious and verbalized) may contradict those at another level of exchange (unconscious and unverbalized). Here we use "unconscious" in the same sense as Kuhn's "paradigms" or Polanyi's "tacit knowledge," that is, a system of implicit beliefs.

Where the homework has been left undone, guilt and discouragement must be prevented, first through an understanding of the reasons (thoughts, emotions, conflicting behaviors) for the client's inaction, and then by planning for future coping in the face of similar resistances. For example, Beck et al. (1979) cite the following client reactions: "It is useless to try," "I can't do it," "I am too weak to do anything," "If I try it and it won't work out, I'll only feel worse." Clients usually accept such reasons as valid, whereas the therapist views these reasons as hypotheses to be tested. The need for such hypothesis testing can be conveyed to the client in many ways, of which the following dialogue is one example:

CLIENT: I didn't try phoning my daughter. I just can't do it.
THERAPIST: Is that true, you never can do it?
CLIENT: That's right. It would be humiliating.
THERAPIST: You would have to feel humiliated?
CLIENT: Certainly! After all I said to her last year? She'd laugh at me for being so weak.
THERAPIST: How do you know that? You made her sound very understanding last week.
CLIENT: Well she is understanding, when she wants to be.
THERAPIST: Then she might be ready to be understanding again, isn't that possible?
CLIENT: It's possible.
THERAPIST: And it's possible that even if she were not understanding, you would not need to feel humiliated by your experiment of calling her. Isn't that possible?
CLIENT: It's only an experiment.
THERAPIST: That's right. Is there something you are saying to yourself then, maybe even right now, that makes you feel humiliated?
CLIENT: Well no, because when I'm with you, here, it sounds silly, you know, when I say "I'm just a weak old fool, having to talk to my family again."

THERAPIST: But you don't think like that in here?

CLIENT: No. When I'm here I see how silly that is.

THERAPIST: And if you phoned your daughter right now, from here, do you think you'd need to feel humiliated?   •

CLIENT: No. (Pause) No I wouldn't. I guess it does depend.

THERAPIST: On your thoughts?

CLIENT: Yes. On my thoughts.

THERAPIST: Do you want to experiment right now then? And call her from here? And see what your reaction is?

CLIENT: Could I?

THERAPIST: Of course.

CLIENT: I never thought I could. (Laughs) Well then, Let's—like you always say—let's check it out.

This dialogue also illustrates, implicitly, that in cognitive-behavioral therapies nonadherence to treatment plans is viewed not as a sign of a personality defect or of stupidity on the part of the client, but instead as a natural consequence of an interfering thinking style, or a set of dysfunctional beliefs, and/or as the result of a set of interpersonal consequences that reinforce resistance. The cognitive-behavioral approach is as much concerned with the environmental consequences that follow client resistances, both within therapy and in vivo, as it is concerned with the nature of both the client's cognitions and his or her affect.

And when homework has been left undone, it is not only the client who should be the focus of our attention. Each therapist, recognizing his or her own potential discouragement, must then work out what might be called *transresistance*: the resistance that is all too easily transmitted from client to therapist and back. Not everyone should be a therapist. The cognitive-behavioral therapist needs actively to expand on a natural reservoir of optimism and creative thinking in the face of countless discouraged patients. To achieve this growth, cognitive-behavioral strategies must continually be applied to one's own thinking and activity, in or out of supervision. It is in this continual self-supervision that one develops the firm inner conviction that a client's resistances *can* be reduced, however discouraging the initial outlook. In this light it is interesting to note that an observer of cognitive-behavioral therapy (as reported in Beck *et al.*, 1979) indicated that a noticeable characteristic of cognitive-behavioral therapists is their persistence, or unwillingness to give up despite repeated client resistance. Each time the client reports that he or she "failed" or "can't change," it is another occasion for the cognitive-behavioral therapist to have the client reexamine the data that lead to such conclusions (invoking the scientist analogy). With the therapist's guidance the client is encouraged to reexamine the nature of the cognitions, feelings, and so on that led to the statements of hopelessness and frustration. Moreover, the therapist must be very sensitive to the client's thoughts and feelings about such failures and must question and challenge the client as to whether such failures mean that the client will always ("must") fail. Such consistent analysis and support provide an important basis for overcoming and preventing client resistance.

Anticipating Relapses and Attendant Resistances

As the client employs the various coping skills in vivo, it is inevitable that there will ensue setbacks and slow progress which will in turn lead to a negative internal dialogue questioning the effectiveness of therapy and the client's own ability to change. The cognitive-behavioral therapist must anticipate and subsume such a negative, self-referent "catastrophizing" reaction into the therapy process. Cameron (1978), from a cognitive-behavioral perspective, has succinctly described these therapy techniques.

> There are a number of things that can be done to prevent over-reaction to slow progress and setbacks. First, the therapist can discuss the time-frame for change with the client at the time interventions are begun. Many clients have unrealistic expectations about how quickly they can change. A person who thinks he is going to change in a month well-ingrained patterns of interaction acquired over a lifetime is almost certainly going to be disheartened by the pace of therapy. Second, structuring therapy so that there are a progressive series of specific intermediate goals rather than a few vague, long-range goals increases the sense of progress. Third, anticipating failures and setbacks may short-circuit over-reaction to them. The therapist can indicate that while these things are normal, people tend to become discouraged in response to them, to have doubts about whether therapy will work for them or whether they can ever change. In anticipating this negative self-monologue, the therapist can note that it is important for the client to expect this so that when the negative thoughts begin he recognizes them as a normal part of the therapy process and doesn't take them too seriously. The therapist can wrap up his statement with a suggestion that he has found that simply anticipating these negative thoughts tended to short-circuit them; the client will likely find that when he has such thoughts he will recall this conversation and this will make it possible for him to dismiss the negative self-talk as normal. (p. 246)

One objective of cognitive-behavioral therapy is to convey to the client that the goal of therapy is to provide him or her with the skills to cope with unavoidable problems as they occur, rather than to attempt to eradicate problems per se. The cognitive-behavioral therapist works to make the client a better problem solver, and a more competent personal scientist.

A number of methods have been used to enhance treatment generalization and maintenance by minimizing client resistance. For example, in some cognitive-behavioral techniques, such as stress-inoculation training, the client is exposed to a host of different coping techniques and is encouraged to pick and choose from this array those that work best for him or her, as determined in an application phase of treatment. This application phase may include actual exposure to graded, laboratory-based stressors, imagery and role playing, as well as in-vivo graduated rehearsal. This approach is always organized in such a way that the client becomes an active collaborator in shaping therapy. (See Turk *et al.* [in press] for a detailed description of how this stress-inoculation procedure has been applied to the cognitive-behavioral treatment of pain.)

Another important technique often used in cognitive-behavioral therapies, one that has particular usefulness for anticipating and dealing with resistance, is the imagery technique. Recent research, summarized by Meichenbaum (1977), confirms the usefulness of these imagery procedures for enhancing treatment adherence and for reducing client resistance. The imagery procedure works by helping the client visualize himself or herself faltering or resisting in a critical situation. Such visualization can and should include the imagery of accompanying negative thoughts in reaction to the event, followed by coping strategies applied to meet these new challenges. The following dialogue illustrates these points.

THERAPIST: Let's practice this a bit more. Imagine that during the job interview next week something happens and your feelings of discouragement start to return. How could that turn out?

CLIENT: Well, it could happen too. For instance if they asked me why I haven't worked in so long, and then they looked angry about that, I'd probably be tempted to give up right there. I mean, I'd feel there was no point in continuing the interview.

THERAPIST: What thoughts might there be?

CLIENT: Well, you know, that nobody wants to hire a person with my history, and so there's no point. And coming here to see you isn't going to change my past history, so again there's no point. And really, all I've done is to get myself into an even more painful situation by that interview, which I'd resent in a way.

THERAPIST: If you did experience thoughts like that, is there something you could do about them?

CLIENT: Yes, of course. But I might not.

THERAPIST: Why not?

CLIENT: Well that's the thing. I'm not sure. I might feel that if I did counteract those thoughts, then something much worse would happen to me. *(Pauses)* I'd think I had no right to stop those thoughts. But I'd just have to say to myself that I could look at that too, I guess. Thoughts can't hurt you by themselves. I'd have to tell myself that it was another experiment, to see if stopping those other thoughts would really produce worse thoughts. And if it did, then I could maybe catch the worse thoughts and look at them. So, yes. If I told myself that, then I could handle a bad question on the interview. It's a chance to make some progress. And that's what I need. So that's why I'm doing it. I could tell myself I didn't need to be discouraged. I'd remember, I didn't have to feel discouraged. That would stop it.

Imagery changes the meaning of future experiences with resistance, so that these come to have a déjà-vu quality: "That is what we talked about in therapy." In short, *it is not the resistance itself, but what clients say to themselves about such resistance—the setbacks, the possible relapses, and so on—that influences the degree of treatment adherence.*

The focus on relapse prevention has received a good deal of attention from Marlatt (1978), who has developed a cognitive-behavioral treatment approach for clients who are addicted to alcohol and other drugs. Marlatt's cognitive-behavioral model focuses on the determinants of relapse: the influence of high-risk situations, the availability of alternative coping behaviors, expectations about the effects of alcohol intake especially after abstinence, and, most relevant to the present discussion, Marlatt focuses on the individual's cognitive reactions to taking the first drink (the "abstinence-violation effect"). The cognitive-behavioral therapist is concerned with what will be the nature of the client's thoughts, images, and feelings in the criterion situation, when the therapy may not work. What is the nature of the cognitions when the client takes that first drink, when the depressed client has new moments of despair, when the obese client gorges, when the client reexperiences intense pain? What clients say to themselves at that moment is viewed as critical in determining the course of treatment adherence. Since the nature of the internal dialogue at this critical period is viewed as so important, it receives a good deal of attention within therapy—as, for example, in the following excerpt.

THERAPIST: What is the worst thing that could happen during the upcoming vacation period?

CLIENT: The worst thing would be if after all this my fiancé broke the engagement.

THERAPIST: That would be a real shock, all right. How would you cope?

CLIENT: I'm not sure I would cope.

THERAPIST: Really?

CLIENT: Well, I'd be tempted to just collapse. I couldn't come here. I'd need a lot of support. What I ought to do would be to accept the fact that I needed some support, and put myself in the care of my sister. She's terrific in a crisis.

THERAPIST: You could do that.

CLIENT: Now I could do that, yes. Then I'd need to cope with the feelings that this proved I'll never ever have a chance to marry. Nobody could love me. All the things we talked about, only now they'd be much worse.

THERAPIST: Those are challenging thoughts.

CLIENT: Yes. And I'd have to tell myself, I guess, that if I didn't get the best of them, they could get the best of me. I'd have to tell myself I have no choice but to fight them.

THERAPIST: How could you fight them?

CLIENT: Well, you know me. I'd start by writing them all down. Then I'd do as much to look at them and to counter them as I could. I mean, I really have learned a lot in here. And then the vacation would be over and I'd consult with you about what to do with the mess from there.

THERAPIST: That sounds very effective.

CLIENT: It does, too.

Termination Phase of Psychotherapy

The concern with the client's resistance processes is also paramount in the termination phase of the therapy. Resistance may manifest itself in the client's reluctance to end therapy and in the client's dependence on the therapist. In order to handle this dependence the cognitive-behavioral therapist once again examines the nature of the client's belief system and the internal dialogue that gives rise to such dependence. The same therapeutic techniques that were used in previous phases of psychotherapy are applied to these final instances of resistance. Note that the typography of the response per se is not the determining factor in deciding whether a client's behavior should be considered resistance. What may be viewed earlier in therapy as treatment adherence may, at a later phase of therapy, be viewed as resistance. Client resistance is defined partly in terms of the therapist's and client's objectives. The following excerpt illustrates how the therapist must walk a fine line between, on the one hand, trying to foster independence, and yet, on the other hand, leaving the door open for future booster sessions and follow-up treatment if warranted.

CLIENT: I'm wondering if we really should stop the therapy next week if my father's business does go into bankruptcy after all.   ٥

THERAPIST: Yes, it's hard to know what would happen. Are you thinking that you wouldn't know how to handle your new feelings then?

CLIENT: Partly, yes.

THERAPIST: Is that all you're thinking?

CLIENT: Well, I'm also thinking about what we talked about. I mean I know that there are some things now I can do. I don't have to feel panicked, if I take control. But I can't help thinking about 2 years ago. I thought I was cured then, and I was wrong.

THERAPIST: Well here again we are back to the thought that the "cure" is in you, that your problems are all your own doing, without the unforeseen playing any role, as if you have no problems except in your head. But does the evidence suggest you are right?

CLIENT: It doesn't, I know. There is always the chance that a new problem will come up.

THERAPIST: Being human, it is bound to come up. And when new problems turn up, what will you do?

CLIENT: I'll cope.

THERAPIST: You'll cope.

CLIENT: And, I'll be able to deal with it, if I hear myself saying I can't cope.

THERAPIST: How will you deal with it?

CLIENT (Laughs): Well if it gets too bad, I'll call you.

THERAPIST: You are the expert on how bad it is. If you did call me in to help you, I'd respect that. I'm impressed by your new coping skills now, which is why I suggested that you set next week as your last session. Like everything else we have tried, it is something of an experiment of course. It isn't only you who is interested in how it turns out. That's why I've asked you to phone me in 3 weeks. On the phone we can evaluate this experiment of working independently.

CLIENT: Yes; I really do think it will go all right, but I have these other worries still too.

THERAPIST: That's only to be expected. And you've been handling them well.

CLIENT: Yes, that's true. I have.

Group Treatment

When cognitive-behavioral therapies are done in groups, many aspects of resistance are minimized and treatment adherence may be significantly increased (cf. Beck et al., 1979; Meichenbaum, 1977; Turk et al., in press). Some advantages of group treatment include: (1) shared disclosure of clients' cognitions; (2) the chance to sample client behavior in a real social setting, in order to explore the clients' internal dialogue

and beliefs; and (3) the opportunity for in-vivo group assignments. Moreover, groups can serve to multiply successful models, and to supply a
realistic data base for correcting any one client's naïve psychology.
Groups enhance the offering of hypotheses for test as well as the means
for testing these hypotheses. Space does not permit a detailed look at
this special aspect of resistance from the cognitive-behavioral perspective, but the references cited above are valuable sources of additional
information.

Conclusion

What is it that resistance resists? In general, all therapies agree
enough in their usage of this term so that we may answer this question:
resistance resists a change. For cognitive-behavioral therapies the significant change that is resisted is a change in the client's willingness to
find and test possible alternative coping strategies, both behavioral and
cognitive. Although the *affective* expressions of resistance—fear of
change, pessimism, hopelessness, hostility—are not ignored, it is the
cognitive and behavioral avenues for changing these affects that are the
focus of cognitive-behavioral therapies. These therapies stress the hypothesis that supporting every resistance are cognitions of this general
type: "Trying to change is only going to risk that very likely possibility
of making everything much worse."

It is difficult if not impossible to convey in this limited discussion
the host of cognitive-behavioral techniques that have emerged during
the last 10 years to deal with client resistance. What is being underlined
is the fact that so-called nonspecific factors such as the initial interview,
the reconceptualization of the present problems, homework assignments, and so on are all central to handling a client's potential resistances. We feel that the failure to consider such variables in planning a
variety of medical and psychological interventions has contributed to
the amazingly high incidence of treatment nonadherence (ranging from
7% to 87% as reported by Davidson, 1976).

The issues of client adherence and resistance are as complex as they
are important. This fact is emphasized by Cameron (1978), who, working
from a cognitive-behavioral perspective, has given a number of caveats
for therapy that are worth repeating. Cameron's caveats provide an
excellent summary of many of the cognitive-behavioral viewpoints we
have considered.

First, whenever possible, the therapist should influence the referral processes so that the timing and content of therapy are realistic. As Cameron states:

> Psychologists may realize substantial clinical dividends if they invest the time and effort required to cultivate relationships with referring agents by providing information about the nature of the therapy, the rationale underlying it, its limitations, data pertaining to its effectiveness, and prompt feedback on all cases referred. (Cameron, 1978, p. 237)

Next, the therapist must take care to establish a therapeutic alliance with the client and to examine the nature of any client cognitions that impede the development of a cooperative working relationship. Cameron goes on to describe some of these cognitions as follows: (a) the client's belief that his or her problem is not psychological in nature; (b) the client's belief that the therapist is an adversary, or the agent of an adversary; and (c) the client's belief that psychological interventions are not effective. In each case the therapist uses the client's own experience to support the case for a psychological intervention.

Cameron also suggests, and we concur, that one can and should develop metaphors, aphorisms, and simple demonstrations to illustrate the feasibility of a particular treatment approach. For example, in the cognitive-behavioral treatment of pain Cameron reports that he was able to have the pain client use a set of distraction techniques to cope with pain. At first the client was somewhat resistant, not quite understanding the potential viability of such a coping mechanism. Given this resistance Cameron (1978) used the following procedure:

> First, I ask the patient to be aware of the sensations in his thighs as he sits in his chair. I note that those sensations are real, and they have a physical basis, but they are not normally experienced because other things occupy his attention. Then I suggest that he think of a TV set: he could block out the channel 9 signal by tuning in channel 11; the channel 9 signal is still there, but not being tuned in. I suggest that while his pain signals are real, he can learn to "tune them out". Tying the conceptualization to an image not only facilitates communication of the conceptualization, but often serves a "bell ringer" function as well. A number of pain patients have reported that they frequently think of the TV metaphor when experiencing pain and take appropriate action to "tune out." (p. 244)

Such examples go a long way toward making the therapeutic suggestions that are offered both more plausible and more credible. Credibility of treatment procedures may be enhanced in other ways as well, thus minimizing resistance. A pain patient, when offered muscular relaxation training, may doubt its potential therapeutic value especially given a history of multiple medical operations. Both Meichenbaum

(1976a) and Cameron (1978) note how the status of the intervention of relaxation can be enhanced by the use of EMG biofeedback training. The level of technology being brought to bear on the problem may then appear more commensurate with the client's perception of the problem. Cameron notes that therapeutic adherence may increase if the therapist selects and presents interventions in a way that allows the client to view them as sufficiently potent to deal with the problem.

A client's beliefs, expectations, self-statements, and images play a paramount role in determining treatment adherence. Since these processes are the central focus of cognitive-behavior therapies, we feel such therapies offer a very promising way for dealing with client resistance.

Epilogue

A discussion of client resistance should end with an important caveat, one that Davidson (1976) has highlighted. Namely, it is necessary for us as therapists to assure the efficacy of a treatment before we start ensuring compliance. Davidson suggests that we tend to view clients' resistance as "vaguely sinful" and as reflecting that something is wrong with the client. One must keep in mind the history of various medical and psychological treatments and wonder whether the client's resistance may reflect perspicacious wisdom and plain good judgment. Turk *et al.* (in press) remind us of the treatment given Charles II of England at the hands of the best physicians of the day.

> A pint of blood was extracted from his right arm and a half-pint from his left shoulder. This was followed by an emetic, two physics, and an enema comprising 15 substances. Next, his head was shaved and a blister raised. Following in rapid succession, more emetics, sneezing powder, bleedings, soothing potions, a plaster of pitch, and pidgeon dung was smeared on his feet. Potions containing 10 different substances, chiefly herbs, as well as 40 drops of extract of human skull, were swallowed. Finally, application of bezoar stones (gallstones from sheep and goats) was prescribed. Following this extensive treatment, the king died.

Or consider the treatment offered George Washington for what was probably a throat infection compounded by pneumonia.

> Because he could afford the best cure available, he was given a mixture of molasses, vinegar, and butter, and then made to vomit and have diarrhea. But he lapsed. In desperation, his physicians applied irritating poultices to blister his feet and his throat, while draining several pints of blood. Then he died. (Power, 1978, p. 24)

One can well imagine the physicians of the day meeting at the local pub or even editing a book on patients' resistance to the current treatment. "If only the king or president had properly adhered to our treatment, then we would have seen the expected improvement." If only Charles II and George Washington had shown some resistance to treatment!

ACKNOWLEDGMENTS

The authors wish to thank Pat Bowers, Ken Bowers, and Roy Cameron for their helpful comments.

References

Bandura, A. Self-efficacy: Towards a unifying theory of behavior change. *Psychological Review*, 1977, *89*, 191–215.

Beck, A., Rush, J., Shaw, B., & Emery, G. *Cognitive therapy of depression*. New York: Guilford Press, 1979.

Berenson, B., & Carkhuff, R. *Sources of gain in counselling and psychotherapy*. New York: Holt, Rinehart & Winston, 1967.

Brush, S. Should the history of science be x rated? *Science*, 1974, *183*, 1164–1172.

Cameron, R. The clinical implementation of behavior change techniques: A cognitively oriented conceptualization of therapeutic "compliance" and "resistance." In J. Foreyt & D. Rathjen (Eds.), *Cognitive behavior therapy: Research and application*. New York: Plenum Press, 1978.

Davidson, P. Therapeutic compliance. *Canadian Psychological Review*, 1976, *17*, 247–259.

Davis, R. Treating adherence. *British Journal of Psychiatry*, 1967, *129*, 513–520.

Frank, J. *Persuasion and healing: A comparative study of psychotherapy* (Rev. ed.). New York: Schocken Books, 1974.

Gurman, A., & Knudson, R. Behavioral marriage therapy: A psychodynamic system analysis and critique. *Family Process*, 1978, *17*, 121–138.

Hebb, D. Science and the world of imagination. *Canadian Psychological Review*, 1975, *16*, 4–12.

Kasl, S. Issues in patient adherence to health care regimens. *Journal of Human Stress*, 1975, *5*, 1–17.

Kuhn, T. *The structure of scientific revolutions*. Chicago: University of Chicago Press, 1962.

Ledwidge, B. Cognitive-behavior modification: A step in the wrong direction. *Psychological Bulletin*, 1979, *85*, 353–375.

Levy, R., & Carter, R. Compliance with practitioner instigations. *Social Work*, 1976, *21*, 188–193.

Mahoney, M. *Cognition and behavior modification*. Cambridge, Mass.: Ballinger, 1974.

Mahoney, M. *The scientist: Anatomy of the truth merchant*. Cambridge, Mass.: Ballinger, 1976.

Marlatt, A. Craving for alcohol, loss of control, and relapse: A cognitive-behavioral analysis. In P. Nathan & A. Marlatt (Eds.), *Experimental and behavioral approaches to alcoholism*. New York: Plenum Press, 1978.

Meichenbaum, D. Toward a cognitive theory of self-control. In G. Schwartz & D. Shapiro (Eds.), *Consciousness and self-regulation* (Vol. 1). New York: Plenum Press, 1976. (a)

Meichenbaum, D. Cognitive factors in biofeedback therapy. *Biofeedback and self-regulation,* 1976, *1,* 201–216a. (b)

Meichenbaum, D. *Cognitive-behavior modification: An integrative approach.* New York: Plenum Press, 1977.

Mitroff, I. *The subjective side of science.* New York: Elsevier, 1974.

Novaco, R. Anger and coping with stress: Cognitive behavioral interventions. In J. Foreyt & D. Rathjen (Eds.), *Cognitive behavior therapy: Research and application.* New York: Plenum Press, 1978.

Polanyi, M. *Personal knowledge: Towards a post-critical philosophy.* Chicago: University of Chicago Press, 1958.

Power, L. *San Francisco Chronicle,* March 15, 1978.

Raimy, V. *Misunderstanding of the self: Cognitive psychotherapy and the misconception hypothesis.* San Francisco: Jossey-Bass, 1975.

Schwartz, R., & Gottman, J. Toward a task analysis of assertive behavior. *Journal of Consulting and Clinical Psychology,* 1976, *44,* 910–920.

Strupp, H. Specific vs. nonspecific factors in psychotherapy and the problem of control. *Archives of General Psychiatry,* 1970, *23,* 393–401.

Turk, D., Meichenbaum, D., & Genest, M. *Pain: A cognitive-behavioral treatment approach.* New York: Guilford Press, in press.

Wilson, T., & Evans, I. Adult behavior therapy and the therapist-client relationship. In C. Franks & T. Wilson (Eds.), *Annual review of behavior therapy: Theory and practice* (Vol. 4). New York: Brunner/Mazel, 1976.

8

The Behavior-Analytic Approach

Ira Daniel Turkat and Victor Meyer

General Introduction

The phenomenon known as resistance represents an experience well-known to clinicians of all persuasions. However, what one clinician labels "resistance" may not be similarly viewed by his fellow clinician. In essence, this discrepancy arises from differing definitions of resistance among and within the various schools of thought. Thus one's ability to identify and modify resistance will be dependent on one's approach to clinical phenomena in general.

In the behavior-analytic approach (Meyer & Turkat, 1979), we attempt to operationalize clinical phenomena. In other words, we try to specify what is happening in as accurate and concise detail as possible, so that all observers can agree when the particular phenomenon is occuring. This approach helps us systematically monitor the phenomenon in order to test variables for its prediction and control. Similarly, in dealing with "resistance," we must first be able to clearly define what it is.

In developing a definition of resistance, it is essential to recognize that the definition must be general enough to encompass all resistant behavior but flexible enough to incorporate the behavioral specificity of each individual case, in each particular situation, in its appropriate con-

Ira Daniel Turkat ● Departments of Psychology and Medicine, Vanderbilt University and School of Medicine, Nashville, Tennessee 37240. Victor Meyer ● Academic Department of Psychiatry, Middlesex Hospital Medical School, London W1N 8AA, England.

text. In other words, there are no behaviors that can universally be labeled "resistance," and the range of specific behaviors that can be labeled "resistance" is infinite. For example, failure to perform a specified assignment may be labeled "resistance" in many cases, whereas such behavior may not be labeled "resistance" by a therapist working with an individual hypersensitive to criticism (i.e., subjecting oneself to therapist criticism). Thus it is the therapist's labeling of behavior that determines what is and what is not considered "resistance." Hence, the following definition: *Resistance is client behavior that the therapist labels antitherapeutic.* We believe this definition is general enough to cover all instances of resistance but must always be operationalized to the individual experience (i.e., when situation A occurs, client B performs behavior C which therapist D determines as therapeutically nonbeneficial for client B).

It is evident from our conceptualization of resistance that it is impossible to list all the behaviors that might possibly be labeled such. However, in order to provide a fuller understanding of the idiographic nature of resistance, we will present some common (but by no means exhaustive or mutually exclusive) resistance-producing situations frequently seen in our clinical practice. Nine general situations with specific examples will be delineated.

A situation that frequently produces resistant behavior involves *reinforcement conditions.* Often the reinforcement available to the client for performing the resistant behavior is far more powerful than any reinforcer the therapist could provide for changing. One of our recent cases is an excellent example.

> A middle-aged woman was referred to us for shoplifting. The basic problem across all her complaints (shoplifting, interpersonal anxiety, depression) involved an excessive need for approval. The etiology of her shoplifting occurred in this context, as her husband restricted his approval of her to her shoplifting success. Furthermore, intrinsic reinforcement was extremely important as the client was a very ambitious high achiever who experienced tremendous feelings of self-approval when she successfully completed a perfectionistically planned caper. Also, the client was negatively reinforced (i.e., an aversive event was terminated) by this habit in that she could quickly eliminate bad feelings by stealing. Finally, the financial and material benefit (at pretreatment) involved a take of approximately $1,000 daily, enabled the client to maintain two apartments, and provided expensive gifts for interpersonal approval. Naturally,

the reinforcement for engaging in this behavior during treatment was far more potent and immediate than the consequences of our treatment strategies. Thus, frequent resistant behavior occurred.

Another situation that frequently produces resistance involves *punishment conditions*. In certain cases, learning control over the primary problematic behavior may result in punishment for such a change.

A female agoraphobic came for help in learning to control panic attacks. A major consequence of these panic attacks was the client staying as close as possible to the husband at all times. An important contributing factor to this client's difficulties involved the husband's reinforcement of her dependence. In fact, the marriage developed on this type of relationship. It became apparent that if the client learned to control her panic attacks and became more independent, the husband would probably leave the marriage. Thus, engaging in "resistant" behavior was one way to avoid massive punishment.

Avoidance situations frequently produce resistant behaviors as well. The classic example is the individual presenting a phobia. This individual organizes his whole life around avoiding exposure to the anxiety-provoking stimuli. He enters therapy with the goal of being able to approach feared stimuli despite a history of continuous avoidance of these stimuli. With the aim of therapy to eliminate all avoidance, one accidental exposure to a high anxiety-producing stimulus may force the client to avoid and thereby strengthen the phobia. Furthermore, planned exposure to anxiety-provoking stimuli in itself often creates opportunities for resistant behaviors to develop (i.e., deliberate avoidance).

Another situation that frequently produces resistance involves the specific *modification methodology*. For example, when a particular client was taught to stop ritualistic washing by exposing him to "contaminated" stimuli while preventing washing, he performed ritualistic thoughts in his mind.

Resistance may also occur because the client may have a specific *skill deficit*. For example, a social phobic assigned to say hello to an attractive, opposite-sex stranger may resist this task because he does not know how to respond after receiving an inviting reply.

Another situation that may frequently produce resistance involves *therapist attraction*. We have had clients who display resistance in order to prolong regular flirtation sessions with us.

When a *goal discrepancy* develops between therapist and client, resistance is quite likely to occur.

> One of our clients was a perfectionistic medical student aspiring to become "the best" surgeon in England. His hands would tremble when he was watched by superiors—the only area in which he wanted our help. The therapist was interested not only in eliminating shaky hands, but in reducing the client's social isolation, fear of females and important others, and in making him more comfortable in other evaluation-type situations. Despite the therapist's presentation of a formulation (interrelating all the client's complaints) and treatment program that the client agreed with, the client insisted on working only on his hand-trembling problem. Every attempt was made to broaden the client's goals but to no avail. Treatment was attempted, the client participated on his own terms, and eventually terminated treatment when the therapist (feeling relatively useless) offered a more comprehensive intervention.

Another situation that frequently produces resistance involves *client misconceptions*. One client reported that previous sex therapy for her husband's impotence by an internationally reputed clinician was a total failure. Apparently, the client believed that sex must be totally spontaneous in order to be pleasurable. Consequently she resisted all detailed instructions by the sex therapist. Unfortunately, she never discussed this matter with him.

A final situation that commonly produces resistance involves *client manipulation*. For example, one client with a basic fear of being out of control would attempt to control therapy to the extent of violating almost all the therapist's instructions.

It is clear that resistant behaviors are many and diverse and may be produced by a wide variety of situations. Most important is the idiographic nature of resistance, in that the label "resistance" represents very different behavior from case to case and situation to situation. Furthermore, the clinical management of resistance will always vary as well. Thus, given the idiographic nature of resistance, any method for its management must be based on a general framework that can be suited to the individual experience. It is here that the behavior-analytic approach has much to offer the clinician, as its idiographic orientation for understanding and modifying clinical phenomena provides important information for managing resistance.

Introduction to the Behavior-Analytic Approach

Many behavior therapists approach their clinical cases with an armamentarium of treatment techniques and try to fit the client to their treatment technology. In the behavior-analytic approach, the clinician seeks to understand all aspects of the client's difficulties in terms of causative and maintenance factors; then adapts the existing technology by innovating treatment procedures to the individual case. The search for understanding involves an operationalization of the clinical phenomena according to the scientific method, namely, specifying independent and dependent variables. It is this approach that provides the behavior-analytic clinician with a systematic method to predict and control behavior, particularly, resistant behavior.

Operationalization and the rejection of the homogenous-disorder concept have important implications for managing treatment and resistance. Let us consider two individuals complaining of dog phobia. The first case experiences rapid heartbeat followed by images of being attacked by the dog, shaky hands, arms, and legs, and runs away when in close proximity to a dog. Increase the proximity and the "anxiety" behavior increases. The second case, whenever a dog barks, experiences the thought, "Oh my God, I must get away before anyone sees me," followed by excessive sweating and then shortness of breath, increased heart rate, feelings of bodily rushes, and then avoidance. Proximity appears to have no effect unless barking occurs. Increase the frequency, intensity, or duration of barking and "anxiety" behaviors increase. Thus, although both cases may be labeled "dog phobia," an operationalized approach indicates that both individuals present different independent and dependent variables and therefore require different treatments. Clearly, an operationalized approach has tremendous implications for clinical practice.

In order to give the reader a fuller understanding of the behavior-analytic approach to clinical phenomena, including resistance, we now turn to an operationalized account of the behavior-analytic procedure.

Behavior Analysis Procedure

The method of behavior analysis in clinical practice can be seen as a three-stage process (1) initial interview; (2) clincial experimentation; and (3) modification methodology. Throughout each stage of behavioral analysis, the clinician's behavior is guided by the experimental method. The framework presented here is just that, a *framework* for clinical activity.

Initial Interview

The goal of the initial interview is to develop a behavioral formulation of the presenting clinical phenomena. This formulation, which has three components, is defined as follows: a hypothesis that (1) explains the relationships of all the client's complaints to one another; (2) explains why these behavioral difficulties have developed; and (3) provides specific predictions of the client's behavior in any situation. Unquestionably, a tremendous amount of information is to be gathered and conceptualized during the initial interview in order to develop a behavioral formulation. Consequently, the behavior-analytic-oriented clinician behaves like an efficient detective, structuring the interview in a logical, systematic, and comprehensive way; and he attempts to avoid wasting any time on irrelevant information.

The clinician's reliance on the scientific method is ever present. The clinician gathers information, creates a hypothesis, tests it out, reformulates his hypothesis, tests it out, and so on from the beginning of assessment to the end of treatment. At the very first contact with the client, the clinician is attempting to obtain enough information to begin the continuous hypothesis-testing process. As the client walks in the door, the behavior-analytic-oriented clinician is assessing the client's manner of movement, style of self-presentation, speech mannerisms, attire, and so on, searching for a clue. The clinician's first question may already be based on a hypothesis derived from this information. As more information is elicited, the clinician's hypotheses are either confirmed or reformulated until a behavioral formulation is developed.

The relationship to the client during the initial interview (and subsequently) is of tremendous importance. In order to get the information he is after, the therapist must be able to create the appropriate environment for the client. Unfortunately, there is no standard approach to the relationship the clinician can take. Instead, on the spot, the clinician must assess (through hypothesis testing) how to react to the client and then modify his behavior accordingly in order to obtain the necessary information. Thus the clinician must display a tremendous range of skills. He must be sensitive, perceptive, empathic, intelligent, flexible, adaptive, creative.

The initial interview itself is structured into four basic stages: (1) exhaustive problem list; (2) developmental analysis; (3) predisposition search; and (4) behavioral formulation.

Exhaustive Problem List. One of the quickest ways to develop a hypothesis is to begin the interview with the client producing a list of all the behavioral problems he is currently experiencing. Problems are defined generally, and the therapist uses this information to hypothesize additional problems the client may be experiencing and/or to develop a hypothesis as to the relationships among the client's complaints. From this information the therapist hypothesizes which problem appears to be the primary or most incapacitating problem and moves into the second stage of the initial interview.

Developmental Analysis. During this stage of the interview, each problem will be examined: (1) in its current manifestation; (2) in its etiology; and (3) in its history. Thus the clinician traces each problem from its beginning through its development to its present status. The order of problem examination is the clinician's perogative. However, from our clinical experience, we have found a ranked order (in terms of incapacitation) to be typically the most efficient.

In conducting the developmental analysis, we attempt to operationalize all terms—including not only the problematic behaviors but the hypothesized determinants as well. The clinician and client together attempt to operationally and exhaustively specify: (1) the antecedents that appear to produce the response; (2) the response components; and (3) the consequences that appear to follow the response. Furthermore, in using a descriptive approach, the clinician examines the antecedents, responses, and consequences across all possible measurable modalities. Thus a stimulus-response-consequence analysis is undertaken of the precise cognitive (e.g., thoughts, imagery), autonomic (e.g., heart rate, galvanic skin response), motoric (e.g., movement), and environmental (e.g., people, places, objects) modalities (Turkat, 1979). Following such an analysis the clinician's ability to identify the determinants of the client's behavioral difficulties is highly improved. Furthermore, therapist–client communication is facilitated.

Predisposition Search. Following the developmental analysis of each individual problem the client presents, the behavior-analytic-oriented clinician investigates the client's behavior prior to the onset of behavioral difficulties. In essence, the clinician is searching for factors that predisposed the individual to develop these behavior problems given the appropriate circumstances. Thus, possible genetic, organic, and/or environmental predisposing factors are examined.

Behavioral Formulation. At this point the clinician combines all the relevant information to formulate the client's behavioral difficulties. Utilizing the antecedent-response-consequence analysis across cognitive, autonomic, motor, and environmental modalities (Turkat, 1979), the clinician formulates the relationships among the client's complaints, explains why these difficulties developed, and uses this information to predict the client's response to natural-environment and analogue-environment situations. It is here where the individually tailored treatment program is initially devised in accordance with the behaviorally formulated independent and dependent variables.

Clinical Experimentation

Following the identification of the precise independent and dependent variables of the presenting psychological phenomena from the therapist's formulation of the client's self-report, the second stage of the behavioral analysis begins. Here the clinician arranges natural and analogue environmental situations to actually test out the independent variables. Furthermore, systematic behavioral recording is used to monitor the identified dependent variable. Throughout this process, the clinician manipulates additional independent and dependent variables that were not identified during the initial interview as new hypotheses are developed and/or previous ones are further evaluated. In short, the clinician performs actual clinical experiments for isolating the relevant independent and dependent variables across cognitive, autonomic, motoric, and environmental modalities. The reader is referred to Ciminero, Calhoun, and Adams (1977) for an excellent review of these procedures and to Hersen and Barlow (1976) for single-case methodology.

Modification Methodology

The development of an efficient, individually designed modification program is dependent on clear delineation of the precise independent and dependent variables. Although the preexisting behavioral (and other) treatment procedures may be used as *methodological guidelines*, every case is treated individually and therefore the clinician must be aple to innovate where necessary. An examination of the Lazarus approach of multimodal behavior therapy (Lazarus, 1976) highlights the more efficient approach of behavior analysis. Whereas Lazarus may bombard the client with a wide range of treatment procedures simultaneously, we would devise a treatment program aimed at managing the precise independent and dependent variables. Furthermore, once treatment is introduced, the independent and dependent variables are continously monitored so that changes in them may be assessed and managed accordingly. The behavior-analytic-oriented clinician always remains a pragmatist. Not only is bombarding the client with a barrage of treatment procedures time-consuming, it is often unnecessary.

As previously mentioned, there are tremendous limitations in doing clinical work of any nature, including behavior analysis. Obviously, one cannot develop an efficient, individually tailored treatment program if one cannot obtain the necessary information. Second, even if one can obtain the information, there are times when the independent and dependent variables are not controllable by the clinician and are beyond manipulation. In such cases one is forced to adjust and to support the client in as practical ways as possible.

Behavior Analysis and Resistance

It should be clear that because the specific independent and dependent variables vary (within and among cases), resistant behaviors will vary as well. As previously mentioned, there are a large variety of situations that appear to produce resistance and each resistant behavior must be approached idiographically. There are certain cases in which resistance appears never to occur, and other cases where it dominates therapeutic interactions. By no means can a clinician have a standardized, successful approach for dealing with all resistant behaviors; similarly standardized treatment is bound to produce treatment failure.

Our approach in behavior analysis is to try to predict resistant behaviors from the behavioral formulation. If they can be predicted, at times they can be averted. If they are unpredictable, the behavior-analytic-oriented clinician tries to understand them from the behavioral formulation. If the formulation cannot yield an understanding, then the formulation is inadequate and must be modified. In any case, the clinician's indications for reacting to (and/or preventing) resistance are based on the behavioral formulation.

To illustrate the use of behavior analysis in understanding and dealing with resistance, we will now present a complex and difficult case seen in our unit in London. Rather than present the smooth-running success story, we have chosen a case that demonstrated many resistant behaviors.

Clinical Illustration

The Client

The client, Mrs. R., was an attractive, 34-year-old, married woman with two children. She lived in a middle-class neighborhood in surburban London.

Presenting Complaints

The client presented the following list of behavioral complaints: (1) vomit phobia (2) difficulties relating to her children (3) marital difficulties (4) lack of sexual pleasure with her husband (5) lack of self-confidence (6) interpersonal difficulties, and (7) depression.

Primary Complaint

The major area of concern to the client was what she described as a vomit phobia. Mrs. R. indicated that she was severely incapacitated by this problem in that her whole life was structured around it. She reported experiencing tremendous anxiety and subsequent avoidance of any possible situation that might lead to her being exposed to someone vomiting, Mrs. R. herself vomiting, or vomit itself.

Stimulus Components. A large variety of stimuli appeared to elicit anxiety and avoidance in relation to Mrs. R.'s vomit phobia. They can best be classified into four major stimulus groupings: (1) stimuli associated with the children possibly vomiting; (2) stimuli associated with the husband possibly vomiting; (3) stmuli associated with Mrs. R. possibly vomiting; and (4) other stimuli associated with vomit.

Mrs. R. was the mother of two attractive daughters aged 3 and 4. We were able to identify 40 different behaviors that when performed by her children in her presence evoked anxiety in Mrs. R. and subsequent avoidance (either reactive or preventive). They were as widely ranging as, for example, looking pale, eating quickly, yawning, and swapping toothbrushes. Mrs. R.'s children, in short, served as a constant source of anxiety stimulation.[1]

A number of stimuli associated with Mrs. R.'s husband also produced anxiety and avoidance in relation to Mrs. R.'s vomit phobia. Fortunately, they did not parallel the range and degree of stimuli that produced anxiety for Mrs. R. when exposed to her children. There were three major stimuli involving Mr. R. that produced vomit-phobic behavior by Mrs. R.: (1) Mr. R. reporting a stressful day at work; (2) Mr. R. experiencing a migraine headache; and (3) Mr. R. drinking too much alcohol. Mr. R., a pleasant, passive fellow, ran his own business in the London advertising industry and consequently would occasionally experience these behaviors which served as vomit-related anxiety-provoking stimuli for Mrs. R.

Mrs. R. Also appeared to experience anxiety and avoidance in relation to a variety of stimuli that she perceived as possibly causing *her* to vomit. Sixteen of these were identified, including traveling by boat, eating creamy foods, being around others with a "tummy bug," and taking new medication.

Finally, there was quite a variety of other anxiety-provoking stimuli related to Mrs. R.'s vomit phobia: (1) actually seeing vomit (e.g., in the toilet); (2) anyone saying anything related to vomit or the act of vomiting "That commercial made me want to puke"; (3) others commenting that Mrs. R. looked ill; (4) knowing that a virus was going around; (5) attending parties with her and others' children; (6) listening to other mothers discuss their children's vomiting experiences while Mrs. R.'s children played with these children; and (7) assessing everyone at social functions where food and drink are available for possible vomiting.

In short, it is clear that Mrs. R. was consistently exposed to a wide variety of anxiety-elevating stimuli related to her vomit phobia.

Response Components. When exposed to anxiety-provoking stimuli, Mrs. R. experienced excessive sweating and (with high anxiety-producing stimuli) stomach knotting followed by: *cognitive:* "Oh my God, I'm getting panicky," "Oh my God, they'll see how terrified I am," "*I mustn't let them see me anxious,*" "How can I hide my fright?", "How can

---

[1] A complete list of the 40 stimuli, as well as a complete list of the other stimuli of which examples are given below, can be obtained by writing to the authors. The lists illustrate more fully the product of our operational approach.

I comfort my child without her vomiting on me?", "I'm such a terrible mother," "Oh my God, I might vomit", followed by: *autonomic:* trembling, shaky legs, increased heart rate, dry mouth, weak voice, nausea, inability to eat, diarrhea, and *motoric:* running away from the stimulus situation (e.g., in the home, Mrs. R. would run to the toilet and/or out of the house).

Given the wide range of stimuli that produced this type of anxiety response, its manifestation can be seen in a variety of contexts. Most important was Mrs. R.'s continuous avoidance of her children. She indicated that she would avoid them as much as possible. Consequently, she had never spent more than 24 hours alone with her daughters. During the day she would perform "disappearing acts" (as her husband called them) whenever she was presented with the responsibility of handling the children while an anxiety-provoking stimulus was present. When the children cried out during the night, Mrs. R. would pretend to be asleep; Mr. R. would provide the comfort. Mrs. R. would rigidly monitor and regulate the children's food and liquid intake. She did so not only in the home, but also prevented the children from having many meals at friends' homes, parties, and so on. Whenever a somatic complaint was presented by either child, Mrs. R. rushed to the bathroom and eventually arranged for the child to visit the family physician.

In terms of the marital situation, being continually exposed to anxiety-provoking stimuli prompted short-tempered, bitchy, resentful behavior toward the husband. Socially, the client avoided many gatherings and when she did attend, she was continually assessing possible vomiters and thereby experiencing much anxiety.

Consequence Components. Once Mrs. R. would avoid or escape an anxiety-provoking vomit stimulus, she would experience an immediate reduction in anxiety, thus receiving a powerful negative reinforcer. Furthermore, Mrs. R. would be *giving up the responsibility of handling the situation*, which would frequently be reinforced by the husband who would take over the responsibility. However, shortly thereafter, Mrs. R. would begin to feel uncomfortable again as she would *criticize herself for her behavior*. Thus, if she exposed herself to the vomit stimuli, she became anxious, and if she avoided the stimuli, she also became anxious. Naturally, her self-confidence for handling various situations was low.

Another important consequence was her inability to relate to others, which was most apparent in her relationships with her children and husband. Furthermore, the anxiety she experienced with them and with others at social functions resulted in a loss of ability to receive reinforcement from others. Consequently, she would often become depressed (see Lewinsohn, 1974). Finally, given her restricted eating habits, she appeared extremely underweight.

Development

The development of Mrs. R.'s vomit phobia may best be understood by first examining a variety of factors that appear to have predisposed Mrs. R. for developing this type of problem and then tracing the origin and development of the vomit phobia.

Predisposition. Mrs. R. was an only child. At age 3 her mother passed away. Mrs. R.'s father, a cold, lonely, isolated man, was a perfectionist who demanded a lot from others, had exceptionally high standards, and was quick to point out the mistakes of others. Mrs. R. indicated that as far back as she could remember, she was always afraid of her father. She hated making mistakes around him as he would constantly criticize her. For example, the client recalled feeling extremely anxious when he attempted to teach her how to tell time (age 3 or 4). *The father would test her at unpredictable times and be very upset when she would make a mistake.* The client worried constantly about being tested for telling time by her father, desiring to please him but afraid of failure.

The client's strong desire to avoid her father's criticism and to gain his approval was exacerbated by the death of her mother. Since she was an only child, Mrs. R.'s search for a source of comfort and security was restricted to her father. Unfortunately, he provided little (if any at all) love, affection, empathy, or support, and instead created an atmosphere of critical evaluation. Furthermore, the father was a pilot and was frequently away from home. Thus, when he was home, the "testing ground" appeared even more important to the client and the fear of father's disapproval grew in intensity. Naturally, the client developed a poor self-image, and was very insecure and hypersensitive to criticism.

Onset. The client's first vomiting experience occurred at age 3 prior to the mother's death. The client was lying in bed and felt very sick. Following a lengthy period of feeling sick, the client warned the housekeeper that she was to be sick and then vomited. The housekeeper matter-of-factly cleaned up the mess and payed no unusual attention to Mrs. R. The client did not appear to experience any anxiety throughout this first occurrence.

The second vomiting experience occurred at age 5. By this time the mother had been dead for 2 years and the father's influence had been well established. The father had returned from flight duty, and was taking the client on a trip to visit a popular cave. During the drive to the cave, they stopped at a little stand to buy a drink. The client was given an orange drink that tasted a bit peculiar. Within a few moments, she experienced chest pains and immediately vomited. The unpredictability and aversiveness of the experience frightened the client, and the father became very angry. He yelled at the person who had sold him the drink, and wisked his daughter back to the car. In an angry tone, the father warned her, "I hope you're not going to be sick again." Mrs. R. began to worry that she might be sick again and remained frightened of that possibility. Before reaching the cave, they stopped for a bite to eat. The client was too afraid that if she ate she might vomit, so she avoided eating. Eventually they made it to the cave. That night while lying in bed, the client began to imagine caves of vomit. She became even more frightened when unable to stop the aversive imagery. There was no one to seek reassurance from; telling her father would have resulted in criticism. The next day she began restricting her diet, refused orange drink, oranges, and so on, avoided new foods, and food and drink offered by friends. Each night for approximately 1 month, and intermittently thereafter, the client continued to experience these aversive images of vomit caves. Clearly, she had begun to display vomit-phobic behavior.

History. At age 6, the client saw some vomit on the floor at school one day. She felt anxious about it and got away from it as soon as possible. At age 8, the housekeeper vomited in a room in which the client could hear but not see. Mrs. R. felt very anxious during this experience and was very concerned for the housekeeper. Furthermore, she interrogated the housekeeper to isolate foods that possibly caused the vomiting. For quite some time thereafter, Mrs. R. continually checked to see if the housekeeper was going to be sick again.

At ages 9 and 10, Mrs. R. was exposed to two boys who vomited at school. In both incidents, she experienced anxiety and strong concern for the boys. When the teacher asked who would volunteer to take the sick child to the bathroom, Mrs. R. felt panicky that she would be asked.

At age 10, the client's father remarried. Prior to the wedding, the stepmother-to-be was exceptionally nice to the client and Mrs. R. was very receptive to having her for a mother. Unfortunately, immediately after the wedding, the stepmother began to pick on the client and constantly criticized her. For Mrs. R. this behavior came to be more than a disappointment, and she became intensely aware of how alone and isolated she was. The client felt she could not do anything right (given the parents' constant criticism), and felt the stepmother was planning to harm her. Mrs. R. feared poisoning by the stepmother and began to closely scrutinize and restrict the food and drink provided for her in the home. After each meal the client would take an Alka Seltzer to avoid becoming sick. She would repeatedly ask friends if she looked pale or ill and would panic if the reply was affirmative. A year later she failed her examinations, (11 plus, a standard English school examination), and was labeled stupid by her parents. The client swore she would never risk another test like that again and consequently lost all interest in school.

During the next few years the client experienced a variety of situations in which she saw vomit. Each time she became anxious and avoidant. She continued preventive self-vomiting strategies as well. Her insecurity grew as she began to realize that she had a problem with vomit and became ashamed of her fear. Because Mrs. R. feared others' criticism for her inability to handle this problem, she continued to hide it. Thus efforts to eliminate the problem (i.e., confiding in someone for help) produced anxiety as well and consequently were avoided.

At age 17, the client attended a hairdressing school following her withdrawal from general education. She decided to leave home and take a job in Brighton. This job was the client's first, and it was also the first time she left home. She was extremely afraid of failure. One night she continued worrying about it to the point that she vomited. She began to brood about the possibility of it happening again; her eating restrictions multiplied. Eventually she moved to Brighton, fearing an inability to cope with her vomit phobia. During her first day at work her hair was being washed and Mrs. R. began to worry that she might suffocate and vomit. She panicked and ran to an aunt who lived in town. She spent a week there, feeling extremely insecure. Eating diminished, diarrhea was frequent, and Mrs. R. began taking antiemetics on a more regular basis. She returned home claiming to be sick and was severely criticized by her parents.

At age 20, Mrs. R. was in a pub one evening when a girl who was drunk began to look ready to vomit. The client's anticipatory anxiety was severely elevated. The drunk girl's boyfriend asked the client to try and help his girlfriend, which produced further anxiety. Mrs. R. became panicky, fearing their criticism of her inability to handle the situation. At this point the drunk girl vomited on the table in front of Mrs. R., and Mrs. R. ran out of the pub feeling anxious, guilty, and inadequate. Following this experience, Mrs. R. became more sensitive to the possibility of others vomiting and began to attend more perfectionistically to potential cues (paleness, etc.) at parties, pubs, on trains, and so on.

That same year the client became pregnant. Because she was terrified of morning sickness, her pregnancy was terminated and Mrs. R. experienced much guilt.

In the next few years a variety of further sensitizing experiences occurred; at age 28 she became pregnant again. She was terrified of being unable to cope with the pregnancy or to manage the child because of her phobia. Pressured by the husband, family, and general practitioner (who assured the client she would "grow" out of her phobia), she succumbed. No morning sickness occurred, but Mrs. R. constantly worried about vomiting and about her inability to be a good mother.

When the child was born, the client was very insecure about being a mother and would become so anxious as to be unable to perform simple tasks. At 3 weeks, the baby began vomiting every day for the next 3 months and intermittently to the present. The phobia grew in intensity, frequency, duration, as did the frequency of exposure to the stimulus, and insecurity feelings multiplied. The client felt too anxious to comfort her child; felt inadequate, and guilty about feeling inadequate; and was terrified of the daughter becoming like her.

A year later a second child was born (because of pressure and other factors). This child was a less frequent vomiter but still a source of intermittent sensitizing experiences.

Other Behavioral Problems

In addition to the vomit phobia, six other behavioral problems were delineated. A brief discussion of them will provide an understanding of their manifestation as well as a more global picture of the client.

One of the client's major difficulties was her lack of self-confidence and poor self-image. She described herself as boring, nonunderstanding, self-centered, selfish, unintelligent, not attractive enough, narrow-minded, and, worst of all, subject to a phobia she could not cope with. She frequently experienced strong guilt, particularly for her inability to cope with her phobia, "like anyone else could." She believed she could not do anything correctly, and that whatever tasks she would undertake would result in failure. On the positive side, she felt she had one good quality: She was a good listener.

The client's relationship to the children was another problem area. Mrs. R. was anxious around them almost all the time and avoided being alone with them whenever possible. She felt unnatural and incompetent as a mother although she strove to be a perfect mother. As a result of her vomit phobia, she restricted their eating, drinking, playing, and other behavior to protect herself from vomit-related anxiety-provoking stimuli.

Mrs. R.'s relationship with her husband was very strained. The couple had used a variety of marital therapy services, but to no avail. The husband resented Mrs. R.'s avoidance of responsibility for the children, continual complaining, and the restrictions her phobia placed on all of their lives. Furthermore, Mrs. R. constantly reminded her husband that she never wanted children to begin with, that he forced her to have children, and that she would never forgive him for what he had done to her. Sex was nonexistent since the birth of the second child.

The client's interpersonal relationships were few and unsatisfying. Mrs. R. always felt that others did not really want her around and that she would have to hide her phobia from them or be criticized and ridiculed. Consequently she felt anxious, avoided many social situations, and never initiated social encounters. She appeared quiet, shy, and passive.

Finally, as a consequence of her predicament, Mrs. R. would become depressed from time to time. With a lack of social, sexual, occupational, marital, or familial reinforcement, she would catastrophize about her situation and inabilities, feel guilty and worthless, and experience changes in sleep, appetite, weight, and activity.

Formulation

The presenting complaints of this 34-year-old woman can be understood in terms of a behavioral formulation. Their origin, development, and present status can best be explained from a historical account.

Mrs. R. was an only child whose mother died when the client was 3. This event elevated the father's influence on the client in a variety of ways. The client's search for security (emotional, etc.) was restricted as there were no other available individuals. Aside from the father, there was little opportunity to develop behaviors for emotional closeness such as warmth, affection, self-disclosure, or requests for reassurance. Furthermore, the father was a cold, isolated, stern, lonely, ambitious, demanding perfectionist intent on raising an orderly, well-controlled, and "perfectly" behaved child. The child's attempts to obtain positive responses from the father were restricted to behaviors that he determined as important: orderliness, achievement, and the like. Thus the client was given an environment of critical evaluation, and she learned that she should always be well-controlled, never make mistakes, achieve as much as possible, and so on. At an early age the client was trained to be a perfectionist.

The development at an early age of the client's perfectionistic (i.e., mistake-free) approach to life was exacerbated by a variety of factors. First of all, the father's job permitted him to be home only intermittently which elevated the importance the client attached to his visits. With the mother gone and with no other individual to provide assurance, support, and affection, the client was apparently on a deprivation schedule. Thus gaining her father's reinforcement through "good" behavior became even more important. Furthermore, the father served as a "perfect" model in the client's eyes, incapable of making mistakes. Naturally, the client felt unable ever to be as competent as her model. Finally, any mistakes the client made were severely criticized. Thus she became fearful of making mistakes, fearful of being criticized, and fearful of not being able to achieve what was expected of her (such as the tasks the father would reinforce if achieved and verbally punish if failed). Consequently, the client developed into an insecure, self-doubting individual, afraid to attempt behaviors that could not be done perfectly and for which she could possibly be criticized.

Given this training, the development of the vomit phobia is understandable. At age 3 the client had not yet developed "sufficient" perfectionistic training, and she did not receive any criticism for vomiting at that age. Furthermore, vomiting was predictable (i.e., preceded by a lengthy period of feeling sick). At age 5, however, the client was well trained to be orderly, "perfect," and fearful of criticism, and her vomiting experience at this age was a disaster. Being taken on a trip by her father was a rare treat; but an outcome was that her vomiting was criticized by him. Furthermore, this time the vomiting was unpredictable and "out of control." Given her fear of criticism, particularly the father's criticism, the client was predisposed to develop anxiety about any unpredictable stimulus that could provide criticism at unexpected times—again, especially his criticism. Thus Mrs. R. developed a vomit phobia: avoiding certain foods, experiencing ruminative aversive imagery about vomit, and so on. The client avoided any attempts to seek help for the fear, as such behavior would be criticized. Thus a conflict developed in which the vomit phobia generated anxiety and attempts to remedy the phobia would generate anxiety. Finally, each attempt to prevent possible exposure to vomiting (and therefore to possible criticism) strengthened the phobic behavior. As we have seen, an examination of the client's history of vomiting experiences appears to reflect the fear of criticism.

The client's insecurity interacted with the vomit phobia throughout its development and grew with a variety of sensitizing experiences: the critical stepmother, failing important school examinations, vomiting in anticipation of leaving home and of failing at her first job, panicking at her first job and returning home a failure, having a pregnancy terminated because of fear of morning sickness, running away from helping a vomiting friend. As we have also seen, an examination of the client's present cognitive anxiety responses highlighted the relationship between vomit and criticism.

The relationship of the client's hypersensitivity to criticism and vomit to the other behavioral difficulties is clear. Her interaction with her children was based on avoiding any interaction that might be criticized (anything that might lead to vomit, providing comfort, etc.). Furthermore, being a perfectionist and having such a poor self-image, she evaluated every attempt she made at mothering as a failure. Thus all interactions were "proof" of her inabilities. Given the frequent state of anxiety she experienced, she blamed the husband for forcing her into a "living hell" (i.e., the children were a constant reminder of her mistakes and failings). After the children were born and the client's inabilities "revealed," the client refused to engage in sex with the husband. Interpersonal situations were another source for the client's faults to be "revealed," and she avoided them as much as possible. When in them, she was avoidant of possibly making mistakes by remaining quiet, shy, and passive. Consequently she was restricted in the number and range of behaviors leading to reinforcement (interpersonal, familial, etc.), and of course became depressed at times.

Thus the presenting psychological phenomena could best be understood in the context of Mrs. R.'s hypersensitivity to criticism.

Given this conceptualization of Mrs. R.'s difficulties, a variety of predictions were possible regarding the clinical course. We will limit ourselves to some of the major ones.

1. If the client remained in her present environment, there would be minimal possibility of improvement. Given the tremendous range of anxiety-provoking stimuli present and her continual avoidance responses, outpatient treatment alone would not appear to be capable of overcoming these obstacles (previous outpatient treatment attempts reinforced this prediction).

2. Treatment aimed only at the vomit phobia would be unsuccessful. Given the client's sensitivity to criticism and its relationship to the vomit phobia, Mrs. R. would continue to avoid possible criticism situations (such as vomit-related stimuli).

3. If the client's hypersensitivity to criticism and vomit were reduced, she would be more able to develop behaviors leading to reinforcement. Thus improvement in marital, parenting, interpersonal areas, and so on could be facilitated and the client's depressive episodes reduced.

4. The client would experience anxiety about having the responsibility to improve during treatment, and would worry about being evaluated and failing. Thus, in the beginning of treatment, all responsibility for progress would have to become the therapist's. Furthermore, the therapist would have to provide a nonjudgmental, nonevaluative environment to minimize the client's anxiety. Thus, in the initial phase of treatment, the therapist explained to Mrs. R. that it was entirely the therapist's responsibility to create the necessary environment for Mrs. R. to improve. Furthermore, the therapist explained that if Mrs. R. did not improve it was the therapist's fault. Even when Mrs. R. admitted being afraid to improve, the therapist argued that it was his responsibility to remove all obstacles to her improvement, whether motivational, fear, and so on. Thus an environment was structured where Mrs. R. would not be exposed to stimuli that emphasized evaluation of her progress as her responsibility.

5. The client would avoid the therapist's criticism wherever possible (withhold information, etc.). Consequently, at first, a totally accepting, noncritical, reassuring therapist was indicated. Thus, for example, when Mrs. R. would "take a chance" and reluctantly admit some of her failings, the therapist would objectively argue that these were obvious outcomes for anyone with her history and that there was no blame or fault involved.

6. If the therapist appeared infallible, the client would experience anxiety and progress would be impeded. Consequently the therapist would have to act as a coping model (see Bandura, 1969): a perfectionist who does not like but appreciates and benefits from making mistakes and being criticized. Here the therapist disclosed many instances where he tried to do the best job possible but did not succeed. The therapist presented the resulting criticism as somewhat unpleasant, but demonstrated how he learned and benefited from it. Thus, from predictions 4 and 6, the therapist would have to accept any lack of treatment progress

as his fault but feel that it was something to be accepted and in some way beneficial—obviously, a very difficult role to take.

7. A very tightly controlled environment was needed for effective treatment. This fact is clear given the tremendous range of stimuli that produced criticism and vomit-avoidant behavior. Treatment would have to be carried out on an inpatient basis.

8. The chances for highly efficacious treatment were not very good. Given the client's 30-year history of organizing her life in this manner and given the infinite range of anxiety-producing stimuli, it appeared unlikely that a "perfectly" controlled environment could be created.

Treatment Strategies

The most important and realistic treatment goal was to make Mrs. R. more functional in interactions with her children. In order to help the client manage the various behavioral difficulites she experienced, the general treatment strategies were as follows. First, the client's reaction to vomit-related stimuli had to be reduced. Second, the client's sensitivity to criticism had to be reduced as well. Following this intervention, parenting and marital behaviors needed to be focused on, and then interpersonal areas. Unquestionably there would be interactions in progress between areas, but the arousal to vomit and criticism would have to be approached first. Furthermore, given the formulation, it seemed that focusing exclusively on the vomit and criticism behavior could possibly bring about far-reaching improvements in the other areas.

Thus the initial treatment program involved: (1) training in anxiety management (see Meyer & Reich, 1978; Turkat & Kuzmierczyk, 1979); (2) hierarchical exposure to vomit stimuli; and (3) hierarchical exposure to criticism. Given the client's operationalized anxiety parameters, treatment progress was primarily assessed via: (1) client self-report, (2) psychogalvanic response, and (3) hierarchical progression.

Client Progress and Resistance

The client was placed in our 11-bed unit, and her behavior on it was consistent with the formulation. During the early weeks, she avoided interactions with patients and staff whenever possible. All spare time was spent alone in her room. She appeared perfectly groomed, moved in calculated ways, and every conversation involved lengthy latencies between one's questions and her answers.

Having gone over the formulation and treatment plan, the client was well aware of which behaviors were therapeutic and which were not. Nevertheless, insight was insufficient to eliminate resistance.

In attempting to provide an initially criticism-free environment, all staff responded in a friendly, accepting way. Any social approach behavior was reinforced with a criterion of progressive improvement. The therapist provided reassurance, served as a coping model, and prompted social approach behavior in "safe" situations (i.e., noncritical interactions). Although obvious improvement occurred (e.g., less anxiety, attended all meals with other patients, teatime, group meetings), the client's fear of failure and rejection remained. Furthermore, our efforts to aid Mrs. R. in this regard served as "proof" in her eyes of her failings. Finally, she experienced guilt for our participation.

Practice in controlling these feelings was also incorporated into Mrs. R.'s anxiety management sessions. With considerable practice over the weeks, she began to be able to bring her anxiety down quickly. However, once anxiety was decreased, Mrs. R. began to worry about being able to keep up the control. Suggesting apathy statements she could say to herself proved helpful ("So what if I'm anxious?", "Who gives a damn?"). Thus, for Mrs. R., not caring about losing control of anxiety appeared to facilitate its control—which came as no surprise given her catastrophic cognitive anxiety responses. Unfortunately, between sessions she worried about the demands of the next session and was only occasionally successful in controlling anticipation. *Improvement meant more responsibility and obviously an increase in the probability of failure and criticism.* Of course, treatment progressed at a slow rate over a number of months.

During the next few months there were significant gains in the client's behavior. She began to interact more with patients and staff. Mrs. R. also began to demonstrate more control over anxiety. She appeared more spontaneous in a variety of situations. The client progressed a number of steps up the criticism and vomit hierarchies (which also contained stimulus elements of both in certain exposures) and experienced a few brief but successful visits with her family. However, there was still much resistance.

The client practiced a number of anxiety control sessions on her own. At one point she appeared to extend these sessions in a perfectionistic fashion (i.e., spending lengthy periods of time alone). Furthermore, this practice resulted in less interaction time with other patients. Time limits were eventually imposed (in a noncritical manner, of course).

Although Mrs. R. did appear to be progressing up the vomit and criticism hierarchies, she was still unable to stop perfectionistically assessing her environment for possible vomiting, despite our interventions. Milk left on the table was thrown away, "pale" patients were interrogated and/or avoided, and Mrs. R.'s diet remained as restrictive as ever.

Our ability to control Mrs. R.'s environment in terms of vomit and criticism stimuli was not as good as we had hoped. One patient had a history of manipulating others through somatic complaints as well as vomiting after meals at times. Another patient interrogated others in order to identify ways to manipulate them for his advantage. Mrs. R. used to be cornered by this patient (we found out later on) late at night and forced to go over her treatment sessions in detail. Eventually he discovered her sensitivity to criticism and used this approach in manipulating her. One "planned" criticism exposure (having the client write an article and read it to a group of patients) turned into a disaster. Mrs. R. wrote about her family, and one patient who was hypersensitive about children became extremely upset. The client interpreted this event as more proof of her horrible mistake-making ability. Thus, just as certain steps of progress would be made, resistant behaviors were forced to continue.

One of the most encouraging signs for the behavioral clinician occurs when the client begins to broaden therapeutic practice experiences on his own. With Mrs. R. that was exceptionally rare. On one occasion the client wrote a poem of her own initiative and asked the therapist to criticize it. The therapist provided the mildest criticism he thought possible and which he felt the client could handle. During the criticism, the client controlled her anxiety very well. However, on her own she began to ruminate about it and she became fearful that if it upset her so greatly, she must be too attracted to the therapist. These thoughts prompted self-doubting and increased insecurity in Mrs. R. Just prior to this experience, pictures of individuals vomiting and other related scenes were introduced into treatment. One of Mrs. R.'s responses was nausea. It appeared that in conjunction with the criticism experience, she started becoming so anxious that she began anticipating and consequently experiencing an inability to eat or drink. All indicated therapeutic responses had little impact and the client began experiencing strong anxiety while eating and drinking and started losing weight.

Since the client was rather underweight already and was experiencing quite a bit of anxiety, we were forced to slow down her vomit and criticism exposure. Eating served as a stimulus for anxiety about self-vomiting but was essential. Furthermore, any attention directed to eating more and putting on weight caused Mrs. R. to feel pressured and therefore less able to do so. Thus very delicate prodding was used with the dietician providing dietary supplements. Anxiety management practice with eating and drinking was gently implemented as well.

Throughout this period, practical problems with Mrs. R.'s family were developing. Mr. R. had previously signed a contract to move, and the move had to occur during Mrs. R.'s hospital stay. Business pressure began to mount for Mr. R. and the responsibility of the children provided additional anxiety. Mrs. R. experienced much guilt for the problems she was "causing" for her family and felt even more pressure to improve.

Over the next few weeks, vomit and criticism exposure remained at basically the same level and Mrs. R.'s eating and weight began slowly to improve. However, the practical difficulties at home began to multiply, particularly when the people taking care of Mrs. R.'s children could no longer do so. The husband began to pressure Mrs. R. to return home. Furthermore, *the longer Mrs. R. remained in the hospital, the more we were strengthening her avoidance of responsibility.* Finally, we began to realize that treatment continuing at this pace would take a very long time in order to be successful. Given the most realistic treatment goal—to help Mrs. R. be more functional with her children—such a lengthy separation might prove detrimental. At this point we felt an urgency to switch treatment *procedure,* though still basing it on the indications of the formulation.

We needed to get Mrs. R. back with her family as soon as possible. However, unless we achieved a more substantial reduction in her autonomic arousal, she would continue to avoid the children and other responsibilities. We concluded that flooding might be a favorable alternative. Our approach would be as follows: (1) Expose Mrs. R. to enough vomiting (without avoidance) until she felt no more anxiety about it; (2) have Mrs. R. vomit a number of times until she no longer felt it was such a terrible experience (note: she had successfully avoided self-vomiting for the past 17 years); (3) expose Mrs. R. to her children for a long enough period (without avoidance) until she was more comfortable and functional with them (note: since their birth she had arranged to avoid them to the extent that she had never spent a full day alone with them); (4) continue hierarchical criticism treatment as an outpatient; (5) consolidate vomit treatment improvement; and (6) follow the initially stated treatment plan.

Mrs. R. was predictably reluctant. Not only was she fearful of exposure to the stimuli, she feared failing as well. Furthermore, she was fully aware (and admitted later on) that she could continue her many avoidances, especially of her children and husband, by continuing on a gradual-exposure inpatient treatment. A week of discussion culminated in Mrs. R. signing a consent form to participate. Flooding would begin in a few days.

Mrs. R.'s dilemma was revealed in the following conflict: Participate in flooding and be exposed to everything she feared, versus avoid treatment, be criticized, and continue experiencing the phobia. Understandably, the client's anticipatory anxiety increased and she threatened discharge. Staff responded empathically but reassured her of possible benefit. The night before flooding was to begin, the senior author received a call at home in the middle of the night from the client's father, who demanded that the treatment not be used. Apparently, the client had become frantic and called him in a last, desperate attempt. The situation was managed accordingly. The client was reminded that she could withdraw from treatment at any time but to understand that such withdrawal could cause a worsening in her phobia and that all reasonable means to prevent withdrawal would be implemented (as stipulated in the consent form). The client continued to claim that she would not participate even as we walked her to the "flooding room."

We had arranged for approximately 50 vomiting experiences to occur (over a 2-day period if necessary). Staff members and actors volunteered to role play the anxiety-provoking stimuli (e.g., "I feel sick," overeating, moaning) and to take a drug (ipecac) to produce vomiting. Mrs. R. was instructed to take responsibility for comforting the sick individuals. She had also agreed in the consent form to vomit herself. Her anxiety was assessed via psychogalvanic response throughout flooding.

In anticipation of the first vomiting exposure, the client demonstrated heightened anxiety across all three response systems: uncontrollable trembling and sweating, standing in a corner of the room on top of a chair (avoidance), and screaming ("Ira you bastard, let me out!"). As individuals began vomiting (10:15 A.M.), Mrs. R. continued these responses for a few hours. She refused self-vomiting, would not eat and would not drink. After a number of vomit exposures, she eventually came off the chair and began to comfort the sick individuals. Her cognitive and physiological responses continued. By early evening she was no longer avoiding vomit or the individuals, but her cognitive and autonomic anxiety continued. She still refused self-vomiting. By late evening she could pick up and throw vomit, was covered with it, and showed no avoidance of it. We stopped at 11:30 P.M., provided reinforcement for her gains, and permitted a shower, dress change, and so on. She ate and went to sleep.

The next day Mrs. R. said she would not return to the treatment room. She felt she was no longer as fearful of others' vomit but still afraid of self-vomiting. Since we were most concerned with helping Mrs. R. be more functional with her children, we negotiated to continue flooding of others vomiting with the provision that Mrs. R. would be given an antiemetic.

Day 2 lasted from 11:15 A.M. until 4:30 P.M. By mid afternoon the client was pouring vomit all over herself, asking people to vomit on her, and evidenced gains across all three response systems. By late afternoon the client cried with joy as she repeated, "After 30 years it's all over."

The next day the client was so overwhelmed with appreciation she felt guilty for not vomiting herself. The therapist utilized this feeling to get the client to attempt self-vomiting. With much reluctance, the client took the drug. Her anticipation of self-vomiting made her extremely anxious. Unfortunately, the drug did not work for her and she developed diarrhea. After this attempt we felt we could not let her not vomit or we might further sensitize her to self-vomiting. We struggled over a 10-hour period with negotiations, food and drink, more ipecac (three different doses), fingers down the throat, and a spatula down the throat but to no avail. It appeared we could not get Mrs. R. to vomit. We tried to salvage the situation by reassuring her of this "proof" of her body's resistance to vomiting, and by praising her for not avoiding. We were still fearful of possibly strengthening this aspect of her phobia.

The next day we began "home flooding." Mrs. R. returned home and took full responsibility for the children while Mr. R. moved out of the house. She was not to avoid them (she was to stay with them at all times on her own, play with them, etc.) and was to practice exposing herself to previous vomit-related anxiety-provoking stimuli (e.g., giving them much more food and drink, giving creamy foods or very cold drinks filled to the top). Furthermore, she was to practice her anxiety control skills concerning criticism (e.g., as a mother) and cognitively rehearse achievements she had made. She was permitted one call to the husband per day and one call to the therapist every other day.

On a behavioral level, "home flooding" appeared successful. Mrs. R. carried out all instructions, took full responsibility for the children, and even comforted her daughter once when she was spitting up. However, on a cognitive level, the client felt inadequate in all her interactions, and doubted herself whenever exposing herself to possible vomit stimuli ("Will I get anxious?") and even after successful handling of them ("Will I keep it up?"). She experienced occasional thoughts of, "If they vomit I can handle it," but these frightened her in that she might not handle it. While the client's autonomic arousal was reduced and avoidances eliminated in terms of her children, she still felt that she wanted to avoid the children and her husband. At one point Mrs. R. admitted that having the phobia provided a means to avoid her larger responsibilities (and thereby avoid more anxiety-provoking criticisms), and appeared intent not to give it up. Thus, although objective data indicated nonphobic behavior, the client's self-doubt and fear of failure and criticism would not permit improvement to be acknowledged and therefore did not permit it to be maintained. Consequently, partial relapse in the vomit phobia developed as the formulated primary behavior problem still required further intervention. Mrs. R. is still being seen in our unit.

Discussion

Throughout this chapter we have attempted to illustrate the behavior-analytic approach to the problem of resistance. The case presented exemplifies our reliance on the behavioral formulation to understand, predict, avert, and react to resistant behaviors. We chose a case that we felt would reflect the realities of doing clinical work (i.e., its limitations) with difficult cases, rather than one of our many smooth-running success stories. It is hoped that this chapter will give the reader a clear understanding of the behavior-analytic framework for approaching clinical phenomena. We also hope that we have sensitized the reader to some of the difficulties of clinical practice and the inadequacy of standardized treatment.

ACKNOWLEDGMENT

We extend our appreciation to Dr. Edward Chesser, who served as consultant psychiatrist in the case of Mrs. R.

References

Adams, H. E. *The psychology of adjustment*. New York: Ronald Press, 1972.

Bandura, A. *Principles of behavior modification*. New York: Holt, Rinehart & Winston, 1969.

Ciminero, A. R., Calhoun, K. S., & Adams, H. E. (Eds.). *Handbook of behavioral assessment*. New York: Wiley, 1977.

Hersen, M., & Barlow, D. H. *Single case experimental designs: Strategies for studying behavior change*. New York: Pergamon Press, 1976.

Lazarus, A. A. (Ed.). *Multimodal behavior therapy*. New York: Springer, 1976.

Lewinsohn, P. M. Clinical and theoretical aspects of depression. In K. S. Calhoun, H. E. Adams, & K. M. Mitchell (Eds.), *Innovative treatment methods in psychopathology*. New York: Wiley, 1974.

Meyer, V., & Reich, B. Anxiety management: The marriage of physiological and cognitive variables. *Behaviour Research and Therapy*, 1978, *16*, 177–182.

Meyer, V., & Turkat, I. D. Behavioral analysis of clinical cases. *Journal of Behavioral Assessment*, 1979, *1*, 259–270.

Turkat, I. D. *The behavior analysis matrix*. Unpublished manuscript, Middlesex Hospital Medical School, 1979.

Turkat, I. D., & Kuzmierczyk, A. R. *Clinical considerations in anxiety management*. Unpublished manuscript, Middlesex Hospital Medical School, 1979.

III

Commentaries by the Authors

9

Behavioral and Psychodynamic Psychotherapies

MUTUALLY EXCLUSIVE OR REINFORCING?

Michael Franz Basch

Patient's Resistance or Therapist's Constriction?

As a teacher of psychiatrists who are doing their postgraduate training in psychoanalysis I have noted over the years, as these students approach the end of their formal training, that they will say something to the effect that they are not quite sure exactly how much they know about doing psychoanalysis, but one thing they have finally learned to do is psychotherapy. Since I said the same thing to my supervisors when I had reached that stage in my professional training, I understand what they mean. Through conducting psychoanalyses they have learned that psychotherapy is not mini or substitute psychoanalysis but a form of treatment that, though profitably informed by the contributions of psychoanalysis, has different goals and therefore requires variations in technique. I have dealt with these issues in some detail in my earlier contribution to this volume as well as elsewhere (Basch, 1980, in press). Many so-called psychoanalytically oriented psychiatry residencies and training programs teach their students to look on the patient's immediate

Michael Franz Basch ● Suite 3605, 55 East Washington Street, Chicago, Illinois 60602.

complaint as only a cover for deep-seated psychosexual conflicts that must be resolved through interpretation. The further assumption is that if successful, such interpretation brings in its wake both the spontaneous resolution of the more superficial problems, and a healthy adaptation to love and to work. It is impressed on these students that any attempt to deal with a patient's immediate difficulty will of necessity fail, in addition to which the possibility of any therapy in depth will have been sacrificed. In this way an approach that does hold true for the treatment of neurotic symptoms is misapplied to the detriment of both the patient's welfare and the would-be therapist's training. Every patient is not neurotic, that is, the focal conflict of his pathology is not necessarily an oedipal one, and, therefore, there is no justification for equating every presenting complaint with a neurotic symptom. The student of psychoanalysis learns the criteria for psychoanalytic treatment and the limits of the psychoanalytic technique. As a result he feels much freer to deal with his patients very much as the cognitive-behavioral therapists do. Eventually, if reasonably talented, he works out for himself some variant of the approach put forward by the representatives of cognitive-behavioral psychology who have contributed to this volume.

In my earlier chapter I tried to show that much of what is called resistance to therapy is actually a result of the therapist's fear to explore the patient's world in accordance with the patient's perception of his circumstances rather than according to a preconceived perceptual set provided by a usually incorrect exposition of Freud's concepts of development, normal and abnormal. Meichenbaum and Gilmore's chapter provides an excellent introduction to the type of therapeutic interaction that I much prefer to the all-too-common attempt to do therapy by looking for a causal explanation for the patient's present problem in his personal history as that is brought out in the anamnesis. Psychoanalysis does not work that way and, predictably, the attempt to foist this kind of pseudotherapy on patients, no matter how well-meaning the student therapist may be, will fail.

Resistance and Transference

What I do miss in Meichenbaum and Gilmore's chapter is a discussion of what I would consider resistance, that is, the patient's active or passive opposition to progress in spite of a capable therapist's best efforts. It is not resistance, in my opinion, when the patient does not respond to the first or second attempt of the therapist to help him. All this lack of response means to me is that the patient and therapist have to keep looking for the right "fit" that will make sense to the patient and let him move forward. What I would like to know about are those cases, and I have had many of them myself, in which, for example, the encouragement to make the telephone call (pp. 145–146) results only in a rationalized evasion of the behavior that is needed to take the first step in resolving the problem. In those situations I think it is the transference relationship between therapist and patient that would have to be taken into consideration, a relationship that Meichenbaum and Gilmore refer to only in passing as the "therapeutic relationship," which they acknowledge is all-important for successful outcome. Here we analysts can make a contribution. Resistance, when it is genuine and not a euphemism for the therapist's lack of understanding, experience, or effort, is resistance in and/or to the transference. Quite correctly Meichenbaum and Gilmore emphasize that the cognitive-behavioral training, what I call the perceptual set, that a patient brings to his problems is what determines his successful or unsuccessful adaptation to life. But let us not forget that these patterns are not abstract entities developed in isolation. These patterns are the result of the experience and training people get from the first day of life and they are inextricably linked to the relationship with the most important trainers in perception that we have, the parents or parent surrogates who constitute the child's world and on whom he depends fo his very life for a good many years.

In the example given by Meichenbaum and Gilmore, a patient was helped to reach the conclusion that it was not only a good idea to call his daughter but that it was an imperative bit of behavior, that is, that the threshold to altering his miserable existence lay not in just hypothesizing about but in acting on his convictions. Here it was the trusting relationship that the client had with his therapist that enabled him to overcome his reluctance, face his fear of embarrassment or humiliation, and contact his family. Indeed the therapist, correctly in my opinion, suggested his own telephone and that very minute to place the call. What went unspoken, however, was the fact that this patient had what is called a positive transference to the therapist: He brought to the therapy the capacity for drawing strength and accepting help from another person. What if he had not had such a mental set? What if the exchange had come to a different conclusion?

THERAPIST: Do you want to experiment right now then? And call her from here? And see what your reaction is?

CLIENT: Oh, I'd like to do that all right, but I'm not going to.

THERAPIST: How come?

CLIENT: Because I see through your ploy, that's why.

THERAPIST: Ploy?

CLIENT: I'd be doing exactly what you wanted me to do under the guise of making my own decision about it. I would be doubly humiliated: first, for crawling on my hands and knees to my family begging for forgiveness, and second, for letting myself be manipulated by you into doing it.

THERAPIST: I'm not trying to manipulate you.

CLIENT: Do you deny that you feel it would be good for me to call my daughter? Do you deny that you would feel satisfaction as a therapist if you got me to do this?

That impasse is what I would call resistance, and it is this kind of situation that I would like to see resolved along cognitive-behavioral lines. Would the approach differ from mine? I do not know; maybe not. As an analyst, sufficiently freed, I hope, from a parochial attitude, I might well do up to a point exactly what Meichenbaum and Gilmore describe, but, failing to achieve what I had hoped, look for an explanation for that failure in the relationship that the patient was recreating with me in the transference.

THERAPIST: Hey! I thought we were working together on this problem and all of a sudden you are making an adversary situation out of it. Of course I would get some satisfaction from seeing you make progress. Even if the phone call didn't work out I would be happy for your having at least tried it. Where is the crime if I were to give myself a pat on the back for being such a clever therapist?

CLIENT: I didn't mean it that way.

THERAPIST: Well, what way did you mean it?

CLIENT: I don't know.

THERAPIST: Yes you do, at least you know more than you are telling me. You can see how you are getting yourself into a situation with me that is similar to the one with your family. There is a misunderstanding, you get your feelings hurt, feel humiliated, and then resolve the situation by leaving it. Next thing you'll be telling me is that you are not coming back to see me.

CLIENT: How, how . . . how did you know that?!

THERAPIST: It's no big trick, that's your pattern, isn't it? If at all possible I'd like to head this off before it happens here.

CLIENT: Well, I don't really want to leave you either . . . but you're forcing me to make this phone call makes me wonder if you are the right therapist for me.

THERAPIST: You see! Now I'm forcing you to do something, instead of you wanting to do something for yourself that you find hard to do. Don't tell me that you didn't know long before I told you that the obvious step for you to make was to contact your family and see if you couldn't arrive at a rapprochement.

CLIENT: I guess you are right about that. My friends have told me to do that many times, but I didn't need them to tell me anyway, I've known it since I left home.

THERAPIST: O.K., so it's something else that's going on. When the mood in here turned from one of friendliness and cooperation to your thinking that I was manipulating you, what were the thoughts, memories, pictures, and what have you, that were going through your mind?

CLIENT: I guess I was thinking about my mother and how she'd talk me into doing what I didn't want to do and then tell my dad that I had decided to do it. That's how I got into business school and gave up the violin, remember?

THERAPIST: I remember very well, but I also remember that you told me that you gave up the violin and the hopes of becoming a professional musician because you realized that you couldn't ever be as good as the great violinists you had heard play. You didn't want to go on if you couldn't be a Menuhin or a Heifetz, so you went into business where you could excel, and have.

CLIENT: Much good it's done me.

THERAPIST: That's not the issue right now.

CLIENT: You mean, I didn't tell you originally that it was my mother who convinced me I'd never be a star?

THERAPIST: Right.

CLIENT: I guess she had me so brainwashed that I don't remember anymore how I came to the conclusion.

THERAPIST: You know now. My urging you to make the phone call was seen as being manipulated by mother. It doesn't matter whether or not I helped you come to a conclusion that would be ultimately helpful to you, because as far as you were concerned your independence was once more being challenged.

CLIENT: I guess I'd rather be independently unhappy than feel pushed into happiness.

THERAPIST: Exactly.

CLIENT: Maybe that's why I always resented my wife's advice. She always said she was only trying to help me. Do you think I ought to make that phone call to my daughter?

THERAPIST: I've got my doubts now. Maybe it would be better if we worked on the material that's coming up now before you try to reunite with the family. I really don't know and I leave that up to you. As you correctly said, it has to be your decision—though, of course, I'm not ruling out our talking about it further and helping you in any way I can to come to a conclusion. I think our job now is to look at this attitude of yours that really puts you in a bind. If people try to help you they are manipulating you and robbing you of your independence; if they don't try to help you they are abandoning you.

CLIENT: How can I ever get out of that mess?

THERAPIST: You have already started to do that by letting us see that something in the relationship to your mother that has gone unexamined has been influencing your life detrimentally without your being aware of it.

CLIENT: That's what you analysts mean by unconscious mental life?

THERAPIST: That's what we mean.

Eclecticism: Is It Worth a Try?

Would the cognitive-behavioral therapist take the tack that I did or would he insist that the immediate problem, the reunion with the family, remain in focus? Much of what is called client resistance stems, in my opinion, from the gaps in technique that a doctrinaire attitude toward theory imposes on a therapist. A theory can serve as a comfortable framework in which to do one's work, but it can also become a set of blinders that shuts us off from whatever else is going on around us. If we expect patients to learn to acknowledge their mistakes without being overwhelmingly humiliated by confronting their shortcomings openly, should we therapists not be able to look at each other's work and learn from one another without thereby feeling belittled, humiliated, or annihilated? I am as much troubled by the behaviorists' seeming disregard of the unconscious motivators of human behavior as I am by the disregard in my circles of what the behavioral approach to problem-solving techniques has to offer us.

A case in point is Turkat and Meyer's detailed, courageous exposition of resistance to treatment. Would their patient's vomiting phobia have responded better to either a psychoanalytically oriented psychotherapeutic approach or to a psychoanalysis? Shouldn't the possibility that the phobia represented a symbolic conflict of an oedipal sort have at least been taken into account? I think so. The patient's phobia could well represent a displacement of the combination of guilt and excitement around fantasies of replacing her mother in her father's affection. That her mother's death and the onset of the phobia all took place during the time of the oedipal phase of development, when competition with the parent of same sex for the parent of the opposite sex is at its height, is very suggestive. It seems to me that when our best efforts at using the techniques in which we have become expert fail to help the patient, we owe it to the latter to at least entertain the possibility that it might be worth having him try an alternative approach. That, by the way, does not imply, as far as I am concerned, necessarily relinquishing our treatment efforts and giving up whatever it is we are doing that is useful but demonstrably not sufficient to achieve the resolution of the patient's problems. I will mention my experience with combined treatment shortly.

Lazarus and Fay take the position that resistance is too often a rationalized excuse for the therapist's failure to take the necessary steps that might help the patient; but they do point out that there are patients who do not respond to even the most skilled and devoted therapeutic efforts on their behalf. It is only the latter patients whom I would label "resistant." These patients, who Lazarus and Fay seem to think should be dismissed for wasting the therapist's time, are the ones that I believe can often be helped if the therapist focuses on trying to understand the resistance rather than demanding of himself or of the patients that it be overcome by being tackled head-on.

As Lazarus and Fay acknowledge, their model for therapy is essentially an educational one. I am not surprised that they run into trouble when dealing with clients whose past experiences preclude their being able to benefit from even the most well-meant educational efforts of the therapist. But why become angry or contemptuous of their clients' failure? Would it not make more sense that such patients, instead of being dismissed and perhaps relegated to living out an unhappy and miserable existence, be given an explanation of what the problem in therapy seems to be and then counseled to see an analytically oriented therapist who might, potentially at least, be able to help them resolve those conflicts that stand in the way of their learning happier and more adequate problem-solving techniques? The future course of the treatment could be decided by what this approach succeeded in uncovering. What do we, or, more important, our patients, have to lose by our utilizing each other's expertise?

I have in recent years had several experiences in which my analytic efforts were frustrated by the patients' pervasive anhedonia that responded only when pharmacological management was instituted. Once the chronic underlying depression was sufficiently ameliorated, some of the patients were able to make progress in their introspective work and their respective analyses could run their course. It never occurred to me that the efficacy of the medication in any way detracted from the value of my analytic work or that the scientific standing of psychoanalysis was thereby diminished. By way of contrast, I have also seen patients in whom medication had been tried without any appreciable beneficial results, but whose difficulties were then successfully resolved when psychoanalysis or psychoanalytically informed psychotherapy was used. However, these experiences did not then persuade me that chemotherapy was useless, only that, as in all the healing arts, there is no panacea and that it is not always easy to match patient and treatment successfully. Are we really still so insecure about the standing of our respective theoretical positions that our self-esteem as therapists and the credibility of our training depends on dismissing what others, using a different approach from ours, seem to have learned about mental functioning and malfunctioning?

Behavior and Its Antecedents

Goldfried stresses that it is the therapeutic relationship that may well determine whether the various technical maneuvers employed by the behavioral therapist will be successful or meet with resistance. I agree with that point as well as with several references to the positive effect of so-called corrective emotional experiences promoted by the therapeutic interaction, provided it is understood that these are not artificially staged attempts to supply the patient with what he may have lacked in childhood, but are instead incidental to the therapist's concern for the patient and his devotion to the therapeutic task. Since I found myself in essential agreement with so much of what Goldfried has to say, I was somewhat chagrined to find him taking an indirect swipe at those of us who take the past into consideration in evaluating the origin of our patients' difficulties. Also, I must say, the example he gives to buttress his position was not particularly convincing to me. He describes a treatment in which an apparently analytically oriented psychotherapist who had become his patient was helped by the application of behavioral techniques to the seeming exclusion of insight into the possible childhood origins of the problem that troubled him. I have no quarrel with Goldfried's choice of technique, nor do I doubt his success with this patient; indeed, I gave a similar example. However, in order to convince the patient of the correctness of his approach Goldfried pointed out to him that the patient had himself told the story of undergoing significant personality changes as a result of a relationship with a woman friend. "Do you mean that all of this happened without any insight into the past?" Goldfried quotes himself as saying, and then states: "This comment had its intended effect, as the client became more willing to proceed with the therapy." If this statement is meant to demonstrate that, in principle, the focus of therapy should be on the here and now rather than on past events, it is a non sequitur. Of course, if maturation is proceeding unimpeded there is no need in or out of therapy to struggle for insight into the past. The past only becomes important if the person under consideration cannot productively utilize the experiences of the present. What would Goldfried have said if the patient had recounted that in spite of the love, interest, and concern of people who had tried to relate to him he found himself increasingly unhappy, and had demonstrated by his behavior that he had not changed some long-established behavior patterns that continued to make him unhappy? Would it not be expected that under those circumstances the patient would also fail to respond to the well-meant efforts and skillfully applied technical maneuvers of the therapist? If reinforcement, flooding, persuasion, and so on was all to no avail, would it not make sense somewhere along the line to explore with the patient what might have taken place in the past that left him so dead-set against trusting anyone, including the therapist who was trying to help him?

I suppose I have a lot of trouble grasping the opposition that exists for so many therapists on both sides of the fence between cognitive-behavioral theory and psychodynamic theory. Why does the demonstrable validity of either one rule out the potential value of the other? That past relationships are of utmost significance for therapy is clearly demonstrated by Goldfried himself. He gives the instructive example of how he enabled a client to overcome a work inhibition through permitting and/or encouraging the client to call him on the telephone to report his progress. The client was thus afforded "a 'corrective emotional experience' that was built on in subsequent weeks." There is no doubt then that this episode influenced the patient's attitude and behavior from then on. Is there any question but that this client will continue to be influenced in applicable situations in the future, even the distant future, by what transpired between him and Dr. Goldfried that day? Since Goldfried acknowledges that the "past" that he provides his client is significantly influential for the client's future behavior, what about the past provided by his mother and father and the emotional vicissitudes of his early life? Would it not matter to the adult-to-be that when he was 5 years old some family crisis preoccupied his parents to the point that for many months no particular attention was given to his progress and that his need for positive feedback and reinforcement was ignored or misunderstood as unseemly demandingness? If anything, wouldn't the behavioral analysis of the present-day coping techniques coupled with this information from his past guide the therapist, no matter what his theoretical "persuasion" might be, more accurately than either the behavioral analysis or the genetic reconstruction alone?

A Suggestion for the Future

We have much to learn from each other, but, given the parochial and doctrinaire atmosphere of our training programs and professional societies, little incentive or opportunity to do so. Therefore I would like to make a modest proposal. In my best of all possible worlds there would be a society that welcomed participation by therapists trained in behavioral, in pharmacological, and in psychodynamic techniques. As is customary, there would be periodic scientific meetings at which papers would be presented and discussed. Each paper would have three formal discussants, one from each discipline. However, I would make it a rule that if, let us say, a pharmacologically oriented therapist were making a presentation, only the discussant also trained along those lines could presume to be negatively critical about his paper—point out disagreements, possible errors, caveats, and so on. The other two discussants, one psychodynamically and the other behavioristically oriented, would only be allowed to say what they found helpful and worthwhile in their pharmacologically oriented colleague's presentation. They would be permitted to raise questions only as long as these were directed to making the particular contribution even more useful to their own work. By arranging it so that we would perforce have to deal respectfully and positively with the work of other disciplines, an atmosphere of mutual understanding would not be long in developing. My hunch is that all of us as well as those we treat could not help but benefit from such an exercise.

References

Basch, M. F. *Doing psychotherapy*. New York: Basic Books, 1980.
Basch, M. F. The significance of self psychology for a theory of psychotherapy. In J. Lichtenberg *et al.* (Eds.), *Reflections on self psychology*. New York: International Universities Press, in press.

10

A Critique of the Concepts of Resistance in Behavior Therapy

Sidney J. Blatt and H. Shmuel Erlich

The chapters in this volume by behaviorally oriented therapists highlight some of the primary differences between our conception of therapy and theirs. The primary image of the behaviorally oriented therapist that emerges is that of teacher, coach, detective, researcher, and scientist. The task for patients (or clients) is to learn specific techniques that will supposedly enable them to solve problems and more effectively cope with disrupted aspects of their lives as they are expressed primarily in a specific, focused symptom formation. The therapeutic techniques are drawn from procedures frequently used by teachers to establish effective learning (lesson plans, homework assignments), by coaches to encourage greater commitment, or by scientists (or detectives) in the search for hypotheses and for experimental procedures that will either confirm, disconfirm, or lead to the refinement of the hypotheses. According to Turkat and Meyer, for example, "the clinician performs actual clinical experiments for isolating the relevant independent and dependent variables across cognitive, autonomic, motoric, and environmental modalities." Techniques are selected on a purely "pragmatic" basis, primarily in terms of whether they will be effective in reducing the specific, distressing, and troublesome symptom. In contrast, we believe that the

Sidney J. Blatt • Departments of Psychiatry and Psychology, Yale University, New Haven, Connecticut 06520. H. Shmuel Erlich • Department of Psychology, Hebrew University, Jerusalem, Israel.

basic mutative factor in therapy is the patient's experience of himself and of the therapist within the context of the therapeutic relationship. Interpretations provide recognition and insight into distorted modes of interpersonal interaction, but it is the entire context of the therapeutic relationship that provides the basic experiences that allow the individual to explore and develop new modes of relatedness.

In general, we believe that interpersonal relationships are the essential ingredient of any human experience. We all develop and experience our pleasures and disappointments, in an interpersonal matrix. The disturbances in living that lead some of us to seek professional therapeutic assistance develop and are expressed in an interpersonal context, and the potential for effective treatment for many of these difficulties exists in the special interpersonal relationship we call psychotherapy.

Natural psychological growth and development, as well as growth and development within the therapeutic context, take place primarily through an ever increasing, complex, and differentiated internalization of the experience of sequences of caregiving relationships. The providing of care, in this broad developmental context, includes not only the more obviously nurturing aspects but also the more subtle forms of nurturing, that is, those that provide a somewhat protected context in which the individual has the opportunity to explore an optimal range of self-enhancing experiences without encroachment. The internalization of the cognitive and affective dimensions of repeated caregiving, interpersonal sequences results in the establishment of cognitive schemata that have a content and a formal structure. These schemata are expressed primarily in the development of the concept of the object—in concepts of the self and of others. This structural dimension evolves toward increasing differentiation, articulation, integration, and complexity (Piaget, 1937/1954; Werner, 1948/1957; Werner & Kaplan, 1963). Serious and repetitive disruptions within caregiving relationships result in disturbances and impairments in the development of these cognitive-affective schemata. Impairments can occur during different developmental phases, and their nature and severity define the type of psychopathology. The issues involved in the disruption of caregiving relationships determine the content of the symptomatic expression of psychological disturbances. The developmental level of the impaired cognitive-affective schemata determines the nature (or structure) of the disturbances. Similar content themes can occur in different cognitive-affective schemata and, likewise, similar impairments in schemata can be expressed with different content.

Although we agree with Meichenbaum and Gilmore about the importance of changes of cognitive structures in therapy, we believe that what
is important to stress is that the disturbances and impairments of these
schemata—of the concepts of self and others—originally evolve, are
expressed, and can best be changed in an interpersonal matrix. Turkat
and Meyer, in their extensive presentation of a single case, provide us
with an opportunity to illustrate some of the immediate consequences
of this difference in orientation.

Although it is important to understand and respond to the symptomatic expression of Turkat and Meyer's client's problem of vomit phobia, it also seems important to us to recognize that this symptom began
at around age 3, about the time of the death of the client's mother.
Nowhere in the case history do we learn the cause of the mother's death,
what the client recalls of this troubled time, or her thoughts, feelings,
recollections, and fantasies about this pivotal event in a young child's
life. We also learn little about her memories and feelings about her
father's relative unavailability during this stressful time. Likewise, we
are told little about the client's stepmother, the client's pregnancy and
abortion at age 20, her marriage, and the quality, nature, and basis of
her relationship with her husband. It seems important to note that when
the patient felt threatened by the anticipation of an impending bom-
bardment in an aversive therapeutic plan, she called her father and not
her husband. The specific content of her phobia—the fear of vomit and
of vomiting—is undoubtedly important, but equally and probably more
important are the interpersonal contexts in which the client has and still
does experience her difficulties. In an exploration of the difficult issues
and interpersonal relationships in her life, the relationship with the
therapist and his empathic and sensitive understanding of her difficulties
become central.

The therapist is not a teacher or a scientist but a relatively neutral
participant—a *compassionate* listener and an *empathic* observer—who has
assumed the task of helping an individual understand the significant
dimensions of his life and how specific symptoms and concerns express
many of his disturbances. The nature of the interpersonal relationship
that the patient and the therapist can establish, and how this relationship
changes over time, will provide firsthand information about significant
aspects of the patient's interpersonal experiences. Furthermore, the quality of the interpersonal relationship that develops in therapy, as patient
and therapist share in the exploration of significant past and current life
experiences, can lead to the building of new cognitive-affective sche-

mata. The patient will, it is hoped, develop new self-concepts, more adaptive conceptualizations of others (including the therapist), and new conceptualizations about the nature of interpersonal relations. Changes in these cognitive-affective schemata are an essential part of the therapeutic process; but unlike Meichenbaum and Gilmore, we believe that these new conceptuatizations occur within the context of the therapeutic relationship and are the result of the recognition and understanding of current and prior maladaptive modes of relatedness and the internalization of aspects of the therapeutic relationship.

Interpretation and insight help the patient to recognize and acknowledge repetitive, limited, and distorted concepts of the self and of others; but, as in normal psychological growth, it is the progressive internalization of aspects of the interpersonal relationship that results in the development of more mature cognitive-affective schemata. As patients become able to recognize and understand the repetitive distortions they bring to their interpersonal relationships, they become increasingly able to appreciate and utilize new aspects of their current relationships, including the therapeutic relationship. They are able to develop more differentiated and integrated concepts of themselves and others and begin to appreciate the range of actual and potential interactions that can exist between people. In this therapeutic context, resistance occurs as an impediment to the exploration of conscious and unconscious repetitive distortions of past and current interpersonal relationships, including the current relationship with the therapist. There can be resistance to the recognition of aspects of the distortions patients bring to interpersonal relationships, and resistance to considering and exploring alternate modes of relatedness. These impasses will often occur in condensed and focused form directly within the therapeutic relationship. Resistant patients are neither people who "do not want help" nor "deliberate saboteurs" (Lazarus & Fay), but instead people for whom exploration and change are difficult, painful, and even dangerous.

Although we share with several of the behaviorally oriented therapists the recognition that the basic resistance is a fundamental reluctance to change, the behavioral emphasis on technique, tactic, and method seems to us to limit their recognition of the importance of resistance as an essential aspect of the interpersonal dimensions of the therapeutic relationship. This point is of particular importance because it is the recognition of the expression of the resistance within the therapeutic relationship that allows the therapist not only to observe resistances directly, but in a context and form that permit the patient and therapist to begin to identify the resistance and to consider its multiple meanings and purposes. Resistance, as discussed in the behaviorally oriented chapters, is seen primarily as noncompliance with the advice and directions of the therapist. Resistance is often viewed as an expression of a lack of commitment to change, and the therapist's task is often to manipulate the clients to get them to believe change is possible and to commit themselves to the sustained effort necessary to produce change. Resistance is generally viewed as something beyond and in addition to the patient's presenting problem rather than as an inherent part of the problem and of the forces that have prevented the patient from moving naturally and spontaneously, in his own right, to more appropriate and satisfying modes of adaptation.

Although resistance may be expressed as apathy, a lack of commitment, procrastination, impatience, and so on, it is essential to understand these phenomena not in isolation but as an essential component of the patient's difficulties. We agree with Meichenbaum and Gilmore that it is essential to identify the meanings of the resistant behavior in the total context of the patient's problems and the therapeutic relationship (e.g., as Meichenbaum and Gilmore put it, "what clients say to themselves about such resistance"). This view is in marked contrast to those of Lazarus and Fay who believe that it is preoccupation with feelings and thoughts, instead of actions, that impedes therapeutic progress. Although we agree with Lazarus and Fay that resistance must be seen as not residing solely within the patient, we disagree that it is necessarily the therapist's task to find ways to get the patient to comply with the therapeutic plan. Instead, we believe that the therapist helps the patient to recognize the resistance, when and how it occurs, and its multiple meanings, particularly the patient's fear and apprehension of change. The behavioral view of the therapist as teacher, scientist, or detective often seems to result in a disregard for the client's experiences—his thoughts and feelings about his resistances. The behavioral emphasis on the manipulation of the client often fails to help the client identify and express his own inherent potential for creating change.

Although resistance is often expressed in noncompliance with therapeutic rules and directions, there are those people who, as Lazarus and Fay point out, adhere to every detail of therapeutic direction but still fail to change. Thus resistance is much more than mere noncompliance, and it is even more than negative therapeutic outcome. Resistance is a basic reluctance to explore, to understand, to grow, and to change. In the context of the therapeutic alliance, the recognition and understanding of resistances plays a central role in the therapeutic enterprise. Resistance is not the failure of a resisting patient or the fault of a therapist who has not used an appropriate technique or experimental manipulation to get the patient to comply. It is not the result of a failure of the therapist to manipulate the patient in order to produce change or to be, as Lazarus and Fay suggest, a highly skilled actor who can change roles and cloaks as he believes the patient requires a new and different form of manipulation. We believe that resistance is a consequence of a failure to be understood—of the patient's failure to communicate clearly and of the therapist's failure to understand effectively. It is the process of understanding and being understood that provides the impetus for a patient to overcome resistance and to relinquish, at times slowly and tentatively, old, repetitive, maladaptive patterns and to move toward growth.

In contrast to a preoccupation with identifying the most effective therapeutic manipulation, we share Goldfried's emphasis on the contextual aspects of the therapeutic enterprise and how the therapeutic relationship can provide important information about the client's resistance as well as being a most powerful force for change. But we disagree with the tendency to exploit the relationship and use manipulative techniques, such as the therapist "construing" for the patient that setbacks in therapy are temporary variations on the way to progress. It seems to us more effective for therapist and client to recognize resistances and to struggle to understand and resolve them. Not only does this approach establish a collaborative enterprise in the attempt to resolve an impasse in treatment, it also establishes a basic attitude that can be useful in dealing with the next layer of resistance when it is encountered.

In conclusion, we would like to comment on a thoughtful and provocative issue raised by Goldfried about the ethical dilemma of attempting to induce change in patients with low motivation and for whom change may produce alterations in their life they may find unacceptable. This dilemma is much more a problem if the therapist assumes responsibility for manipulating the patient to change than if the issue of change is a shared responsibility between therapist and patient, with the ultimate decision always with the patient. We believe that the task of therapy is to help patients become as fully aware as possible of their options and of the reasons for and the consequences of their decisions. We feel that the ultimate resistance, which must be understood and resolved in therapy, is the patient's reluctance to accept and assume responsibility for the conduct of his own life.

References

Piaget, J. *The construction of reality in the child*. New York: Basic Books, 1954. (Originally published, 1937.)

Werner, H. *Comparative psychology of mental development*. New York: International Universities Press, 1957. (Originally published, 1948.)

Werner, H., & Kaplan, B. *Symbol formation: An organismic-developmental approach to language and the expression of thought*. New York: Wiley, 1963.

11

A Psychoanalytic Critique of the Behavioral Contributions

Paul A. Dewald

An overview of the four behavioral therapy chapters indicates how far some present-day therapists have moved away from the original models of behavior therapy. All these authors emphasize the importance of the therapist–patient relationship; the search for particular meanings of the behavior in question; the concept of multiple determination of manifest behavior; the concept that there are "causes" that need to be discovered and understood; and the recognition that the manifest behavior of the patient in a therapeutic setting may be contradictory to his consciously avowed purpose in seeking help.

It is not surprising to a psychoanalyst that such a shift in emphasis and conceptual understanding has occurred among behavior therapists. Anyone who observes patients in a clinical setting with a reasonably open and naturalistically observant point of view sooner or later recognizes in the clinical data some of the irrationalities and complexities of manifest behavior that psychoanalysts have described for decades. It was the clinical observations made in the therapeutic situation that forced Freud repeatedly to revise his basic theoretical assumptions and to bring his theoretical and conceptual understanding into greater harmony with his clinical findings. The chapters in this volume suggest that a similar evolution is occurring in the thinking and observational orientation of behavioral therapists.

Paul A. Dewald ● Department of Psychiatry, St. Louis University School of Medicine, St. Louis, Missouri 63104.

However, in all these four chapters the authors are content to restrict themselves to descriptions of manifest behavior at the level of the patient's conscious explanation or awareness, without ever asking the further question of why such behavior is occurring. Their emphasis is on pragmatic trial and error in regard to the prescription of technical interventions, without any attempt at a cohesive and generalized conceptual understanding. They are content to settle for improved behavior without seriously examining or exploring why and how such improvement occurred. In several of the chapters, although the vocabulary may be different, the authors arrive at or make use of concepts long since described and defined in the psychoanalytic and psychodynamic literature, without either recognizing or acknowledging such similarities.

Taken as a whole the four chapters describe various aspects and forms of what I would call (from the psychodynamic perspective) reasonable supportive psychotherapy (Dewald, 1976). Among the limitations of the chapters is the failure to recognize multiple different forms and levels of therapeutic intervention and the failure to correlate observations and definitions regarding resistance with the overall goals and strategies of the therapeutic process. In other words, when the goal of therapy is supportive and symptom oriented, a particular behavior by the patient must be conceptually observed and defined differently from when the goal of therapy is the uncovering of underlying causes or the encouraging of increasingly self-determined and independent levels of function and motivation.

From a psychoanalytic and psychodynamic point of view all four chapters suffer from the narrow definition of resistance that is offered and used. The chief emphasis is on the patient's failure to carry out the therapist's requests, suggestions, or prescriptions, and resistance is seen as something in the way of progress and something over which the patient has a conscious, volitional control. The chapters fail to recognize manifestations of resistance that are more subtle and characterological, as well as instances and manifestations of resistance that occur outside of the patient's awareness. They also fail to recognize that important elements of the therapeutic process occur when the therapist is able to interpret the meanings and manifestations of a resistance in ways that permit the patient to overcome, reduce, or bypass his own resistances. The patient thereby gains an increasingly detailed and effective understanding of the nature and operation of his own mental processes. From a psychoanalytic and psychodynamic point of view, resistance is a far more complex, multidetermined, layered, and variously interesting process than is acknowledged by the authors of these behaviorally oriented chapters.

To make my critique more specific, I now turn to the individual contributions.

Resistance or Rationalization? Lazarus and Fay

Throughout their chapter Lazarus and Fay emphasize that therapists who make a diagnosis of resistance are seeking to rationalize their own failures in the treatment process. They correlate resistance with noncompliance and the negative outcome of therapy: a narrow and incomplete understanding of the concept.

At the same time, in their discussion of the varieties of resistance they do acknowledge a significant component to be the "individual characteristics" of the client. They do mention the cognitive abilities, genetic endowments, and cultural heritage of patients as contributing to the manifestations of resistance; yet for the most part they offer only pragmatic, trial-and-error clinical recommendations without any rational or cohesive explanation of the phenomena.

In another place they make a distinction between "the *patient* being resistant and the *problem* being resistant." This concept is a naive one in which the individual is separated from his behavior patterns and the manifestations of his neurotic disabilities. Such separation is a kind of resistance that many patients themselves will use in a therapeutic setting to disclaim their own responsibilities for their own limitations and/or neurotic suffering (Schafer, 1976).

The authors describe various behaviors exhibited by patients who for one reason or another are reluctant to reveal unpleasant aspects of themselves. They seem to imply that searching for specific reasons and forces contributing to such difficulty, or for the possibility that the difficulty could be related to the therapist's attitude toward the patient, represent unique cases or are not considered in psychoanalytic thinking. Similarly, they imply that rapid remission of specific symptoms is automatically looked on with suspicion by the psychodynamically oriented therapist. The question in such a case is not the manifest relief of symptoms *per se*, but the goal of therapy and the nature of the therapeutic process in which such a rapid remission of symptoms has occurred.

In their attempt to catalog the varieties of resistive behavior, the authors indicate a number of factors to which dynamic psychotherapists have long been directing attention, although using different terms. For example, when Lazarus and Fay speak of compliance as being "threatening," they are alluding to the concept of intrapsychic conflict, fantasy, and anxiety as a motivational stimulus to avoid discomfort and displeasure. When they speak about the therapeutic relationship being at fault and the patient displaying "passive-aggressive behaviors toward the therapist," they are in a superficial way alluding to the role of the therapeutic relationship and the transference of characteristic behaviors to the interactions with the therapist. The question of the patient's social network and secondary gain from maladaptive behavior was addressed by Freud (1926/1959) in his original discussion and classification of resistance.

Although they emphasize the potential failures and mistakes by the therapist as responsible for "most treatment impasses," the authors do indicate a recognition that there are patients by whom "the desired outcome is not valued highly enough." They make a point of avoiding the use of the term "motivation," but "a rose by any other name . . ." They also admit that there are patients who withdraw from therapy when basic issues are about to be confronted or when "substantial changes [are] in the offing," and they do refer to those individuals who seem to participate and cooperate with the therapist and yet "may be highly accomplished 'passive-resisters' who derive an enormous sense of power and gratification from the therapist's frustration." The shortcomings of their approach are manifest in the fact that although they can describe such behaviors they have no theoretical, conceptual, or motivational framework with which to explain or understand these phenomena.

In their discussion of interpersonal systems or family processes they illustrate the essential superficiality of their conceptual approach. Patients receiving intermittent reinforcement from significant individuals in their environment or family must have some kind of "fertile soil" within them on which such reinforcement acts. In regard to the case they describe of the woman whose "marital interactions were an exact copy of her parents' style," they are content to emphasize that her reluctance to change "had little to do with resistance as traditionally conceived, but was integrally tied to her own values and those of her social milieu." They fail to ask why she maintains those values, what are the internal motivational processes that lead her to repeat the parents' marital style, identifications of this patient with the earlier figures in her life, and so on, all of which would more adequately begin to explain the nature of this individual's behavior.

The emphasis on the role of the therapist and the possibility that the therapist is educationally or experientially deficient or is himself resistant represents an issue dealt with far more completely in the psychodynamic framework, in the concept of countertransference. The authors quote Franks and Wilson to the effect that

> If a person as a child has been able to maintain his identity only by resisting or fighting parental authority, there is no reason why we should not suspect that he will attempt to treat his behavior therapist with similar defensive tokens.

This quotation is merely a rephrasing of the important but well-described concept of transference; and when Lazarus and Fay go on to talk about therapists unwittingly reinforcing certain kinds of behaviors in the patient, they are likewise talking about transference gratification and possible countertransference forces within the therapist.

They emphasize that "to lump a myriad of different behaviors under the heading "resistance" or "countercontrol" misses the fact that specific messages have specific meanings and call for specific (different) interventions." That is an obvious truism, and in the psychodynamic approach to the concept of resistance the issue of the specific meaning of a particular behavior pattern and its relationship to the current context of the therapeutic process, as well as its shifting meanings during the course of therapy, or from one patient to another, is an obvious and repeated therapeutic necessity.

Resistance and Clinical Behavior Therapy: Goldfried

In his introduction Goldfried indicates that although many early behavior therapists ignored the issue of resistance, continuing clinical experience requires a recognition of its presence and significance in the therapeutic process.

In describing the client's role in behavior therapy, he suggests that clients must: (1) believe that change is possible; (2) accept the reality that the change process will be a gradual one; (3) accept the fact that the therapist will not do anything *to* or *for* them; and (4) have a favorably disposed attitude toward the articulated therapeutic strategy outlined by the therapist. In my own perception of the therapeutic process there is a significant difference between the patient's conscious and unconscious attitudes regarding these four points, and the full acceptance of these issues frequently occurs as a result rather than as a precondition of treatment.

Goldfried admits to one of the limitations of the behavioral model when he says that "there is nothing intrinsic to the behavioral model of change—at least in principle—to suggest that difficulties in implementing the therapeutic procedure are to be anticipated." In the psychoanalytic and psychodynamic model resistance *is* anticipated, and is recognizable and understandable in the basic clinical and conceptual formulations. The needs to account for repeatedly observed resistances in the clinical setting were some of the clinical data that forced Freud's revision of psychoanalytic theory from the topographical to the structural model.

In describing his general clinical strategy Goldfried discusses four major issues, each of which is also addressed in psychodynamic therapies, although from significantly different perspectives.

For example, Goldfried discusses "creating a positive context for change." Here he emphasizes the importance of the therapist–patient relationship, and how it influences the patient's responses to the treatment process. His focus is predominantly on positive rapport and a "good" relationship with the client, in which the therapist seeks to maximize his direct suggestive influence. From a psychodynamic point of view, he is describing only one element of a total relationship. The relationship includes not only rapport and the therapeutic alliance, but also multiple transference elements. And if the patient is to explore and resolve deeper levels of ambivalence, it must also include competitive, hostile, suspicious, and aggressive components that are eventually dealt with as part of the therapist–patient relationship and the interactions between them.

He describes specifying between-session assignments and providing positive reinforcement and feedback; and he suggests a "method of increasing the accountability of clients for their agreed-on homework assignments." Such techniques put the therapist in the role of a judging parental figure and keep the patient in the position of the dependent child who continues to seek rewards and to avoid criticism from that external figure. Whereas these strategies may be compatible with dynamically oriented supportive psychotherapy, the aim in an analytic approach is to have the patient develop and assume his own internalized, judging superego functions and to avoid having the therapist serve in that role.

Goldfried points out that the form of the resistance does not by itself give sufficient information, and that the therapist must try to understand the reasons for it; he emphasizes that similar behaviors may have different meanings for different clients; and that the therapist must take the initiative in dealing with the relevant determinants of a particular resistance when it occurs. These points were described long ago in psychoanalytic technique (i.e., Fenichel, 1941).

In his comments about "resistance as a sample of [the] client's presenting problem" Goldfried is actually describing the phenomena of transference and the repetition with the therapist of typical behavior patterns that had been evolved with other important people in the individual's life. Even his comment that "such forms of resistance are indeed a mixed blessing in that they interfere with the course of therapy but at the same time provide the therapist with a firsthand sample of the client's problem" is a restatement of the analytic therapeutic use of the transference as a paradigm and prototype of how the patient relates to others outside the treatment situation. And his comments about the therapist's response to the patient's behavior are again analogous to the analytic concept of countertransference and the therapeutic use of the therapist's personal feelings and reactions to enhance his understanding.

In discussing "resistance resulting from [the] client's other problems," Goldfried makes use of a concept that is similar to the analytic one of signal anxiety and the occurrence of intrapsychic fantasy as a determinant of maladaptive behavior. In his recommendation that "inquiring about the thoughts, feelings, and behaviors that preceded the client's unsuccessful attempt at following through on the homework assignment, it is often possible to *uncover* [italics mine] those determinants that then need to be the focus of change," he is describing a therapeutic technique that, focused at preconscious levels of conflict and change, is similar to psychodynamic psychotherapy.

In dealing with the fear of changing, he again is describing a source of resistance known since Freud's (1926/1959) original definitions, and his recommendations for dealing with this fear are all in keeping with analytically oriented, supportive therapeutic techniques.

Unlike Lazarus and Fay, Goldfried is willing to use the term "motivation to change," and has accepted the concept that some patients have minimal conscious motivation for change and that this issue needs more attention in the behavioral literature.

His theory of psychological reactance is understandable from a psychodynamic perspective as relating to conflicts over passivity and dependence, and the multiple adaptive and/or defensive ways by which patients attempt to resolve such difficulties. The description of internal versus external individuals deals with character types described long ago in the psychoanalytic literature. The suggestion to tailor the therapeutic procedure in keeping with such particular preferences points to a means of supporting the patient's characteristic adaptation and resistance to change, and thus again carries a supportive rather than a basically changing orientation as a therapeutic goal.

The same is true regarding Goldfried's emphasis on environmental factors, and his statement about secondary gain from neurotic disturbance, a subject dealt with by Freud (1926/1959). The technical recommendations for the therapist actively to intervene to change environmental factors imply that the patient is too immature or inept to do it himself and needs parental protection. Once again this intervention is acceptable as a supportive maneuver, but contraindicated in an analytic attempt to promote maturation and independence.

The Behavior-Analytic Approach: Turkat and Meyer

After emphasizing that resistances are well-known to all clinicians and that the behaviors in question occur in an infinite variety, the authors describe nine situations that frequently activate and produce resistance. These situations are described in superficial terms, and no attempt is made at conceptual or explanatory unification or understanding. This superficiality is illustrated in their discussion of "therapist attraction," where they say only that "we have had clients who display resistance in order to prolong regular flirtation sessions with us." What they are observing is one descriptive variant in the whole complex process of conscious and unconscious transference and transference resistance, as well as the enormous significance of the therapist–patient relationship.

The discussion of the initial interview strikes me as naive, inasmuch as many patients have not yet established a sufficient degree of confidence and trust to permit them openly and directly to share even the more difficult conscious sources of their complaints and problems. Furthermore, at such an early phase the patient is frequently unaware of the underlying difficulties, even though he may be trying his best to be candid. Experience has shown dramatically and repeatedly that much of the material presented by the patient in an initial interview represents unwitting and unconscious distortion, omission, defensive experience and expression, and so on, and therefore the capacity of a therapist to arrive at more than a general formulation is limited at best. The capacity of the therapist to tell what is relevant and what is irrelevant is even more limited, and therefore I question Turkat and Meyer's statement that the therapist "attempts to avoid wasting any time on irrelevant information."

The authors' emphasis that "possible genetic, organic, and/or environmental predisposing factors are examined" seems to be in a more dynamic vein than much of the behavioral literature, which tends to emphasize that past history is of relatively little significance, and that the only important issues are the current ones in a patient's pathological functioning. The same is true of their comments that "the clinician formulates the relationships among the client's complaints, explains why these difficulties developed, and uses this information to predict the client's response to natural-environment and analog-environment situations." They recommend a continuing process of hypothesis testing and modification as the relationship and the therapy unfold, and the therapist formulates a developmental analysis relating the present manifestations of difficulty to past issues.

Even though Turkat and Meyer are focused at levels of conscious awareness, their general recommendations regarding the meanings of the patient's material and the connections between past and present suggest that their clinical experience has forced them away from a usual behavioral model.

The bulk of their chapter is devoted to an extensive case history of a patient treated by the behavior-analytic method. It is always a problem for the presenter to document and demonstrate his clinical work as a case history and still be inclusive. It is also always tempting for the reader to supply his own interpretation of those data that are presented, which may or may not be compatible with the data that were omitted. In this instance it is striking that the authors (both in their presentation and, presumably, in their clinical approach to the patient) give so little importance to the death of the patient's mother when she was 3 years old, and that no account of this event is made either in the formulation of the case or in the therapeutic process. Furthermore, the emphasis in the relationship with the father is on the possibility of his being critical of the patient. All other components of the parent–child relationship, as well as the impact of the father's remarriage, the repeated separations from the father, the sexual and aggressive impulses and fantasies that the patient would have toward him, and so on are essentially ignored.

Furthermore, in the description of the therapeutic process itself, there are so many additional factors and variables that contribute to the final picture, to say nothing of the multiple ways by which the therapists tend to support many of the patient's resistances, that it is difficult to see how the presentation of this case can serve the illustrative functions the authors intended. That most of the original predictions proved incorrect and that eventually the patient was treated by a method diametrically the opposite of the one that was begun demonstrates the difficulties, described above, of basing too specific predictions on early conscious material offered by the patient.

Resistance from a Cognitive-Behavioral Perspective: Meichenbaum and Gilmore

Of the four chapters this one is closest to the conceptual model of psychodynamic therapy, although the authors in no way voluntarily recognize their indebtedness to psychoanalytic thinking. Examples of such similarity include their statements that resistance is a motivational construct that "can carry information that is conscious, preconscious, or unconscious"; that all therapists have felt "the irresistible resistances of the most dedicated clients"; that their therapeutic approach has to do with having the client "identify, reality test, and correct maladaptive, distorted conceptualizations and dysfunctional beliefs"; that they help the client "become aware of and monitor the role negative and involuntary thoughts play in the maintenance of maladaptive behavior, by recognizing the connections among cognition, affect, and behavior together with their joint consequences"; and that

> behavioral change is a reflection of the intimate interrelationships among the client's cognitive structures (schemata, beliefs), conscious cognitive processes (automatic thoughts, internal dialogue, images), interpersonal behaviors, and resulting intrapersonal and interpersonal consequences.
>
> Much of our work in therapy will attempt (1) to have our clients come to view their cognitions as hypotheses that are to be subjected to reality testing and evaluation; (2) to help our clients become open to anomalous "data"; and (3) to have them examine the nature of those beliefs or "paradigms" that give rise to their maladaptive behavior.
>
> A key goal of cognitive-behavioral treatment is to facilitate the emergence of a new conceptualization over the course of therapy, thereby permitting the

client's symptoms to be translated into difficulties that can be pinpointed and viewed as specific, solvable problems rather than as problems that are vague, undifferentiated, and overwhelming. . . Moreover, the therapist does not present the conceptualization with certainty, but offers it as reflecting his or her current view of what is going on.

In these passages the authors are describing a form of therapy that has to do with personal meanings that are subjected to critical reappraisal, and with therapeutic activity that involves the process of interpretation of specific meanings by the therapist to the patient in hopes that the latter can begin to modify his previously automatic and stereotyped patterns of thought and behavior.

They also emphasize that resistance is closely bound up with affect, and they stress the importance of affect in the development and maintenance of psychopathology. Furthermore, they say that

affect (like belief) is not under direct voluntary control. To modify affect one must change thought and behavior patterns. And to change thought and behavior patterns it is not sufficient just to reason with or "persuade" one's clients.

Essentially, the authors are presenting formulations very similar to those based on psychodynamic principles. They even imply something of a genetic perspective by stating that "much more than psychology has hitherto stressed, affect is largely controlled by previous affects through the mediating links of cognition."

They point out that in the therapeutic process resistance itself can be informative and can provide additional occasions for examining the nature of the client's cognition, affect, and behavior. In other words, resistances have a dynamic meaning that must be understood.

In cognitive-behavioral therapies nonadherence to treatment plans is viewed not as a sign of a personality defect or of stupidity on the part of the client, but instead as a natural consequence of an interfering thinking style, or a set of dysfunctional beliefs, and/or as the result of a set of interpersonal consequences that reinforce resistance.

Furthermore, the therapist should anticipate resistant affects, and in a sense "every resistance signals a new beginning phase of therapy, and every beginning in therapy signals a change in the vicissitudes of existing resistances."

They even describe some elements that can be conceptualized as transference when they mention the "client's internal 'dialogues' (expectations, attributions) concerning both his or her presenting problems and the accompanying expectations about treatment." And the significance of empathy is mentioned: "Insofar as the therapist can accurately and empathically perceive and share the client's expectancies, the therapist is more likely to be able to make sense out of the client's unproductive, resistant behavior."

The authors also recognize that "the therapist must be sensitive to the fact that interventions and contracts established at one level of exchange (conscious and verbalized) may contradict those at another level of exchange (unconscious and unverbalized)," and they even begin to approach the issue of countertransference in their discussion of "transresistance," "continual self-supervision," and "consistent analysis and support" in regard to resistance.

The authors even emphasize the specifically reactivated resistances of the termination phase of treatment, and the importance of applying the same therapeutic techniques used in previous phases of therapy to these final instances of resistance.

Meichenbaum and Gilmore have evolved a descriptive and empirically-based set of precepts for the conduct of psychotherapy. In this they emphasize a variety of natural observations which are similar to analytic findings, but they combine these with other therapeutic interventions that from an analytic perspective are supportive and manipulative. They do *not* offer a comprehensive or internally consistent conceptual framework within which to understand or formulate their experiences.

Summary

What I have tried to point out in this discussion is that as illustrated by the four chapters in question, anyone who works with patients in a therapeutic setting for a considerable time comes gradually to recognize certain clinical phenomena, one of which is the occurrence of behavior patterns that seem to be contradictory to the patient's avowed purpose in seeking treatment. Each of the authors has apparently recognized such phenomena, some more completely and directly than others, and each has prescribed technical procedures by which to alleviate, bypass, reduce, or cope with the behaviors in question.

However, none of these chapters has offered a comprehensive, internally consistent, clinically applicable conceptual understanding of what resistance means, how and why it has been developed, and what are its implications in the overall mental life of the patient. In this sense each of these authors has partly rediscovered the wheel and each (wittingly or unwittingly) has failed to acknowledge that psychoanalytic clinical observations of resistance long precede those made in the behavioral literature. Furthermore, clinical psychoanalytic theory (in contrast to metapsychology) offers the most elegant, comprehensive, and internally consistent explanation of this aspect of a patient's behavior. The various attempts at formulations by the authors of these four chapters have included only a partial understanding of the problems, meanings, processes, and manifestations of the complex issue of resistance. Up to now, at least, only psychoanalysis has been able to offer a comprehensive and systematic description and clinical explanation of the multiple meanings and functions of resistance in psychotherapy.

References

Dewald, P. A. Toward a general concept of the therapeutic process. *International Journal of Psychoanalytic Psychotherapy*, 1976, 5, 283–299.
Fenichel, O. *Problems of psychoanalytic technique*. New York: Psychoanalytic Quarterly, 1941.
Freud, S. Inhibitions, symptoms and anxiety. *Standard edition* (Vol. 20). London: Hogarth Press, 1959. (Originally published, 1926.)
Schafer, R. *A new language for psychoanalysis*. New Haven: Yale University Press, 1976.

12

Psychoanalytic Resistance and Behavioral Nonresponsiveness

A DIALECTICAL IMPASSE

Allen Fay and Arnold A. Lazarus

As the editor of this book can attest, we displayed a high degree of resistance to writing this commentary. But Paul Wachtel, able clinician that he is, eschewed an insight-oriented approach and employed an effective cognitive-behavioral style, replete with an awesome arsenal of assertive responses. He did, however, experience several harried months over our procrastination.

Why were we reluctant to write this commentary? Why did it prove so difficult for us? We had looked forward to a lively exchange with our psychoanalytic confreres; yet, as we read through their material, we found it difficult to select cogent points for discussion. First, their writings, like the psychoanalytic process itself, often defied objective, specific, and dispassionate assessment. Second, we found that their basic assumptions about people, about the nature of psychological distress, and about the active ingredients of change (and the barriers to change) are so much at variance with our own clinical perceptions and judgments that meaningful dialogue is virtually precluded. It would be senseless to comment on specific issues without challenging the very fabric from

Allen Fay • Department of Psychiatry, Mount Sinai School of Medicine, City University of New York, New York, New York 10029. Arnold A. Lazarus • Graduate School of Applied and Professional Psychology, Rutgers—The State University, New Brunswick, New Jersey 08903.

which their ideas emanate. To ask what scientific evidence lies behind an observation such as "his homosexuality was a defensive regression against unresolved oedipal strivings" (Blatt & Erlich), or to question the postulated connection between the taking of tranquilizers by an analytic patient and "the wishes and fears regarding oral incorporation of the analyst" (Dewald) would merely perpetuate the futile controversies that have been raging for more than half a century. It is as if a fundamentalist who understood only English and a nuclear physicist who understood only Chinese were asked to comment on each other's chapters. Although one of us underwent an orthodox Freudian analysis and was trained in psychodynamic theory and methods, we find analytic constructs unnecessarily cumbersome, analytic assumptions illogical, and analytic techniques largely irrelevant.

In perusing the chapters in question, we became more aware than ever that in psychoanalysis and analytically oriented psychotherapy resistance exists not as a clinical entity, but virtually by definition. As Schlesinger states, "It is one of my articles of faith, or at least a heuristic assumption, that in psychotherapy defense and transference and hence resistance are *always* present."

Another problem for us arises from our abiding conviction that what a therapist says and does is more relevant to treatment outcomes than what he or she writes about or claims to do. Thus our difficulty lies mainly with psychoanalysis, not so much with psychoanalysts. We have had many fruitful collaborations with analysts, having worked in a complementary fashion with the same patient. We have known analysts who used behavioral methods, and behavior therapists who used insight-oriented methods. We have known therapists of both "camps" who were warm, empathic, and disclosing, and others who were austere, nondisclosing—indeed, noncommunicative. Yet we have serious reservations about integrating psychoanalysis and behavior therapy, despite efforts to do so by Birk (1970), Feather and Rhoades (1972), Wachtel (1977), and Marmor and Woods (1980) among others. We feel there are fundamental theoretical incompatibilities, although we have espoused *technical* eclecticism for many years (Lazarus, 1967). We agree with Messer and Winokur (1980) that "psychoanalysis and behavior therapy embody alternate visions of life that imply different basic possibilities in existence." Despite the fact that within the last decade, phenotypically, behavior therapy has become more cognitive and psychoanalysis more behavioral, genotypically the chasm remains. The need for a better-integrated, comprehensive, and coherent psychoeducational approach will not be satisfied, we feel, by coupling psychodynamic and social learning theories. The broad and systematic base of multimodal therapy offers a solution that avoids paradigm clashes and epistemological incongruities (Lazarus, 1976, 1981).

Basch

To illustrate our basic concerns, we will start with Basch's chapter. It begins with one of the cardinal tenets of psychoanalytic therapy: "Freud demonstrated that psychological symptoms serve a purpose . . ." What Freud demonstrated was that *some* psychological symptoms *may* serve a purpose, since behaviorists have demonstrated even more convincingly that many symptoms may be fortuitously acquired. From the basic Freudian premise, it follows that "clearly, in most cases these coping mechanisms will not readily be given up." Thus both demand characteristics and self-fulfilling prophecies are there at the beginning of a protracted therapeutic undertaking.

Later Basch states, "Thus in our field we should not hope or demand that our patients will respond to our efforts to help them as they might in the case of a physical disturbance—and yet we tend to do so." Noncompliance rates in medical patients are staggering, and although noncompliance is not synonymous with resistance, the problem of resistance is clearly not the sole province of psychology.

The cited view of Freud that resistance is not an interpersonal problem but an intrapsychic one seems benevolent enough in its attempt to avoid pejorative implications; yet it is seriously deficient in light of the more recent emphasis on the social system and the role of interpersonal networks in defining, understanding, and resolving so many of the problems we encounter.

We have strong reservations about Basch's handling of the first patient he presents. As we understand the transaction, Mr. Hoheit poses a problem that he feels is straightforward: "I need advice regarding my children. I want to know whether, in your professional opinion, my getting a divorce would hurt them." Basch, it seems, never attempts to deal with the stated problem but instead converts this man into an analytic patient, whose therapy extends over 4 years. This conversion starts with the initial response; "I don't think that's a question I can answer. If you'll tell me about your situation I may be able to clarify your thinking." And later:

> I would like to hear from you about your children, their personalities, and the effects you think a divorce will have on them because that will help me get a better picture of what's going on with you.

This response by the therapist reminds one of us of his first day of training, when a patient in a ward community group said, "You know how it is with these doctors. If you ask them 'Is it raining outside?' they say, 'What do you think?' " Basch's patient protests repeatedly: "Sounds to me like you're trying to set something up for yourself, Doctor." And

> Well, I asked you a simple question. I came to get a professional opinion from you as I would from a dentist, a lawyer, or a surgeon. I'm perfectly willing to pay what it costs to get it, but you are already making me into a client or a patient . . .

The ultimate resolution of this man's problem seems to be revealed in the following statement, which strikes us as arcane, irrelevant, and preposterous even if in some idiosyncratic sense it contains an element of truth:

> On a much deeper level, material recovered only after several years of analysis revealed that his aggressive attitude concealed the repressed wish and fear to compensate his father for the loss of his wife by offering himself as the passive participant in anal intercourse.

We are not suggesting that Basch's patient's difficulties were confined to the stated or presenting problem, but we do believe that a more parsimonious approach could have produced results of comparable or better quality in much less time. If one uses Erickson's idea of *starting where the patient is* and adopts a systems approach rather than the individual-psychopathology model, we feel there is a much better chance of more quickly effecting a favorable resolution. In fact, without interviewing and working with various members of the social network, Basch would be unable to answer Mr. Hoheit's question even if he wanted to. The handling of this case illustrates what is most troubling about psychoanalytic therapy (not psychoanalysis as a theory of personality, nor all psychoanalysts, nor even this psychoanalyst at all times). In our opinion, its methods are a major cause of the militant antipsychiatry/antitherapy movement of the past decade. A therapist is a patient's consultant; the patient is not the therapist's ward. Sometimes the therapist must use a firm hand and provide strong direction, but we feel Basch exceeded his mandate. Using Basch's transcript of this case, we would like to offer an alternative way of handling the initial exchange.

Basch's Version

THERAPIST *(Walking into the waiting room and offering his hand):* Mr. Hoheit? I am Dr. Basch.

MR. HOHEIT *(Indifferently shaking the proffered hand):* I have to be out of here by 2:00 and you are 5 minutes late, Doctor.

THERAPIST: Come in, please.

MR. HOHEIT *(Settling down in the designated chair):* Will we be done by 2:00, Doctor? I have to be at a meeting by 2:15.

THERAPIST: Will we be done with what?

Fay–Lazarus Version

THERAPIST *(Walking into the waiting room and offering his hand):* Adam Hoheit? Hi, I'm Michael Basch. Sorry I'm late. [If the therapist is late, it is appropriate to acknowledge it in advance rather than wait for the patient, who clearly is already uncomfortable, to bring it up. Many analysts have expressed the view that anxiety is not only desirable but essential to effect a favorable outcome. We prefer, if the patient is uncomfortable, to put him at ease rather than let him "twist in the wind," to quote a prominent Watergate figure.]

MR. HOHEIT *(Indifferently shaking the proffered hand):* I have to be out of here by 2:00 and you are 5 minutes late, Doctor.

THERAPIST: My sessions run 45 minutes. I hope that will get you out in time. Please tell me why you have come.

Basch's Version

MR. HOHEIT: Right. I guess you don't even know what I'm here for. Actually it shouldn't take too long. Abner Tatum was your patient and he is my client.[1] We were talking at lunch the other day and I mentioned my problem to him. Abner said he wanted to stay out of it, but he said you had been of great help to him during his divorce, so I thought perhaps I could use some of your counsel in my circumstances too.

THERAPIST: I'd be glad to be of help if I can be.

MR. HOHEIT: It's not really for me. I need advice regarding my children. I want to know whether, in your professional opinion, my getting a divorce from my wife will hurt them. I have a boy age 6, and two daughters, 16 and 14. The older ones will be leaving home to go to college fairly soon anyway, but the 6-year-old worries me a little.

THERAPIST: I don't think that's a question I can answer. If you'll tell me about your situation I may be able to clarify your thinking.

MR. HOHEIT: You mean if I can give you more information about him then you

---

[1] If Mr. Hoheit is as tense as he sounds, a short digression might make it easier for him relate to the therapist: "How is Abner?"

can tell me how my boy will be affected? I suppose it does differ with each personality.

THERAPIST: No.[2] I would like to hear from you about your children, their personalities, and the effects you think a divorce will have on them because that will help me get a better picture of what's going on with you.

Fay–Lazarus Version

MR. HOHEIT [Same].

THERAPIST: I'll be glad to do what I can. [This version, omitting "if," seems a little more positive and optimistic than Basch's version.]

MR. HOHEIT: It's not really for me. I need advice regarding my children . . . the 6-year-old worries me a little.

THERAPIST: Tell me a little about *him*.

MR. HOHEIT: You mean if I can give you more information about him then you can tell me how my boy will be affected? I suppose it does differ with each personality.

THERAPIST: Perhaps I can, but I could be much more helpful if you would bring your children and your wife to a session. [This suggestion could have been made on the telephone prior to the first visit.]

In contrast to the way Basch handled Mr. Hoheit, the following illustrates our response to another individual.

PATIENT: I have decided that I really don't need therapy, but as a courtesy I thought I would come and tell you so myself instead of simply canceling my appointment at the last minute. So, if you would let me know how much I owe you . . .

THERAPIST: You don't owe me anything. I have provided no service and I do not expect a fee.

PATIENT: Well, you could have scheduled someone else in my place if I had given you sufficient notice.

THERAPIST: That's OK. I appreciate your honesty, but I would feel uncomfortable charging you for nothing. When you set up the appointment you must have wanted therapy. Since then, you have changed your mind. So, let me merely say, thank you for letting me know, and all the best to you.

PATIENT: Do you ever use hypnosis in your work?

THERAPIST: Yes, when it seems to be indicated. Why do you ask?

PATIENT: Well (*pause*), perhaps I should reconsider the whole matter. Let me tell you why I called for an appointment and let me ask you to react to my problem and say whether or not you think you can help.

THERAPIST: Sure. I'd be glad to.

---

[2] We generally prefer something a little softer, such as "Not quite" or "To some extent." We want to avoid contributing to the man's feeling of being an ignorant, incompetent, sick person.

Basch demonstrates considerable flexibility in the treatment of different cases. When his patient Mr. Ilge states, albeit "with a hint of sarcasm"—which may have been more his anticipation of the therapist's negative reaction than anything else—"Perhaps I should keep a diary," Basch admirably though perhaps unwittingly uses two standard behavior therapy techniques, self-monitoring and positive reinforcement of adaptive behavior. We also welcomed his comment that "the primary issue [is] the need to look at what is going on today," as well as his statement, "My emphasis when I function as a psychotherapist is on activity, mine and the patient's." He then asks the $100,000 question:

> If there is no difference between the results the two forms of treatment achieve and the methods they use, would it not make sense to treat everyone by the shorter, less demanding, and less expensive method?

Unfortunately, without providing any supporting arguments, he gives the 10¢ answer: "Of course it does not work that way." In our experience, it *does* work that way. Even if it does not work better in terms of the overall percentage of favorable outcomes, it certainly works as well and takes less time (Sloane, Staples, Cristol, Yorkston, & Whipple, 1975).

Dewald

In Basch's chapter, except for a passing mention, one does not see acknowledgment of errors, failures, or limitations—in contrast to Dewald, who, faithful to Wachtel's directive, discusses failures and reveals a willingness to recommend that a patient work with a colleague who may be more suited to his or her particular needs or personality.

Nevertheless, in Dewald's chapter we again find totally alien goals and methods. Dewald states:

> In psychoanalysis the therapeutic goal and the task for the patient and the analyst is to uncover and resolve the basic infantile and early childhood core of the patient's unconscious wishes and fantasies and the conflicts that arise from them, as well as the attempted solution and/or improved adaptation to those conflicts.

We are not concerned with the correctness of analytic assumptions. We are concerned with their value in promoting positive results (less distress, more satisfaction, freedom from irrational constraints, enhanced growth, more adaptive functioning) in the least amount of time.

Our view is similar to that of the French mathematician, Laplace, who when asked what was the place of God in his system, replied, "I have no need for such a hypothesis." Dewald says further,

> But in both forms of treatment [psychoanalysis and psychoanalytic psychotherapy] the therapist must recognize that only the patient can modify, reduce, or eliminate a particular resistance.

This outlook totally negates such powerful tools in modifying "resistance" as operant conditioning and paradoxical strategies.

Although Dewald has a nonjudgmental attitude, he still explains resistance in terms of the neurotic disturbance of the patient. It is disconcerting to read that it took a patient 6 months to disclose his phobia about public toilets. Another of his patients revealed only in the eighth month of therapy that she had a sexual problem. We feel that this kind of delay often says more about the therapist than about the patient. In the case of the man with the toilet phobia, rather than interpreting the meaning of the patient's behavior, Dewald would have been better advised to employ behavior rehearsal, participant modeling, self-disclosure, social skills training, guided imagery, and cognitive interventions with regard to shame, guilt, embarrassment, criticism, and rejection. It seems to us that the months and years it takes to understand the meanings of problems are a terrible waste. Dewald's presentation of this case concludes with the following comment:

> This vignette illustrates the limitations in the therapist's capacity directly to influence the reduction of resistances, and the fact that this capacity ultimately rests with the patient. The therapist can only point them out, create a therapeutic environment. . .

It seems to us that the limitations exist in this particular "therapist's capacity directly to influence the reduction of resistances." In addition, putting the responsibility on the patient and pointing out his or her resistances is probably the last thing we would want to do because, as we see it, such interventions generally lower self-esteem and impede problem solving.

Dewald, as did Basch, makes reference to a behavior therapy technique. A therapist "eventually" recommended to a patient with compulsive hand washing, "after a long period of work without progress," that he deliberately refrain from the hand washing for 5 minutes at any time when the impulse occurred and that he instead try to become aware of thoughts and feelings during the 5-minute delay.

Thus we see an adumbration of *response prevention*, one of the *only* effective techniques in the treatment of such problems. Unfortunately, it is clearly subordinate to the recommended introspection. This instruction strikes us as akin to using a combination of penicillin and carrot juice in the treatment of pneumonia and then stressing the importance of the carrot juice.

Schlesinger

Schlesinger emphasizes a "paradoxical" view of resistance that may help therapists cope with their own antipathy toward "resistant patients" and may forestall an unproductive frontal assault. He stresses *going with the resistance,* starting where the patient is, but his case histories do not illustrate such an orientation. He does not exploit the rich possibilities of paradoxical intervention, one of the most important methods for overcoming resistance (Fay, 1976; Haley, 1973, 1976; Rabkin, 1977; Watzlawick, Weakland, & Fisch, 1974). When he says, "I shall call this stance 'going along with the resistance,' " he seems unaware of earlier work on the subject in which the very term "siding with the resistance" is used (Sherman, 1968).

We also agree with Schlesinger's most important point—that the therapist must look at the cognitive, affective, and behavioral components of resistance. This notion is consonant with our own multimodal orientation, in which seven dimensions of personality are covered in assessment and therapy: behavior, affect, sensory experience, imagery, cognition, interpersonal relationships, and biological factors. It seems to us that Schlesinger has a number of creative ideas, but is operating within a conceptual model and a technical repertoire that do not allow their fullest expression. He avers that a goal of psychotherapy is "to promote a patient's own activity." The problem for us is that he sees *interpretation* as the major vehicle for achieving that goal. Even if interpretation were effective, we still feel that it is usually circuitous. How about direct suggestion, in vivo practice, participant modeling, role playing, direct cognitive disputation of irrational beliefs, imagery training— and dozens of other cognitive-behavioral techniques?

Blatt and Erlich[3]

In Blatt and Erlich's chapter, we applaud statements such as:

[3] Fay and Lazarus's commentary is based on an earlier version of Blatt and Erlich's chapter than the one appearing in this book.—Editor

> Resistance, in this expanded psychoanalytic model, can no longer be viewed
> as an occurrence exclusively within the patient . . . instead resistance must
> be defined . . . as occurring within the therapeutic dyad, as something
> between the patient and the therapist that interferes with the flow of the
> therapeutic process.

And, again, "Resistance is a conscious and unconscious opposition to the continuity and progress of treatment, an opposition to active inquiry, exploration, and growth within the therapeutic dyad."

However, throughout the chapter the authors emphasize patients' intrinsic limitations and pathology, leading us to feel that they are merely paying lip service to the dyadic concept. Expectedly, they completely fail to consider the identified patient's social network as a factor in resistance.

We have serious reservations about the way they handle their case, a 23-year-old man who had "concerns about homosexuality." In our view "homosexual problems" are problems created by definitions and social biases. The precise determinants of homosexuality itself have not yet been elucidated, but we regard the authors' attitude as unenlightened and counterproductive, if not actively deleterious. They write: "Homosexual patients are generally considered to have poor prognosis in all forms of psychotherapy, including psychoanalysis, because of their fundamental resistance to change." Apart from the logical circularity of this statement, such a pessimistic attitude is likely to create a self-fulfilling prophecy. It is not clear from the history whether the patient wanted to change his sexual orientation, and, if so, whether it was exclusively out of concern about social consequences. If he did not want to change (as is the case for the large majority of homosexuals) but was struggling to deal with the social reality, he needed a repertoire of cognitive and social skills. While reading this detailed case history, we kept wanting to say to the therapist, "Do something!" Assertiveness training frequently came to mind ("he would become tense and uncomfortable if he had to initiate contact"), as did cognitive techniques to rid the patient of shame and guilt. All the homosexual stereotypes are contained in Blatt and Erlich's presentation, including the dominating-mother/ passive-father constellation, which, even in this last quarter of the twentieth century, is referred to as a "serious role reversal." Other putative causes include the patient's mother's preoccupation with his hernia and her giving him enemas, which are part of a list of "a number of factors that can lead to the formation of homosexuality." Throughout, homosexuality is clearly seen as a negative or sick activity: "Mr. K's homosexual activity became more intense during times when he was trying to deal with separation." To us the issue is whether he enjoyed his sex life—if not, why not, and what might he want to do about it—whether he was relatively free from negative self-concepts, and whether he was coping with the social prejudices in an effective way. We will not waste the reader's time by quoting more extensively from this case history, but a simple reading of the original (Chapter 4) will surely give pause to all but the staunchest partisans of the authors' viewpoint.

We have seen several similar cases.

> One patient, also a 23-year-old man, clearly had a homosexual orientation (sexually attracted to men exclusively, masturbated to homoerotic fantasies) although he had never had homosexual relations because of fear of social consequences. He had found many women physically attractive but not sexually appealing. One evening he saw an "expert" on a television talk show and "learned" that he had an illness. He made an appointment with that well-known psychiatrist and was told that he indeed had an illness, that the only effective treatment was psychoanalysis four to five times a week probably for 3 or more years, and that there was only a 33% chance of cure even with treatment. He wanted a second opinion and, in a most anguished state, called us. He came for three visits, during which we endeavored to disabuse him of what we regarded as misinformation, to define the artificially designated problem as a nonproblem, to reduce his shame and guilt, and to provide him with information about available methods to change sexual orientation. He was markedly relieved of his distress, and most satisfied with the information he was given. He called many months later to say that he had had a number of homosexual experiences and was very comfortable with his sexual orientation and pleased about other areas of his life as well.

We are not wise enough to know how this man would have fared with some other form of therapy or with another therapist; but we try not to complicate problems, bewilder patients, or impose awesome financial burdens, especially in the absence of convincing data to justify such measures.

Conclusions

We have found that flexibility in a therapist's personal style as well as a full technical armamentarium will facilitate the disruption of resistant patterns and permit a smoother course of therapy. We have experienced dramatic breakthroughs in a variety of clinical problems by such unexpected therapist actions as:

- Selective self-disclosure
- A middle-of-the-night emergency session in response to a patient's acute distress
- An unsolicited telephone call by the therapist to follow up on something that was discussed in the session
- Shifting the locus of therapy outside of the office, such as outdoor walking sessions or a session in the park, or, under certain circumstances, a home visit by the therapist
- Providing a cotherapist for extensive in vivo work (to facilitate desensitization, provide reinforcement of adaptive responses, offer helpful modeling experiences); at times this technique has entailed recommending a surrogate sex partner
- Shedding a tear with a patient about some personal misfortune
- Sharing a mutual avid interest such as playing tennis or chamber music together

Often, doing something that is out of character or out of the patient's ordinary experience of therapy can initiate a major change. Conveying a clear message that the patient is not sick has often resulted in a positive therapeutic response, particularly in people who have not improved during many years of prior therapy. What we must not do is continue making the same mistakes with patients who are not responding, repeat the mistakes other therapists have made, or in general fit the patient in a procrustean fashion into a unimodal framework. A dramatic change in the therapist's style or actions will sometimes have an electrifying effect. Acting "crazy"—yelling at a patient, threatening suicide oneself, lying down on the floor, walking out of a session, talking to oneself— can at times force the patient into a "healthy" posture. The possibilities for overcoming resistance and achieving favorable results in a short time are often limited only by the therapist's imagination and capacity to shift into different behavioral and affective modes. Dramatizations, metaphors, examples from clinical practice as well as the therapist's personal life, and the deliberate use of humor, including joke telling, can all have a most salubrious effect.

What ultimately matters is what we say and do in the therapeutic setting.

References

Birk, L. Behavior therapy: Integration with dynamic psychiatry. *Behavior Therapy*, 1970, *1*, 522–526.

Fay, A. *Making things better by making them worse.* New York: Hawthorn Books, 1978.

Feather, B. W., & Rhoades, J. M. Psychodynamic behavior therapy. I. Theory and rationale. *Archives of General Psychiatry*, 1972, *26*, 496–502.

Haley, J. *Uncommon therapy.* New York: W. W. Norton, 1973.

Haley, J. *Problem-solving therapy.* San Francisco: Jossey-Bass, 1976.

Lazarus, A. A. In support of technical eclecticism. *Psychological Reports*, 1967, *21*, 415–416.

Lazarus, A. A. *Multimodal behavior therapy.* New York: Springer, 1976.

Lazarus, A. A. *The practice of multimodal therapy.* New York: McGraw-Hill, 1981.

Marmor, J., & Woods, S. M. (Eds.), *The interface between the psychodynamic and behavioral therapies.* New York: Plenum Press, 1980.

Messer, S. B., & Winokur, M. Some limits to the integration of psychoanalytic and behavior therapy. *American Psychologist*, 1980, *35*, 818–827.

Rabkin, R. *Strategic psychotherapy.* New York: Basic Books, 1977.

Sherman, M. H. Siding with the resistance versus interpretation: Role implications. In M. C. Nelson, B. Nelson, M. H. Sherman, & H. S. Strean (Eds.), *Roles and paradigms in psychotherapy.* New York: Grune & Stratton, 1968.

Sloane, R. B., Staples, F. R., Cristol, A. H., Yorkston, N. J., & Whipple, K. *Psychotherapy versus behavior therapy.* Cambridge, Mass.: Harvard University Press, 1975.

Wachtel, P. L. *Psychoanalysis and behavior therapy: Toward an integration.* New York: Basic Books, 1977.

Watzlawick, P., Weakland, J., & Fisch, R. *Change: Principles of problem formation and problem resolution.* New York: W. W. Norton, 1974.

13

A Perspective on the Dynamic Contributions

J. Barnard Gilmore and Donald Meichenbaum

The chapters in this volume underline the fact that healthy changes in personality and behavior are as yet highly unpredictable events. This point holds true in every consulting room and with every type of client. The effect of this truth is both discouraging and challenging. Yes, we do need to be realistic about the limits of our existing therapeutic powers and insights. And yes, we do need to be realistic about unknown opportunities for new therapeutic and theoretical advances.

In this volume we see highlighted the two distinct aspects of the task we all address. As scientists we wish to understand the determinants of resistances. As therapists we wish to discover the interventions that can help the client overcome resistances. If, as has been implied in many chapters in this volume, there are a number of species belonging to the genus *resistance*, then it is important to stress that there is no *one* way to understand, or to intervene in a case of, resistance. And yet we are more than ever struck by what may be common principles for overcoming resistances, principles that are implicit in a number of the techniques described in the foregoing chapters. At the most general level these principles involve motivating and nurturing the search for those "data" that can change the client's hypotheses about his or her inner and outer worlds.

J. Barnard Gilmore ● Department of Psychology, University of Toronto, Toronto, Ontario M5S 1A1, Canada. Donald Meichenbaum ● Department of Psychology, University of Waterloo, Waterloo, Ontario N2L 3G1, Canada.

Information produces change. That was as much Freud's answer to the question, "How can merely talking help me?" as it is the implicit premise behind our cognitive-behavioral approach. It is important to realize that affect is, and should be, information. Behavior is information. Thoughts are information. All three are important sources of the data that may enable the scientist-client to adopt hypotheses that will make affect, behavior, and thinking more productive and less debilitating. Although the work of the therapy session is one important source of information, we are struck by the extent to which most of the case material described in these chapters shows the importance of that information that is gained between sessions in influencing resistances. Thus it seems to us that there can be great utility and great generality in the metaphor of the personal scientist, characterizing the work of the client as well as of the therapist, in all forms of general psychotherapy. One way or another, homework is carried out, new information brought to bear, new hypotheses formulated, and behavior, thought, and affect changed accordingly. Although these processes can be partly nonconscious and/or emotional, they take place nevertheless. When they are conscious, rational, and guided in a supportive manner, change is more likely to be effected. When the therapist determines that "resistance" is caused by lack of information, then clearly information can enable change. When resistance is more complex, it may well be that first the client needs information about information, that is, the client needs the motivation to look at new data and new hypotheses.

On the surface it would appear that the "personal-scientist model" is least in accordance with the psychodynamic view of resistance as the expression of transference. But in our view a set of hypotheses is precisely that which is transferred from previous to current relationships. Thus even the most classic expression of transferred resistance, unconscious and denied, can be understood as being embodied in a set of hypotheses about internal dynamics and external contingencies that are felt by the client to be unquestionable. One can "treat" these transferences by providing hope and information that things are not what they seem, that new interactions, new feelings, new responses, and new thoughts are within reach. The right "experiments" in the right settings can make this information clear to the client. The art in psychotherapy is to create such settings and such experiments. The therapist who is found not to be the critical or hostile or adoring person who has been supposed has arranged the "experiments" that convinced the client otherwise. It is a different kind of experiment that can provide evidence about our general theories of possible psychodynamic sources for transference phenomena, both resistant and facilitative transferences. There need be no quarrel between cognitive-behavioral and psychodynamic perspectives on the realities of transference.

Thus we would again urge a careful operational analysis of the meanings of past relationships, past experiences, and past feelings for the client's existing hypotheses about self and world. A similar analysis is frequently needed to understand specific resistances to gathering the data pertinent to such general analyses, and pertinent to testing hypotheses about self and world. When a client carries an unrecognized hypothesis such as "If I am mistaken, or if this 'shrink' can 'teach' me that, then I would be a failure deserving of punishments and pain," then the treatment of such a hypothesis must of course have priority. And to have priority it must be uncovered.

Reading the chapters in this book and listening for what was not being said (including in our own chapter), we have been struck by a noticeable silence that carries considerable scientific significance. What we as scientists are not looking at closely (so far) are case histories and treatments where resistance has been notably absent. To evaluate any good theory of resistance we need to look at the conditions surrounding its absence as much as at those surrounding its presence. Otherwise we easily fall prey to a confirmation bias in any hypothesis about what does and does not influence resistance. Is resistance inevitable? We think not. If it is not inevitable, then when is it not evident? And *why*?

Finally, we would like to close by again asking if "resistance" does not in fact often express a healthy unwillingness to adopt a new hypothesis while the evidence is still unclear or of doubtful relevance. We argue that it *can* be healthy; and clients are helped by knowing that a therapist recognizes this truth. Thus both client and therapist can quite honestly say, in effect, "I really don't know about that hypothesis. Let's find out in this case, together."

14

Thoughts on the Resistance Chapters

Marvin R. Goldfried

I must confess to having experienced considerable resistance in writing my comments on the psychoanalytically oriented chapters. Although initially I was very enthused over the prospect of reading about the thoughts and experiences of Basch, Schlesinger, Dewald, and Blatt and Erlich on the topic of patient resistance, the actual task proved far more difficult than I had anticipated. In reading and then rereading these chapters, I found it very difficult to point to anything specific that I could comment on. I looked closely for guidelines on how to deal with patient resistance, but was unable to find any that I could readily comprehend. Not surprisingly, my first reaction was to attribute the cause of this difficulty to the individuals who wrote these chapters. It took very little reflection to realize, however, that to do so was not appropriate, as the authors could in no way be faulted for their clinical sensitivity, experience, or sophistication. I then began to blame myself for being obtuse in not being able to comprehend what a group of experts in psychoanalytically oriented therapy had to say about resistance. On further reflection, however, I had to remind myself that my original training was psychoanalytically oriented and that I still retained some familiarity with the relevant writings of Freud, Reich, and Fenichel. My interest and motivation were not a factor either, as I have recently become more involved in the search of common therapeutic principles that cut across all theoretical orientations (Goldfried, 1980, in press).

Marvin R. Goldfried • Department of Psychology, State University of New York, Stony Brook, New York 11794.

Despite the limitations inherent in analyzing the motivations/determinants of one's own behavior, the best answer I was able to offer myself for this dilemma was that the difficulty I was experiencing was attributable to a fundamentally different way in which I, as a behavior therapist, think about clinical problems, as well as the nature of these problems themselves. Specifically, the main difference between my own chapter—and, I might add, those by Lazarus and Fay, Meichenbaum and Gilmore, and Turkat and Meyer—and those written from a psychoanalytically oriented framework involved the *structure* of the way the information was communicated, the assumptions about what *motivates* a client's or patient's behavior, and the specific *content* associated with resistance.

Structure of Chapters

It seems to me that the structural differences that characterize the chapters written from the behavioral and psychoanalytic viewpoints reflect styles of thinking that differentiate the two orientations. Behavior therapy, which originally was based on extrapolations from experimental psychology to the clinical situation, tends to be more systematic and operational in nature. This fact is manifested in the four behaviorally oriented chapters in the way they are more tightly organized and specific than the psychoanalytically oriented chapters. That is not to say that the material in the behaviorally oriented chapters is necessarily "more correct," but that it is probably more likely to be helpful to the clinician who needs to know something about how to deal with resistance.

Motivational Assumptions

As I was taking notes for and subsequently organizing my own chapter, it became most apparent to me that my subject was as much behavioral assessment as it was resistance. As I read the other three behavioral chapters, this realization became even more striking. As with any other clinical problem, adequate handling of resistance from the behavioral vantage point requires a knowledge of those determinants that are likely to be maintaining the difficulty. Lazarus and Fay have clearly organized such potential variables as those related to the client's characteristics and interpersonal relationships, those having to do with the therapist or therapeutic relationship, and those that are a function of our current state of the art. The determinants or motivations associated with patient resistance as reflected in the psychoanalytically oriented chapters, on the other hand, are typically viewed as a function of the patient. It seems to me that one of the differences between the two orientations is the scope of determinants that one looks for in trying to explain any particular action pattern, and that behavior therapists are more likely to look at variables beyond those associated with the particular patient.

What I very much missed in the four psychoanalytically oriented chapters was a consideration that resistance and treatment failures may be a function of the therapist's inability to effectively bring about change—either because of characteristics of the therapist, or because of the state of the art. I was particularly pleased to see this caution dealt with in the chapters by Lazarus and Fay and by Meichenbaum and Gilmore. It is important to underline the point, as this broader context may help keep us from falling into the trap of concluding that resistance is always the "fault" of the patient or client. After all, patients and clients are good citizens of nature, in that they always obey the laws of human behavior. The dilemma that we all encounter, of course, is to be able to comprehend precisely what these laws may be, and then to apply them in any given case.

Content of Chapters

It is also evident that our chapters differ in regard to those clinical phenomena we place under the rubric "resistance." For the most part, behavior therapy, which is more action oriented and places a great emphasis on having the client try out new behaviors in real-life settings, finds that resistance occurs most often in the individual's difficulties in carrying out specific homework assignments. In the four psychoanalytically oriented chapters, on the other hand, resistance is more typically seen in the patient's difficulty in facing up to certain thoughts, wishes, and fantasies, as well in attempts to resolve such underlying conflicts. In essence, resistance represents the patient's defensive maneuvers and is consequently intrinsic to any therapeutic intervention that deals with such defenses.

It should also be noted that behavior therapy does not deal only with homework assignments, nor psychoanalytically oriented therapy solely with insight. Behavior therapists will at times focus directly on the client's thinking processes (Goldfried & Davison, 1976), and psychoanalytically oriented therapists will at times encourage novel extratherapeutic behaviors that may help patients obtain "corrective emotional experiences" (Alexander & French, 1946). Indeed, the clinical strategy of encouraging patients or clients to engage in fear-related activities probably represents one of the more striking commonalities between psychoanalytically oriented and behavioral treatment. A sampling of prominent representatives of each orientation will illustrate this point. For example, Fenichel (1941), on the topic of fear reduction, noted that

> when a person is afraid but experiences a situation in which what was feared occurs without any harm resulting, he will not immediately trust the outcome of his new experience; however, the second time he will have a little less fear, the third time still less. (p. 83)

This very same conclusion was reached by Bandura (1969), who observed:

> Extinction of avoidance behavior is achieved by repeated exposure to subjectively threatening stimuli under conditions designed to ensure that neither the avoidance responses nor the anticipated adverse consequences occur. (p. 414)

It is perhaps unfortunate that our two sets of chapters did not sufficiently deal with such points of commonality.

What Our Chapters Did Not Deal With

So far I have dealt more with the differences between our two approaches than the potential similarities. Unfortunately, I found it most difficult to specify any common elements between the two sets of chapters. I believe that they *do* exist, however, and that they may ultimately represent the most robust of our intervention strategies. As suggested by Wachtel (1977), there clearly exists a clinical "underground," constituting what experienced and sophisticated clinicians of various persuasions have observed over the course of their practice, and on which they may readily agree when stated in nontheoretical terms.

Although I am not familiar with the contemporary mainstream in psychoanalytically oriented circles, it is most clear to me that over the past 10 years clinical behavior therapy has undergone some very significant changes. Behavior therapy began with the assumption that all our therapeutic procedures could be firmly rooted in basic research findings. Nothing was to go on clinically unless it had an empirical basis. As behavior therapy became more and more popular, and more therapists were trained from within this orientation, clinical experience quickly led many of us to recognize that the empirically based "technique" was not always sufficient. The therapeutic relationship began to receive a stronger emphasis, and was viewed as a necessary, indeed essential, ingredient in behavioral intervention. Cognition has also received more emphasis in recent years, and behavior therapists who rely solely on principles of classical and operant conditioning are getting to be an ever-dwindling minority. As we have become more aware of cognitive factors in behavioral interventions, many of us are becoming more appreciative of the complexities and subtleties associated with cognitive processes. Indeed, such "cognitions" may not be readily obtained by direct report, and may at times necessitate associative techniques for assessing a client's implicit ways of viewing the world (Goldfried, 1979; Landau & Goldfried, 1981). It is difficult to predict the course that behavior therapy will take over the next 10 years. We may very well ultimately find ourselves working with many of the same phenomena that psychoanalytically oriented therapists have dealt with for some time, although I suspect the operational and systematic emphasis of behavior therapists will be retained regardless of the subject matter at hand.

Neal Miller, when questioned by Bergin and Strupp (1972) several years ago, predicted that as behavior therapists started to deal with more complicated types of problems, and as psychoanalytically oriented therapists began to emphasize ego mechanisms and the working-through process, both schools of thought would converge in some interesting ways. More recently, Strupp (1978) has suggested that such convergence is already taking place. Certainly, in the field of sex therapy (Kaplan, 1974, 1979), behavioral and psychodynamic procedures have been integrated to enable the clinician to deal with the wide variety of sexual dysfunctions likely to be seen in the clinical setting.

It is most important for both psychoanalytically and behaviorally oriented therapists to leave themselves open to the possibility that the intervention procedures currently at hand might not be the most effective. Probably, much of what we do clinically involves a fair amount of superstitious behavior on our part. In his recent book on the possible effective ingredients that cut across all therapeutic approaches, Garfield (1980) refers to Charles Lamb's essay "A Dissertation of Roast Pig" particularly as it relates to the current status of psychotherapy. As the story goes, the practice of eating roast pig, as opposed to raw pig, was accidentally discovered when a fire occurred in a swineherd's cottage. As one might imagine, this discovery had a dramatic impact on the eating practices of the time. However, numerous houses had to be burned down until it was finally realized that this delicacy could be prepared by simpler methods.

Now that we have been involved in the practice of psychotherapy for close to 100 years, it is not inappropriate to try to move toward some sort of consensus. In looking for the points of agreement that cut across various theoretical orientations, it is also reasonable to consider the possibility that other viewpoints may have unique contributions to make to our own. To engage in such a dialogue, however, may mean that our future ways of approaching clinical problems will look very different from our current ones. As is true of most attempts to change basic thinking and behavioral patterns, a certain amount of "resistance" may be anticipated. Nevertheless, amid growing demands for therapists to be accountable for the cost and efficacy of their methods, the time may be increasingly ripe for us to begin such collaborative efforts.

References

Alexander, R., & French, T. M. *Psychoanalytic therapy*. New York: Ronald Press, 1946.

Bandura, A. *Principles of behavior modification*. New York: Holt, Rinehart & Winston, 1969.

Bergin, A. E., & Strupp, H. H. *Changing frontiers in the science of psychotherapy*. Chicago: Aldine-Atherton, 1972.

Fenichel, O. *Problems of psychoanalytic technique*. Albany, N. Y. Psychoanalytic Quarterly, 1941.

Garfield, S. L. *Psychotherapy: An eclectic approach*. New York: Wiley-Interscience, 1980.

Goldfried, M. R. Anxiety reduction through cognitive-behavioral intervention. In P. C. Kendall & S. D. Hollon (Eds.), *Cognitive-behavioral interventions: Theory, research, and procedures*. New York: Academic Press, 1979.

Goldfried, M. R. Toward the delineation of therapeutic change principles. *American Psychologist*, 1980, *35*, 991–999.

Goldfried, M. R. (Ed.). *Converging themes in psychotherapy : Trends in psychodynamic, humanistic, and behavioral practice*. New York: Springer, in press.

Goldfried, M. R., & Davison, G. C. *Clinical behavior therapy*. New York: Holt, Rinehart & Winston, 1976.

Kaplan, H. S. *The new sex therapy: Active treatment of sexual dysfunctions*. New York: Brunner/ Mazel, 1974.

Kaplan, H. S. *Disorders of sexual desire*. New York: Brunner/Mazel, 1979.

Landau, R. J., & Goldfried, M. R. The assessment of semantic structure: A unifying focus in cognitive, traditional, and behavioral assessment. In S. D. Hollon & P. C. Kendall (Eds.), *Assessment strategies for cognitive-behavioral interventions.*New York: Academic Press, 1981.

Strupp, H. H. *Are psychoanalytic therapists beginning to practice cognitive behavior therapy or is behavior therapy turning psychoanalytic?* Paper presented at the symposium on "Clinical-Cognitive Theories of Psychotherapy," American Psychological Association, Toronto, 1978.

Wachtel, P. L. *Psychoanalysis and behavior therapy: Toward an integration.* New York: Basic Books, 1977.

15

Behaviorists, Cognitive Behaviorists, and Behavior-Analytic Writers

Herbert J. Schlesinger

In the behaviorally oriented chapters resistance varies from a *trait* of the patient who subtly or flagrantly opposes the purposes of the therapy to *instances* of behavior that seem to thwart these purposes. The distinction is important. If some persons are too willfully oppositional, lack "motivation," refuse to cooperate, or are for some reason unable to do so, one may reluctantly have to conclude that they are not suitable for the therapy. If, on the other hand, one regards the patient either for some reason consciously withholding his cooperation or more or less involuntarily reacting to some factor in the therapist, the treatment method, or himself, then a much more complex and discriminating set of possibilities emerges. Neither extreme point of view characterizes the range of behavior therapies or the range of dynamic therapies. Many of the statements about resistance in the behavioral chapters, and indeed a fair portion of the advice about how to handle resistance is quite consistent with a dynamic, psychoanalytic point of view.

What may be more distinguishing is that the behaviorists seem to see resistance as a sometimes thing, an untoward event interrupting the smooth flow of therapy that must be dealt with in order to restore the patient to a cooperative frame of mind. At least some of the behaviorists are evenhanded in assigning the blame for the resistance. Some make

Herbert J. Schlesinger ● Denver V. A. Medical Center, Department of Psychiatry, University of Colorado School of Medicine, Denver, Colorado 80262.

a particular point of blaming the therapist, blaming the patient for only a small portion of resistant behavior. What is lacking in this point of view, however, is awareness that the behavior we call resisting is not an occasional phenomenon, although some of its more flagrant manifestations appear only intermittently to confound therapists. The psychodynamically oriented authors see resistance as a manifestation of the phenomenon of defense and, as such, as a constant presence, like transference, in the therapeutic situation. By the same token, resistance is not the enemy of the therapy but the major business of the therapy. Most dynamicists think that without resistance there would be no need for therapy; what most therapies are about is the patient's more or less unconscious self-defeating, self-deceiving behavior of which resistance to the sought-out therapy is a manifestation. Both groups of therapists give a broad range of advice for "handling" resistance. From the behaviorists we have advice to persuade, educate, manipulate, and in other ways outsmart the patient or convert him to the therapist's way of thinking. Throughout their chapters I observe that techniques proposed to handle resistance do not seem to be linked to any theory about the therapeutic process or the workings of personality. It is the behavior itself that is the target of the intervention. Yet, in contrast, there are statements that have more of a dynamic ring—"the client is never wrong," all behavior is lawful whether defiant or nondefiant. Indeed, the latter point of view is characteristic of all dynamic therapies (but not all self-declared dynamic therapists), and both the more sophisticated behavior therapies and the dynamic therapies seem to regard resistance as an opportunity to learn more about the patient and the conscious and unconscious reasons that govern his behavior.

In several places I found a number of convergences between the behaviorists' views and my own. It is gratifying to read, in Meichenbaum and Gilmore's chapter, that cognitive-behavioral therapies make no significant distinction between the work of assessment and that of therapy. Their descriptions of the plight of the patient at the beginning of therapy—hopelessness, demoralization, fear of going crazy—are exactly like those I have made in my writings. As they point out, an important task at the beginning of therapy is to "convey a sense of both hopefulness and learned resourcefulness to replace the sense of helplessness."

Later they state that "insofar as the therapist can accurately and empathically perceive and share the client's expectancies, the therapist is more likely to be able to make sense out of the client's unproductive, resistant behavior." That is precisely my point of view: The therapist has to find the sense in the nonsense. There is some way in which the client's behavior is *not* unproductive. The therapist's task is to find out in what way it is productive and what it does *for* the patient, not just what it opposes in the therapy.

Meichenbaum and Gilmore's description of the beginning of treatment as involving a reconceptualization of the patient's difficulties, and their goal of further refining this reconceptualization over the course of therapy are quite consistent with the analytic point of view. Trying to understand, conceptualize, and refine the statement of what bothers a patient—that is, to formulate a statement with which the patient can agree—is where they begin. Still, they do seem to ignore that simply reconceptualizing the problem in a way that the patient can accept may lead to significant change, or that the patient may have his own ideas about how to proceed now that he understands the problem differently.

Meichenbaum and Gilmore distinguish their point of view from the dynamic one, which "eventually point[s] toward a correction of the unconscious origins of neurotic affects." What they miss, I believe, is that such corrections take place in the transference, that is, in the present, in a process that comes very close to what they claim for themselves: "Cognitive-behavioral therapies initially focus on the interruption of such affects, after these first arise and well before they have expanded into dysfunctional complexes."

Meichenbaum and Gilmore seem to regard resistance as something to be overcome, whose appearance is disappointing but must be accepted as inevitable. Even though they mention that "resistance itself can be informative," it is something to be coped with. They quote Beck as telling the patient that resistance is essentially a technological problem for the therapist, who must find the best method to resolve it. If one does not work, we will try another. Obviously, success must be the elimination of resistance.

Goldfried too, although he recognizes that patients are not fully rational, nevertheless requires them to behave as if they were. In his view, patients must hold certain optimal attitudes if the treatment is to succeed. They must believe that change is possible, that it will be gradual, involving learning and effort on their part, and that the therapist will not do anything to or for them. They must also "be favorably disposed toward the particular therapeutic strategy" and hold "at least a moderate amount of optimism that it will prove effective"—that is, they must believe in the therapy and in the therapist. It sounds as if the patient is required to subscribe to a credo in order for the treatment to work. Unfortunately, this attitude is not confined to behavior therapists. Many dynamic therapists similarly insist that the patient must be "motivated."

At the same time, Goldfried believes that "the client is never wrong" and that all behavior is lawful whether defiant or nondefiant. But he traces any difficulties to the therapist's inadequate or incomplete evaluation of the case, blaming the therapist rather than the patient for having insufficient "motivation."

The references to hypnotic technique also illustrate that resistance is viewed as an obstacle to be overcome, not necessarily to be understood, and that the patient can be manipulated out of the resistance— sometimes by incorporating the resistant behavior in the "hypnotist's" suggestions.

In fact, somewhat similar techniques are quite applicable in psychoanalytically oriented psychotherapy though with a different rationale. The anxious patient of Goldfried's chapter may have been helped when the therapist not only commented on it empathically but made room for the anxiety in the patient's experience by noting that he could hardly feel otherwise under the circumstances. But for the psychoanalytic therapist the anxiety is not to be treated "away" but to be understood in situ; "it belongs," and its function must be understood.

In presenting the rationale for structure in behavior therapy, Goldfried states, "It should go without saying that, unless therapist and client are working toward the same set of goals and can agree on the means for achieving these goals, therapy has little chance of succeeding." The experienced psychoanalytic therapist will take for granted that he and his patient are probably *not* working toward the same set of goals, and will be suspicious of any seeming agreement on the means for achieving them. It is an article of faith that the patient has a whole hierarchy of goals only some of which he is aware of, and that therapeutic change as we conceptualize it is the last thing the patient wants. Nearly all patients want to be free of pain at the least possible cost. For the analytic therapist the process of therapy can be conceptualized as discovering and dealing with the differences between the patient's emerging awareness of his goals and what he thinks the therapist's goals are. This "dealing with" amounts to clarifying and interpreting. The analytic therapist expects to find contradictions between the conscious agreement the patient makes to work with the therapist and the unconscious "finger crossing" that is expressed in what we call resistance. Resistance, thus, is the main subject matter of psychoanalytic psychotherapy, not a sometime thing.

The description of treatment Goldfried gives in his subsection on structure would be acceptable, so far as it goes, to an analytic therapist. The therapist is proceeding from the general to the specific, trying to find out precisely what is troubling the patient and what kind of things might make his life different. He suggests the opportunity for "behavior rehearsal" (for which we might, at least to give part of its meaning, use the term "working through"), and then he says that "rather than suggesting that the client go out and attempt to behave differently, specific behavior patterns are then dealt with in greater detail." The eschewing of suggestion in favor of the exploration of behavior patterns could describe much of analytic therapy as well. "Role playing" would probably not be used as a studied technique in analytic therapy, but it might well be used *in effect* in the course of discussions with the patient. The admonition to "be with" the client—not to pursue goals or procedures without the client's acknowledgment of their relevance—applies to all good psychotherapy.

Goldfried describes an interesting technique of asking the patient to telephone the therapist after a certain amount of struggling with his homework. He laudably stresses that this not be done in a coercive context, but in such a way that it will be seen as expressing the therapist's concern. It may well be, however, that those patients for whom this tactic does not work do not share the definition of the therapist's behavior as concerned rather than coercive. It is interesting that the author looks for causes outside the therapeutic interaction when the telephone technique does not work rather than investigating what this intervention might have meant.

Goldfried notes sadly that when the behavior pattern that brings the patient to treatment also shows up in the treatment situation, it makes for a difficult form of resistance. He is right; it is also a ubiquitous form of resistance—transference. Part of the problem is that the therapist becomes involved in maintaining the resistance by becoming frustrated and angry. Interestingly, he advocates that the therapist observe his own behavior and emotional reaction—in order to use the countertransference as a source of information and as a means of refocusing on what the client is trying to do to create such feelings: a quite advanced psychoanalytic point of view in the heart of behavior therapy. Thus "the noncompliant behavior patterns then become the particular focus of the intervention"—or, the point I have been making, resistance is the focus of treatment, not an obstacle to treatment.

Goldfried discusses "psychological reactance"—the resistance some individuals show to being influenced by others. The advice is to make the patient think he is changing on his own. In marked contrast, the best psychoanalytic advice is to *let* the patient change on his own and not try to force him to do something that he wants to do anyway. Goldfried makes an interesting reference to some research showing that coping styles or reacting styles interact with the amount of directiveness in the therapy. Here is another point where matching the patient and the style of intervention may pay off.

Environmental problems and the possibility that the patient is overburdened with homework are also mentioned as factors making for resistance. Clearly, no distinction is made between unconscious and conscious sources of opposition. The behavior therapists seem to fall back on Freud's earliest definition of resistance as anything that impedes the progress of treatment. In contrast, my view, in common with other analytic therapists, is that resistance is what the treatment is about, not an occasional obstacle to the treatment.

16

Behavior-Analytic Considerations of Alternative Clinical Approaches

Ira Daniel Turkat

The illuminating chapters in this volume indicate the tremendous variance in approach to the phenomenon of resistance. In the behavior-analytic approach, we attempt to operationalize clinical phenomena and thereby develop a formulation to: (1) label the behaviors in need of modification; (2) identify the precise cause—effect relationships in terms of etiology and current manifestation; (3) label resistant or antitherapeutic behaviors; (4) predict resistant behaviors; and (5) devise a conceptualization to guide the therapist in reacting to and averting these behaviors. In our view, the behavior-analytic approach to resistance is considerably different from the psychodynamic and behavioral approaches presented; we will address ourselves to some of these differences.

First and foremost, we see little utility in discussing the relationship between the behavior-analytic and the psychodynamic approaches to resistance. We see the psychodynamic and behavior-analytic conceptualizations as completely incompatible: Unconscious processes cannot be operationalized. Furthermore, we hope to avoid redundancy in criticism of the psychodynamic approaches; we expect our behavioral colleagues' comments to be sufficient. Finally, we feel we can make a more useful contribution by focusing on the other behavioral approaches.

Ira Daniel Turkat • Departments of Psychology and Medicine, Vanderbilt University and School of Medicine, Nashville, Tennessee 37240.

The behavioral chapters by Lazarus and Fay, Meichenbaum and Gilmore, and Goldfried raise a variety of issues relating to resistance. These can be organized in four rough categories: (1) the relationship between assessment and treatment; (2) the technological approach to resistance; (3) the therapeutic relationship; and (4) miscellaneous.

Relationship between Assessment and Treatment

There is little question that any approach for managing resistance will be greatly influenced by the particular clinician's view of the relationship between assessment and treatment. Furthermore, the purpose and methods of clinical assessment differ across clinicians and have direct implications for resistance management.

In their provocative chapter, Meichenbaum and Gilmore state that the "cognitive-behavioral therapies make no significant distinction between the work of assessment and that of therapy." Instead they view the client's internal dialogues as "the immediate concern of the therapist." Assessment and treatment are seen as a single process: modifying faulty cognitive styles. From our view of clinical activity, such an approach would be likely to facilitate resistant behaviors.

First, by focusing exclusively on cognitive activity, Meichenbaum and Gilmore fail to comprehensively examine the motoric and autonomic response systems. Often these response systems are *not* under cognitive control (e.g., tics, compulsive handwashing). Consequently, treatment aimed at modifying internal dialogues will naturally lead to resistant behaviors. Second, in that it provides cognitive treatment to every case, the system seems to be a standardized approach to clinical activity. As the impressive literature on specificity of conditioning indicates, a standardized approach may lead to resistant behaviors in many cases. Finally, our conceptualization of the relationship between assessment and treatment suggests a number of difficulties in handling resistance from the cognitive viewpoint.

In the behavior-analytic approach there is a clear distinction between assessment and treatment. Furthermore, we specify two different types of assessment: preintervention and continuous. In preintervention assessment, our goal is to develop a formulation that utilizes the client's history and current problem dimensions to *predict* future behavior. In this respect we attempt to predict which behaviors are resistant and when they will occur. This type of assessment provides strategies for managing resistant behaviors. We do not feel comfortable in devising treatments without preintervention behavioral assessment. Continuous assessment refers to the ongoing measurement of targeted behaviors prior to, during, and following intervention. If resistant behaviors develop, they will be detected during continuous assessment and new hypotheses will be tested. Thus the behavioral formulation—a continuous hypothesis-testing process—guides the therapist in managing resistance.

Our dependence on the behavioral formulation (i.e., clinical phenomena operationalized in terms of cause—effect relationships) for managing resistance is inescapable. A conceptual bias (e.g., cognitive mediation as the omnipresent independent variable) may prevent the discovery of precise cause—effect relationships. Without clear specification of the relevant independent and dependent variables, predictive power diminishes. Thus, from the behavior-analytic viewpoint, a behavioral formulation is imperative to facilitate successful resistance management.

It is interesting to note that in their chapters Lazarus and Fay, Meichenbaum and Gilmore, and Goldfried do not appear to conceptualize their clinical activity in terms of a formulation to guide the therapeutic process. Instead their approaches seem to concentrate on a "technological fix" of the client's complaints. Differences between behavior-analytic and technological therapy have direct implications for resistance management, and will now be addressed.

Technological Approach to Resistance

Our major criticism of the behavior therapy literature is its advocacy of a technological approach to clinical activity. In this volume and elsewhere we have outlined differences between the behavior-analytic and technological approaches (Meyer & Bartlett, 1976; Meyer & Turkat, 1979; Turkat, 1979). In short, the technological behavior therapist attempts to match standard treatment procedures to client complaints whereas the behavior-analytic clinician formulates the client's problems, develops a predictive model, and implements idiographically designed treatment. When resistance occurs, the technological behavior therapist implements a new technique; the behavior-analytic clinician employs tactics derived from the formulation[1] (if the resistant behavior has not already been prevented by the treatment strategies indicated by the formulation). We will discuss examples of the technological approach to resistance in this volume in relation to the behavior-analytic viewpoint.

In the previous section we pointed out some general shortcomings of the cognitive-technology approach to resistance; we will now take a more detailed look. When the client believes that he is a worthless person and that no one likes him, the cognitive-technology approach is to "test out these hypotheses" and subsequently teach cognitions incompatible with the present ones (e.g., "I'm not so terrible," "It could be worse,"). From the behavior-analytic view, these self-deprecating thoughts are often very appropriate. Some clients frequently engage in behavior that others evalate negatively, thereby setting up social criticism and isolation. In such cases, teaching these individuals to dispute these accurate "hypotheses" is similar to setting up a delusional system. Furthermore, by modifying internal dialogues and not the social behavior, these individuals will continue to receive social punishment. Another example is the case Meichenbaum and Gilmore reported of a man who "resisted" discussing his thoughts and feelings in fear of possibly being hospitalized and receiving ECT. In such a case we would consider this client's choice appropriate and not resistance. In our experience, clients who have presented this "resistance" have typically verbalized bizarre thoughts and feelings in the past and consequently were labeled schizophrenic, hospitalized, and given ECT for doing so. In such cases we often conceptualize these behaviors as a result of an attention deficit and teach appropriate discrimination, attending, and focusing skills including nonverbalization of bizarre thoughts (see Adams, 1981). Thus one's conceptual approach (e.g., cognitive technological versus behavior analytic) will determine which behaviors are labeled resistant, and what strategies will be used for resistance management. From our viewpoint, nonverbalization of bizarre thoughts is often an appropriate behavior, whereas the cognitive technologist would routinely view it as resistance.

In Goldfried's approach to ensuring beween-session homework compliance, he states that "each therapy session should begin with a discussion of the client's homework, so that it is very clear that this aspect of the change process is an essential part of the therapy." In behavior-analytic approach, the formulation would indicate whether

---

[1] In certain cases the resistant behavior may not be understood from the formulation, which indicates the necessity of a new formulation.

such a strategy was appropriate for a specific case. For example, in an individual phobic of criticism, anticipatory fear of the therapist's evaluation of homework performance may provoke excessive anxiety, thereby preventing the task from being performed. Thus the therapeutic relationship (i.e., in-session behavior by the therapist) would parallel the treatment procedure, and sessions may not necessarily begin with (or even cover) discussion of the homework assignment. From the behavior-analytic view, each case should be handled differently and there is no effective standardized method for managing resistance.

A final example of the technological approach to resistance is the "passive-resister" described by Lazarus and Fay. These individuals are defined as totally compliant but seemingly unable to change, and are conceptualized as deriving "an enormous sense of power and gratification from the therapist's frustration." Lazarus and Fay advocate using paradoxical procedures with these individuals. In the behavior-analytic approach, the formulation would indicate why this behavior occurs and how it should be managed. Furthermore, these determinations will differ across cases. If the client lacks social skills and can only gain reinforcement by passive-aggressive behavior, appropriate skill training and non-reinforcement of passive-aggressive behavior are indicated. If another client is fearful of losing control and complies in such a way as to manipulate the therapist's frustration (for evidence that the client is still in control), obviously a different treatment is called for. The essential point is that resistant behaviors vary across clients and cannot be successfully managed by a standardized technique (e.g., paradoxical procedures). Instead a formulation must be developed to guide resistance management.

Resistance and the Therapeutic Relationship

Throughout this chapter we have emphasized the importance of the behavioral formulation in guiding the management of resistance. In discussing the role of the therapeutic relationship in facilitating resistance management, we again find ourselves at odds with our behavioral colleagues' approaches.

Goldfried, Lazarus and Fay, and Meichenbaum and Gilmore all advocate providing a warm, supportive, empathic therapeutic relationship. In essence the therapist plays a Rogerian role in relating to the client—a standardized approach. In the behavior-analytic approach, the therapist continually tests hypotheses about cause—effect relationships, develops a formulation, and creates the appropriate environment (i.e., treatment and therapeutic relationship) to modify the client's behavior. We do not provide a standardized therapeutic relationship; instead the relationship is based on the indications of the formulation and parallels the treatment program.

In certain cases warmth and empathy may be conceptualized as positive reinforcers and therefore must be used cautiously. Reinforcing all the client's in-session behavior would naturally strengthen certain resistant behaviors and is not indicated from the behavior-analytic view. Instead the behavioral formulation dictates when warmth and empathy are appropriate therapist behaviors. The essential point is that warm and empathic therapist responsivity should not be standardized; such behavior should be used selectively according to the indications of the behavioral formulation.

Miscellaneous Points

We have outlined how the behavioral formulation guides the management of resistance in terms of assessment, treatment strategies, the relationship between assessment and treatment, and the therapeutic relationship. We will now address some other issues raised by our behavioral colleagues.

The number and length of therapeutic sessions is unquestionably an issue of prime importance. Goldfried, Lazarus and Fay, and Meichenbaum and Gilmore indicate that they typically see their clients for 1 hour once a week. We find that we rarely see clients on such a schedule. Our scheduling of sessions is primarily determined by the indications of the behavioral formulation. In modifying existing cause—effect relationships, we attempt to control the individual's environment (in and out of session) as much as is necessary and possible. Thus, for certain clients, we may schedule daily 4- or 5-hour sessions. In other cases we may hospitalize clients or work within their natural environment. Occassionally we may see cases for 1 hour a week. Overall, the number and length of sessions vary considerably across clients as well as during the course of assessment, treatment, and follow-up for a particular client. Although we try to modify existing cause—effect relationships as quickly as possible, there is no standardized allotment for scheduling sessions.

Another issue related to managing resistance is the therapist's conceptual framework for conducting clinical activity. We cannot overemphasize the need to recognize the complexity of life, the diversity of cause—effect relationships, and the limitations of clinical work. The clinician needs to be as open, unbiased, flexible, sensitive, creative, perceptive, and innovative as possible. Theoretical bias (e.g., unconscious conflict or cognitive mediation as the omnipresent independent variable) leads to treatment bias (e.g., interpretation, cognitive modification). The behavior-analytic approach is idiographic and so is its conception of resistance management.

Conclusion

Our ability to control resistant behavior is inescapably dependent on the behavioral formulation. The more accurate identification of cause—effect relationships, the greater the clinician's predictive power and the better the chances for successful intervention. We cannot overemphasize the need to recognize the idiographic nature of clinical activity.

References

Adams, H. E. *An introduction to abnormal psychology.* Dubuque, Ia.: William C. Brown, 1981.

Meyer, V., & Bartlett, D. Behaviour therapy: Technology or psychotherapy? *Scandinavian Journal of Behaviour Therapy,* 1976, *5,* 1–12.

Meyer, V., & Turkat, I. D. Behavioral analysis of clinical cases. *Journal of Behavioral Assessment,* 1979, *1,* 259–270.

Turkat, I. D. The behavior analysis matrix. *Scandinavian Journal of Behaviour Therapy,* 1979, *8,* 187–189.

Author Index

Subject Index